Visitor's to Burgundy and Beaujolais

Don Philpott

Don Philpott has specialised in writing on travel, food and wine for thirty years. He has travelled the world extensively and written numerous travel guides and several books on wine, including *Vineyards of France*. He is a member of the Circle of Wine Writers and Circle of Food Writers. He now spends most of his time writing guide books and living in Florida with his wife and two sons when he is not on the road or checking a new vintage.

Published by:
Moorland Publishing Co Ltd, Moor Farm Road West, Ashbourne,
Derbyshire DE6 1HD England

Published in the USA by:
Hunter Publishing Inc, 300 Raritan Center Parkway, CN 94, Edison, NJ 08818

ISBN 0 86190 5687

British Library Cataloguing in Publication Data:
A catalogue record for this book is available from the British Library.

Colour origination by: GA GRAPHICS
Printed by South China Printing Co. (1988) Ltd., Hong Kong

Cover photograph: Château Corton-André at Aloxe Corton.
Back cover: *(left to right)* Cluny Abbey, the Hôtel Dieu in Beaune, Château
at Rully. *(centre)* The Abbaye de la Bussière sur Ouche.
Page 3: Glorious fields of sunflowers amidst the vineyards near Chablis.

MPC Production Team:
Editorial: Tonya Monk
Design: Debbie Gaiger
Cartography: Mark Titterton
Typesetting: Stella Porter

Photo Credits:
All photographs by Lindsey Porter except for:-
Page 15 *(top)*, page 16 *(left)* Don Philpott, page 71 *(top)* E. Smith
page 110 *(top)* J.L. Guerier, Rhône Alpes Tourist Board, *(below)*

Visitor's Guide
to Burgundy and
Beaujolais

Don Philpott

MPC

Table of Contents

An Introduction to Burgundy   7

Geography   8
History   9
Art and Architecture   16

Touring Burgundy   19

Tour One 400 miles   20
Tour Two 375 miles   21
Gazetteer   21
Towns within Burgundy are listed in alphabetical order with a number inserted
after each entry indicating which tour they relate to.

Touring Beaujolais   91

The Haut Beaujolais   96
The Valley of the Azergues   101
The Lower Azergues Valley   104
The Monts du Beaujolais   106
Additional Information on Beaujolais   108
Tourist Offices   109

Lyon and the Surrounding Area   111

Things to see around Lyon   116
Additional Information on Lyon   118
Places to Visit   118
Tourist Information Offices   119
Hotels and Restaurants   119

Eating Out in Burgundy and Beaujolais   121

The Gastronomy of Burgundy   121
The Gastronomy of Beaujolais   128

The Wines of Burgundy   131

The Wine Districts of Burgundy   135
Chablis   135
Côte de Nuits   137
Nuits-St-Georges   145
Côte de Beaune   146
Savigny-lès-Beaune   148
Côte de Beaune Villages and Côte de Beaune   156
Chalonnaise   157

Mâconnais 160
A Wine Tour of the Burgundy Region 161
Dijon 161
Marsannay to Nuits-St-George 161
Tour of the Beaune Area 163
Pommard to Santenay 165
Chagny and Chalon to Mâcon 168

The Wines of Beaujolais 171

The Districts and Villages of Beaujolais 173
A Wine Tour of the Beaujolais Region 177

Useful Information for Visitors 184

Hotels and Restaurants in Burgundy 184
Youth Hostels in Burgundy 201
Boating in Burgundy 203
Castles, Museums, Sights and Monuments in Burgundy 204
The Vineyards of Burgundy 213
Hotels and Restaurants in Beaujolais 242
Castles, Museums, Sights and Monuments in Beaujolais 244
Vineyards and Tasting Cellars in Beaujolais 245

Facts for Visitors 247

Accommodation 247
Annual Fairs and Events 249
Banks 250
Boating 250
Climate 253
Embassies and Consulates 254
Insurance 254
Maps 254
Measurements 255
Museums 255
Passports and Visas 255
Postal Services 255
Public Holidays 255
Safety 256
Shopping 256
Telephones 256
Time 256
Tipping 256
Tourist Offices 257
Travel 257
Driving 257
By road 258
By train 258
By air 258
Rules of the Road 259
Speed Limits 261
Fuel and Garage Services 261
Car or Bicycle Hire 262

Maps

Route One 22
Route Two 23
Dijon 55
Haut Beaujolais 95
The Valley of the Azergues 102
Monts du Beaujolais 107
Lyon 114
Chablis 134
Côte de Nuits 139
Côte de Beaune 146
Chalonnaise 158
Mâconnaise 162
Chagny to Mâcon 167
Beaujolais 174

Symbols

🏃 Recommended Walk

ᴛᴛ Archaeological Site

⛷ Skiing

❀ Garden

▲ Mountain

🦅 Cave

⛪ Church or Ecclesiastical Site

🏛 Building of Interest

🏰 Castle or Fortification

🏛 Museum or Art Gallery

✤ Beautiful View or
   Natural Phenomenon

✳ Other Place of Interest

Topography

| Road | Town | Itineraries | Towns whose names represent a guaranteed Vintage | Major Road |

About This Guide

There is so much to see in this fascinating and compact region that two itineraries are provided to cover all Burgundy. Each itinerary defines a route and is followed by a detailed gazetteer of everything there is to see and do. Several touring routes through the smaller and lesser-known areas of Beaujolais are included. This book also guides you on foot through the wonderful cities of Dijon and Lyon visiting many beautiful sights and interesting places.

The **Useful Information** section is a comprehensive chapter, listing details on hotels and restaurants, with price ratings, addresses and telephone numbers. Further detailed information listing opening times, addresses and telephone numbers of points of interest are also included and will prove invaluable when touring and exploring.

Also included in this section is a listing on Burgundian wines, best producers, all vineyards and cellars open to the public, including those offering tastings and speaking English.

Distinctive margin symbols in the text and on maps, plus places to visit highlighted in bold, enable the reader to find the most interesting places with ease.

At the back of the guide the **Facts for Visitors**, arranged in alphabetical order, gives practical information and useful tips to help you plan your visit before you go and when you are there.

An Introduction to Burgundy

Just the name Burgundy conjures up wonderful images of good food, fine wines, great hospitality and a spectacular and rich history which spans thousands of years.

Burgundy lies midway between the rich farming cereal plains of Northern France and the industrialised valley of the Rhône. It is a land of gentle, undulating hills, woods and forests, meandering rivers, criss-crossing canals and lakes, lush vineyards and scores of picturesque villages, historic towns and fairytale châteaux.

The location of Burgundy accounts for its long and fascinating history. The network of rivers — Armançon, Yonne, Seine, Ouche, Saône, Loire and Arroux — offered relatively easy access both within the region and from the Mediterranean northwards. The Loire, Yonne, Seine, and Saône radiate out from Burgundy providing further travel north, south, east and west.

Henri Vincenot, a writer from Burgundy, expressed it well when he said that Burgundy was the 'roof of the Western world' because whenever six drops of rain fell on the region, two found their way to the Atlantic, two to the English Channel and two to the Mediterranean. A boat cruise through Burgundy, with its 800 miles (1,288km) of rivers and canals, is a great way to explore.

Burgundy was on the ancient tin route from the Roman tin mines in Cornwall to the Mediterranean, and on the main Roman road from *Lugdunum* (Lyon) to *Trevae* (Trier), part of the road which ran from Italy to Flanders.

This ease of travel and transportation increased considerably when the canal network was built, and then again in the 1850s when Dijon became a major junction for the new railway linking Paris and the Mediterranean. Today, high speed trains and autoroutes make Burgundy more accessible than ever.

There were settlers in the area at least 12,000 years ago and their artistry can still be seen, the Greeks planted the first vines, the Romans brought order to an area of warring tribes, Charlemagne became a great Champion of Burgundy, the Kingdom sided with England against France in the Hundred Years War, and for the last 500 years it has been part of France.

The area is perhaps most famous for its wines which are undoubtedly among the finest in the world. Perhaps it is the greatness of the wines that has led to the creation of so many great dishes to accompany them, and Burgundy's deserved reputation for hospitality. Some of the feasts given for visiting dignitaries in the past were of huge proportions and could last for days.

The antiquity of the area is immediately obvious as you travel through Burgundy with well-preserved centuries-old buildings everywhere. A thousand years ago, Burgundy was the seat of fabulously rich monasteries, and their impact can still be felt today amidst many of the region's finest vineyards.

Burgundy has long been a trading nation, and not just for its wines. It is noted for its mustard and has long been famous for its timber and stone. Trees for fuel were floated down the Seine to Paris, and stone from Burgundy was carried by barge to the capital and used to build many of the city's finest buildings and monuments.

This guide to Burgundy aims to allow you to get the most out of your trip to this wonderful region, whatever your interest. It will help you plan your journey in advance, giving advice on hotels and restaurants, tips on best-buy wines and visiting the vineyards, and is packed with information on things to see and do.

Burgundy is not a large region, barely more than 150 miles (242km) from north to south, but it is essential to have your own transport to explore it fully and freely. A car is most convenient, but cycling and boating can be fun, and many towns and areas are best explored on foot, especially if you are planning to do some wine tasting along the way. If you are travelling by car in a group, take it in turns driving so that everyone can enjoy being a passenger and wine taster. It is both illegal and dangerous to drink and drive.

GEOGRAPHY

Burgundy consists of many geographic parts, but is mostly flat in the north and west, has sloping plains in the east, consists of a plateau in the centre of the region and rolling hills to the south. The Loire marks its western boundary and the Saône its eastern limits. Many of the areas within Burgundy have very distinctive characteristics, such as Morvan, La Côte, the Mâconnais and Charolais. The highest area is the Morvan, although nowhere does this exceed 3,000ft (915m), La Côte is the long thin limestone plateau, on which many of the world's most famous vineyards are planted, and the Mâconnais is characterised by the rolling hills which follow the Saône southwards and run into the Beaujolais Hills. East of this are the Bress plains sandwiched between the Mâconnais and Beaujolais Hills and the Jura mountains.

The creation of Burgundy started hundreds of millions of years ago when the entire area was submerged under a massive sea. Then, more than 500 million years ago, a period of massive uplift began which created the Massif Central to the southwest, the Ardennes to the north-west and the Morvan hills to the south. These mountains were mostly granite and volcanic rocks but erosion wore them down massively, especially in the Morvan. Layers of dead vegetation compressed into rock, created the coal deposits found around Autun and Blanzy.

About 250 to 200 millions years ago the area was again submerged. During this time, layer upon layer of dead marine life was deposited on the sea bed, over the granite base, and over tens of millions of years this was compressed into layers of limestone rock, one of the most important ingredients of Burgundy's wine success. When the waters retreated, much of the exposed limestone was eroded, and this was the time of the dinosaurs and other reptiles.

The third and most recent period of uplift, the one that created the Alps, occurred around fifty to sixty million years ago. The Massif Central was split and the eastern end was broken into a number of sections which now form the hills of Autun, Charolais, Beaujolais and the Mâconnais. The Morvan was also further uplifted during the same period, and erosion ever since has created the plains and rolling hills that can be seen today.

HISTORY

The old kingdom of Burgundy occupies a very strategic position in the east of France, lying between Chablis in the north and Villefranche-en-Beaujolais in the south. It is close to Germany, Holland and Switzerland, and from the earliest times was on the main trading routes and constantly attracted visitors, whether traders, refugees, pilgrims or invading armies.

The region can trace its history back almost one million years and the first evidence of man's presence is from isolated flints dating from one million BC. There are scattered remains of early palaeolithic sites dating from 500,000BC, and there were cave dwellers around Aze during the Acheulean epoch between 200,000 and 100,000BC. Further evidence of cave dwellers has been found near Arcy-sur-Cure and Genay, dating from around 50,000BC. Man was certainly hunting in the area 20,000 years before Christ, and at least five successive hunting civilizations between 35,000 and 10,000BC have been discovered, notably at Arcy-sur-Cure, Solutre and Nuits-St-Georges. The last small tribe of hunters is thought to have occupied the Seille valley around 6,000BC.

By 4,000BC the first agricultural settlements had been established in the Yonne by settlers moving up from the Mediterranean, and the oldest metal objects found date from this period.

Between 1800 and 725BC, the Bronze Age, there were settlements at Ouroux-sur-Saône and Chalon-sur-Saône, and by 600BC there were established trading links with Greek and Italian merchants via the Mediterranean, and works of art from the sixth century BC have been discovered. Gallic tribes ruled the area, although it became increasingly threatened lying as it did, on the northern border of the Roman Empire.

When the Romans invaded Gaul,

it took six years before they finally overcame the tribes of what is now Burgundy in 52BC. Vercingetorix was the man chosen to lead the armies of Gaul against Caesar, and he led the resistance until the battle and siege of Alésia, near Semur-en-Auxois. After six weeks under siege and with no hope of rescue, Vercinguetorix surrendered after extracting a promise that his army would be spared. He was paraded through the streets of Rome and then kept prisoner for six years before being executed. His defeat brought an end to Gallic resistance to Roman occupation and marked the start of a period of great growth. Many splendid buildings and fascinating reminders of the Gallo-Roman era can still be seen throughout the region.

The first vines had been introduced by the Greeks who had travelled northwards from their settlements around the mouth of the Rhône, but the Romans brought order to the area, replanting the vineyards, introducing new wine making techniques and greatly improving quality. In AD312, the Emperor Constantine received a speech praising the wines of the Côte de Nuits and Côte de Beaune and thanking him for reducing the taxes. Because of its nearness to the border, the region now known as Burgundy was constantly under attack from the warring Germanic tribes. Many Roman buildings were destroyed, and the locals built fortified sites for protection. The remains of one of these sites can still be seen above Beaune on the Mont-St-Désiré.

The Roman Empire collapsed in AD410, and its provinces fell victim to further attacks. Burgundy was invaded by the Goths and Vandals, who pillaged and then left the countryside. The Franks and Burgundians took over and the Burgundians from Germany gave the name Burgundia to their new kingdom. The Burgundians originally came from the Danish island of Bornholm. The wandering tribe are believed to have settled around Geneva in AD433 from where they expanded north into Germany and then into France.

They were originally known as Burgundarholmers, and gave their name to Burgundy. They quickly adopted Christianity, and with the Franks, ruled for almost a thousand years.

The Franks overcame the Burgundians in AD534. Charlemagne became ruler of the Frankish Empire in AD800, was King of Burgundy and a great champion of the region, especially its wines. He owned his own vineyards in the region and passed laws to improve the quality of the wines. There is still a vineyard that bears his name Corton Charlemagne, which produces marvellous white wines. Another innovation, for which Charlemagne was famous, was his edict banning the pressing of grapes in the traditional manner — by foot — because he considered it unhygienic.

After Charlemagne's death in AD814, Louis the Pious took over but his family were unable to agree on a

Above: The twelfth-century chateau at Le Rochepot was restored in the nineteenth century.
Below: The ancient St. Andrew's Gate at Autun.

successor. The sons of Emperor Louis battled for 25 years over the succession until AD841 when Charles the Bald defeated his brother Lothar at the battle of Fontanet (Fontenay). Two years later, the kingdom was divided into three under the terms of the Treaty of Verdun, between Charlemagne's grandsons: Charles the Bald received the western part of the territory, and this became the Dukedom of Burgundy.

Apart from a fourteen-year period at the beginning of the eleventh century when Burgundy was occupied by the French King, the Duchy was to prosper and expand over the next six centuries, thanks not only to the power and influence of the Dukes but also to the support they received from a powerful church, and the many religious orders in Burgundy.

In AD587 there is a record of a parcel of land being presented by the King of Burgundy, Gontran, to the Abbey of St Benigne in Dijon. The land contained vineyards, and the Church's involvement in vines and wine has continued ever since. It became fashionable for the lords and members of the court to make gifts of land to the Church, and the wine produced as a result was sought after throughout Europe. There are records of wine being produced at Aloxe in AD696, Fixey in AD733, Santenay in AD858, Chassagne in AD886, Savigny in AD930 and Pommard in 1005.

In AD910 the Duke of Aquitaine established the religious order of Cluny, which on many occasions proved itself more powerful than the King. At one stage, the order controlled 1,450 monasteries and 10,000 monks. They established hospices for travellers, and rapidly gained great wealth and power. The other powerful religious order of that time was Cîteaux, established in 1098. It was started by three former monks from Cluny who wished to return to the austere style of monastic life. They lived in the marshes, among the water holes and reeds opposite the Côte de Nuits. The wells were called cisterns and this led to the monks becoming known as Cistercians. St Bernard, the son of a local lord, became abbot in 1115, and while he encouraged a return to a more austere monastic life, he also realised that the abbey needed income. The Cistercians became experts in agriculture, stock-breeding, fisheries, forestry and wine making. They were also innovators in mining and smelting, and one of their many technological achievements was the invention of the camshaft. This pioneering spirit ironically led to enormous wealth and the Abbey owned huge estates, forests, mills and mines across Europe, from Ireland to Russia. The Cistercians also had a profound influence on architecture, believing that the beauty of the building lay in the simplicity and symmetry of its lines, rather than ornamentation and decoration. The twelfth-century Abbey of Fontenay is a magnificent early example of this.

The many religious establishments attracted tens of thousands of pilgrims every year. These people came to learn or prey at the abbeys and monasteries, or gathered here before setting off on the pilgrimage road to Santiago de Compostela in Spain. Vézelay was a very important pilgrimage site. It was here that St Bernard launched the Second Crusade and Richard the Lionheart launched the Third. Vézelay also prospered because the Holy Shrine contained the relics of Mary Magdalene, and pilgrims, including heads of state from across Europe, who came to pray here. Vézelay went into steep decline, however, when the Avignon Pope ruled that the Saint's relics were in another church, in southern France. The bones are still in the shrine and still sanctified by Rome.

Both monastic orders prospered during the Crusades, obtaining more land and vineyards and winning further acclaim for the quality of their wines. The Cistercians planted vines when they created a new Chapter at Clos de Vougeot, and nuns of the order from the Abbey of Notre-Dame du Tart bought a vineyard in Morey, the now world famous Clos de Tart.

Although Burgundy is in what is now France, it was for many years a separate kingdom and was constantly feuding with the French king. On many occasions the Dukes of Burgundy proved themselves to be more powerful than the French monarch.

During the Hundred Years War (1337-1453), Burgundy was allied to England, and between the eleventh and fifteenth centuries, the Burgundian Dukes increased their 'empire', usually by marriage, but occasionally by war, until it covered much of what is now northern France, Belgium, Holland and Luxembourg, and was the biggest 'country' in Europe.

In 1363 the King of France put his son Philip the Bold (1364-1404) on the Burgundian throne and the reign of the three succeeding Valois Dukes — John the Fearless (1404-19), Philip the Good (1419-67) and Charles the Bold (1467-77) — which lasted until the death of Charles the Bold, saw the heyday of Burgundy's political and artistic achievements.

Philip reputedly earned his title of 'the Bold' at the Battle of Poitiers in 1356, after being captured while fighting alongside his father, King John the Good of France. Although injured and little more than a boy, he is reputed to have struck an English soldier for insulting his father. His marriage to the fabulously wealthy Margaret of Flanders in 1369 made him the most powerful and richest noble in Christendom. Flemish artists and craftsmen were imported to decorate his palace, and he ordered the building of the family mausoleum — the Chartreuse de Champmol in Dijon. It cost so much money to build that his heir, John the Fearless started his reign with huge debts to pay off. John's reign was dominated by his arguments with Louis d'Orleans, whom he had assassinated. This sparked a feud with the House of Orleans and their leader Count Bernard VII of

Armagnac, which subsequently erupted into civil war between the Armagnacs and Burgundians. John the Fearless agreed to a parley on the bridge at Montereau with the Dauphin, later to become Charles VII, but it was a trap and he was murdered. It was because of this treachery, that his son Philip the Good joined forces with the English to seek revenge. And, it was Philip the Good, who in return for a fortune, handed over to the English Joan of Arc, who he had captured at Compiègne. The dispute between Burgundy and France was resolved by the Treaty of Arras. The Dukedom of Burgundy was enlarged greatly, and peace allowed Philip the Good to concentrate on the finer things of life. Burgundy became a great centre of the arts again, and Philip, on the day of his wedding to Isabella of Portugal, founded the Order of the Golden Fleece. Today it is still one of the most prestigious and exclusive orders in France. Charles the Bold was an enigma, a man who loved fighting and hunting, yet was a great scholar. He had two passionate aims, to enlarge Burgundy as much as possible and to reduce the influence of the King of France. He died during one of his campaigns, while laying siege to Nancy during an ill-fated bid to recapture Lorraine. He had no male heir and so the Duchy was claimed by King Louis XI of France.

Apart from the international reputation of its wines, the Burgundians were famous for the lavishness of their hospitality — and still are. Gargantuan feasts lasting hours and sometimes days, were not uncommon. Burgundy is also reputed to be the first place to use a menu, so that guests could know in advance what they were eating. The menu is said to be the creation of Queen Isabeau of Bavaria, wife of Charles VI, the King of France, who was a frequent visitor to Dijon.

Burgundy continued to wield enormous influence, even after the French King resumed authority over it; the Dukes exerted great powers until the French Revolution. Throughout this time they exercised control over every aspect of life, and took a special interest in the cultivation of vines and production of wine. They banned some grape varieties, ordered poor quality vineyards to be uprooted and many of the wines have not changed their style since that time. It was their commitment that created the world famous wines of Burgundy that we know today.

The Dukes were also great lovers of the arts, and Burgundy enjoyed its own spectacular Renaissance. The greatest Dutch and Italian artists, sculptors and craftsmen were employed, and Dijon was one of Europe's most artistic centres. Mozart was introduced to France by the owner of the Romanée vineyards.

During the French Revolution, however, many of the lords and large landowners were executed, the power of the church curbed, and much of the land confiscated.

Above: The thirteenth-century wine press at the Abbaye de la Bussière sur Ouche, near to Chateauneuf.
Below: There are many fine examples of elegant architecture throughout Burgundy including the vine-clad Château Corcelles.

Instead of a handful of hugely powerful landowners, the land was divided into thousands of small plots which still exist today, and which have shaped the Burgundian countryside since the 1870s.

ART AND ARCHITECTURE

Both art and architecture figure prominently in Burgundy's history and an abundance of both survive to further add to the pleasures of visiting the region. During the Middle Ages, the Church largely dominated both artistic and architectural developments. The abbeys were great seats of learning and teaching. Clairvaux, under St Bernard, was famed for the size of its library in the twelfth century, and this period also marked the age of chivalry, inspiring great epic works and plays. There were strolling minstrels and their *chansons de geste* (ballads) were very popular in the courts. The Renaissance flourished under the Dukes of Burgundy, and many of Europe's greatest artists, sculptors and craftsmen were hired to embellish and adorn many of the châteaux, churches and other buildings. Bossuet was born in Dijon in the seventeenth century and became a literary giant, and other writers of this period included Vauban, Madame de Sévigné, and Bussy-Rabutin. The eighteenth century was famed for Réstif de la Bretonne and Piron, the nineteenth century boasted Lamartine, born in Mâcon, and Burgundy's literary

giants of the twentieth century include Colette, Henri Vincenot, Marie Noël, Jacques Copeau, Achille Millien and Maurice Genevoix.

The art of Burgundy falls generally into four categories — Gallo-Roman, Romanesque, Gothic and Renaissance, and many fine examples of all four can be seen throughout the region. Great efforts have been made to preserve the character of the region, and many more recent buildings were designed to harmonise with their older neighbours. There are examples of classical art incorporated into buildings in the sixteenth and seventeenth centuries, and the most obvious examples of more recent architecture are to be found in bridges and other metal structures, reflecting the work of designers such as Eiffel.

Gallo-Roman art

There are many examples of Gallo-Roman buildings and monuments dating from the first century BC to the third century after Christ. The Roman town uncovered at Alésia is worth a visit, as are excavations at Autun, Alesia, Châtillon-sur-Seine, Dijon, Entrains, Saint-Père-sous-Vézelay, Sens and Vertault.

Romanesque art

Many of the best examples of Romanesque art are seen in the numerous splendid churches found throughout the region. Pre-Romanesque buildings from the eighth and ninth centuries and earlier, were frequently made from rough hewn stones with almost crude carvings. It was around the ninth century that the capitals at the top of the columns were first decorated, sculpted in situ, and this art form was taken to exceptional levels during the Romanesque period which started in the tenth century, and was at its height in the eleventh and twelfth centuries. The Romanesque period was important not only because of the richness of its art, but also because this was manifested in the buildings as well. It was a time of great revival and scores of new churches were being built or restored to a new splendour.

One of the first examples of early Romanesque architecture was the basilica over the tomb of St Benigne which was started in 1001 and unfortunately, totally destroyed by fire a hundred years later. The Church of Saint-Vorles in Châtillon-sur-Seine is still standing and the earliest parts date from the tenth century with its rough stonework and primitive decorations. The Burgundy Romanesque style first appeared in Cluny, with its typical broken barrel vaulting, much stronger than traditional arch vaulting, and allowing much greater flexibility of design. This new style also allowed churches to be much taller and lighter, and three storeys of vaulting and openings are common throughout Burgundy. Cluny was also important because it started a new school of sculpture which led to lifelike representations of people and animals as well as motifs, especially on capitals, tympanums

and doors. Gislebertus, the Burgundy master stonemason, was one of the finest exponents of this religious sculpture. Romanesque painting also flourished, although less survives today. Fine examples, however, can still be seen in the crypt at Auxerre, in the choir at Anzy-le-Duc, and at Cluny and Berzé-la-Ville. There are many striking similarities between Romanesque and Byzantine art.

Cistercian architecture, typified by Fontenay, appeared in the first half of the twelfth century, and while part of the Romanesque school, is noted for simplicity and symmetry of design rather than ornaments and decoration.

Gothic art

Typical Gothic architectural features such as pointed vaulting, gargoyles, flying buttresses and rose windows, started to appear from the mid-twelfth century. It was first used at churches in Vézelay although the flying buttresses were added nearly 200 years later. A more specific Burgundian Gothic style appeared in the thirteenth century, characterised by apsidal chapels, high apse, and pillars of different thicknesses made possible by the use of sexpartite vaulting, and often a gallery above the triforium. External decorations include cornices. As the thirteenth century progressed the architects' skill increased, and the churches became much taller, thanks to the builders' skill in constructing vaulting which although thinner, was able to support greater weights. This new vaulting construction made the churches appear even lighter and more elegant. Even more flamboyancy was introduced into Gothic architecture in the fourteenth century, but little of this was implemented or remains to be seen in Burgundian architecture. Gothic sculpture can best be described as more earthy than Romanesque, so much so, that most of it was destroyed during the puritan wave that followed the Revolution. Examples can still be seen, however, in churches in Vézelay, St Père, Dijon, Auxerre and Semur-em-Auxois. One of the best examples of the even more flamboyant realism of the fourteenth century style of sculpture is the Charterhouse of Champmol, which is so ornate and cost so much that it almost bankrupted the Duchy. By the fifteenth century, things had calmed down, and sculptures were simpler and lifelike, without unnecessary embellishments.

There are still lots of very good examples of secular Gothic architecture to be seen, especially in Dijon, Flavigny-sur-Ozerain, Sens, Beaune and Châteauneuf. Ornate galleries and balconies involving intricate working in stone or wood are often a sign of this style of architecture.

Renaissance art

The sixteenth century saw the birth of the Renaissance in France, and it was particularly noticeable in Burgundy because of its close ties with Italy. The church of St Michel in Dijon is a fine example of the transition from Gothic to Renaissance with its Gothic nave and magnificent Renaissance façade. Architecturally, the Renaissance style was exemplified by majestic horizontal lines, semicircular arches and sculptures drawing on Greek and Roman traditions for their inspiration. In the second half of the century, highly ornate decorations were incorporated in building designs and one of the best examples of this is the beautiful gateway into the Law Courts in Dijon.

It is said that a tour of Burgundy is a journey through the last 1,000 years of architecture. It is a journey well-worth making.

Opposite: The elegant Château at Meursault. The region is the largest white wine producer in the Côte d'Or.

The Burgundy region is so compact and so well serviced by main roads that it is very easy to tour by car, even from a central base. The following two itineraries, however, have been developed to allow you to comprehensively tour Burgundy staying at different places each night. A full list of hotels and restaurants is provided to allow you make reservations where necessary. Both tours take about a week but can be adjusted to suit specific interests and timetables. The first tour starts and finishes in Auxerre, and the second begins and ends in Dijon. Together, they provide a thorough exploration of Burgundy — cultural, historic and gastronomic and, of course, allowing every opportunity to enjoy the magnificent wines of the region. Not everyone will want to do the entire tours so the itineraries list all the sights and towns met along the way, as well as suggested detours. Additional information is given in the gazetteer which follows each chapter.

Tour One
400 miles (640km)

Starts from Auxerre. Take the N6 north to Joigny and Sens. Return to Joigny and take the D943 and D3 and then south on the D955 to Toucy. Continue south on the D955 through St Sauveur-en-Puisaye to the major crossroads at St-Amand-en-Puisaye. Then head north on the D90 through St Fargeau and Bléneau, past the seven river locks at Rogny and on to Châtillon-Coligny. Take the D37 north through Châteaurenard and on to the N60. Turn right for a short distance on the N60 and then turn left on the D34 and then the D32 for Ferrières, then head south on the N7 to Montargis. Take the N7 south through Les Bézards to Briare, Cosne, and La Charité-sur-Loire to Nevers, and then follow the D977 to Prémery and then the D977B to Corbigny, and then either the D34 or D985 to Clamecy. You can then either take the N151 north through the Yonne Valley to Auxerre and then the N6 south-east to Avallon, or cut across by taking the D951 east, through Vézelay to Avallon. From Avallon take the N6 east for a short while, and then the D954 to Semur-en-Auxois and Alise-St-Reine, and then the D19 via Fontenay to Montbard. Take the D980 north to Châtillon-sur-Seine. Then take the D965 to Laignes, D953 south to connect with the D905 and head north-west through Ancy-le-Franc to Tonnerre, and follow the D965 through Chablis back to Auxerre.

This tour takes in Auxerre, Joigny, Villeneuve, Sens, La Ferté-Loupière, Toucy, St Saveur-en-Puisaye, Sreigny, St Amand-en-Puisaye, St Fargeau, Châtillon-Coligny, Châteaurenard, Ferrières, Montargis, Briare, Cosne, La Charité, Pogues les Eaux, Nevers, Prémery, Varzy, Corbigny, Clamecy, Avallon, Semur-en-Auxois, Alise-St-Reine, Fontenay, Montbard, Châtillon-sur-Seine, Laignes, Ancy-le-Franc, Tonnerre, Chablis.

Tour Two
375 MILES (600KM)

From Dijon take the D905 west, then the D977B south past Commarin and a turning to the left to the abbey at La Bussière-sur-Ouche, to Châteauneuf and then north-west to Pouilly-en-Auxois. Stay on the D977B to Saulieu, and then take the D6 west and then D20 and D10 north to Avallon. Follow the D957 to Vezelay, and then the D36 and D944 south, through Lormes to Château Chinon. Continue south on the D27 past Mont Beuvray to Luzy and take the N81 north-east to Autun, then south on the N80 to Le Creusot. You can cut the trip by driving east on the N80 to Chalon-sur-Saône, and north on the A6/A31 back to Dijon, or continue south into the Mâconnais.

From Le Creusot take the N80, then the D28 and D983 and D980 which runs north-west through Mont-St-Vincent to Montceau-les-Mines. Follow the N70 south to Paray-le-Monial, then the N79 east through Charolles to Mâcon, and on to Bourg-en-Bresse. Take the D975 north to St-Trivier-de-Courtes, then the D2 west through the Pont-de-Vaux. Follow the D15 to Cluny, then the D981 north to Cormatin, then the D14 east through Brancion to Tournus. The route then heads north following the N6 through Sennecey-le-Grand to Chalon-sur-Saône. From Chalon you can take the A6 to Beaune and back to Dijon, or the D19 to Beaune, and then the wine route N74, or A6 to return to Dijon.

This route takes in: Dijon, Châteauneuf, Pouilly-en-Auxois, Saulieu, Avallon, Vézelay, Lormes, Château-Chinon, Autun, Le Creusot, Montchanin, Bianzy, Montceau-les-Mines, Paray-le-Monial, Charolles, Mâcon, Bourg-en-Bresse, Montrevel, St-Trivier-de-Courtes, Pont-de-Vaux, Cluny, Cormatin, Tournus, Sennecey-le-Grand, Chalon-sur-Saône, Chagny, Meursault, Beaune, Nuits-St-Georges and Gevrey-Chambertin.

Gazetteer

The numbers 1 or 2 after each entry indicate in which tour they can be visited. This gazetteer is arranged in alphabetical order.

Alluy *(1)*

The town is worth a visit because of its church with an unusual twelfth-century crypt. The arch bands of the sunken vault rest on short embedded shafts. There are thirteenth-century paintings over the altar.

Alise-St-Reine *(1)*

10 miles (16km) north-east of Semur-en-Auxois, on the slopes of Mount Auxois 1,335ft (407m) and overlooking the site of the Battle and siege of Alésia in 52BC. The town is named after Alésia, an ancient settlement of Gaul. In 52BC the Roman legions under Caesar had been defeated by the Gauls further south, near Clermont Ferrand. As they moved north to regroup, they were surprised by the Gauls under Vercingétroix on the plain of Les

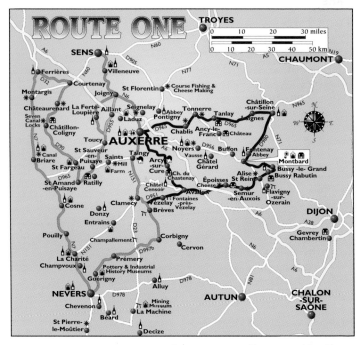

Laumes, close to Alésia, and although heavily outnumbered, the Romans were victorious. The Gauls fled into Alésia and were then besieged. The Romans completely surrounded the settlement with two defensive lines of mounds, trenches and moats. The line closest to Alésia was to prevent Vercingétroix from breaking out, and the second, outer line was to protect Caesar's troops from attacks from any Gauls sent to try to break the siege. The defences were so strong that Caesar's legions were able to hold off an attack by a huge force sent to relieve the Gauls. The relief army, estimated to be 250,000 strong, eventually withdrew and Vercingétroix surrendered, and

was eventually executed by Caesar having been held prisoner in Rome for six years.

There has always been great debate about the location of the battle and siege site and in 1861 Napoleon III ordered excavations in the area to try to resolve the argument. The four-year excavation unearthed the Roman fortifications and a huge amount of artefacts associated with a large military presence. There is now a statute to Vercingétroix, and close to it, a landmark indicator shows the map of the site, indicating the site of the Gallic fortress and the Roman positions. There is a great viewpoint over the area from the summit of

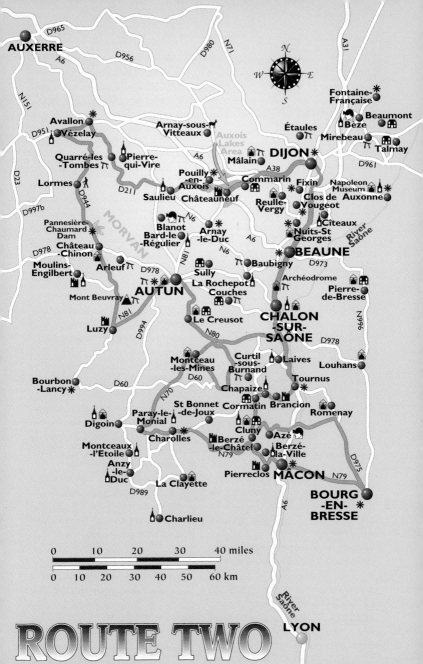

AUXERRE

D965
A6
D956

D880
N71
A31

N
W E
S

Fontaine-
Française
Beaumont
Étaules
Bèze
Mirebeau
Avallon
D951
Vézelay
Arnay-sous-
Vitteaux
Auxois
Lakes
Area
DIJON
Talmay
Quarré-les
-Tombes
Pierre-
qui-Vire
Mâlain
Commarin
A38
D961
Lormes
D211
Pouilly
-en-
Auxois
Saulieu
Châteauneuf
Fixin
Reulle-
Vergy
Napoleon
Museum
Auxonne
D23
D944
D997b
Pannesière-
Chaumard Dam
Blanot
Bard-le
-Régulier
N6
Arnay
-le-Duc
A6
Clos de
Vougeot
Cîteaux
Nuits-St
Georges
River Saône
Château
-Chinon
D978
MORVAN
N6
BEAUNE
D973
Moulins-
Engilbert
Arleuf
D978
Sully
La Rochepot
Baubigny
Archéodrome
Pierre-
de-Bresse
AUTUN
Couches
Mont Beuvray
N81
Luzy
D994
Le Creusot
CHALON
-SUR-
SAÔNE
N80
N996
Montceau
-les-Mines
D60
Curtil
-sous-
Burnand
Laives
D978
Louhans
Bourbon
-Lancy
D60
N70
Chapaize
Cormatin
Tournus
Brancion
St Bonnet
-de-Joux
Romenay
Digoin
Paray-le-
Monial
Charolles
Cluny
Azé
Berzé-
la-Ville
D975
Montceaux
-l'Etoile
Anzy
-le-
Duc
Berzé
-le-Châtel
N79
La Clayette
D989
Pierreclos
MÂCON
N79
BOURG
-EN-
BRESSE
Charlieu

0   10   20   30   40 miles

0 10 20 30 40 50 60 km

River Saône

ROUTE TWO

LYON

Purgatory Mountain, reached from Mussy-la-Fosse. There have been excavations in the town itself. The heart of the Gallo-Roman town which has been uncovered dates from the late first century AD Frankist era. It is on the centre west slopes of Mount Auxois and discoveries include the theatre, forum, commercial and crafts districts, with sanitation and a Merovingian church. Further excavations are trying to find traces of the earlier Gallic settlement. The museum contains many fascinating exhibits from the excavations. Both museum and the excavation sites are open from spring to October. This battle is said to be the finest fought by Caesar.

Sainte-Reine was a young Christian woman, beheaded in the third century, after refusing to marry the Roman Governor. The Fountain of Sainte-Reine is said to have sprung up on the spot where she died, and its waters were claimed to have curative properties which still attract pilgrims.

Ancy-le-Franc (1)

Eleven miles (18km) south-east of Tonnerre, the town is noted for its fine Renaissance château, with beautiful inner court and lavishly decorated apartments, which were fully restored during the nineteenth century. Most still feature their original furniture and fittings. The château was built in 1546 by Antoine III of Clermont-Tonnerre, Grand Master of Waters and Forests, and was designed by the Italian Sebastiano Serlio. The interior was decorated by Il Primaticcio, who also worked on Fontainebleu. In 1684 the château was sold to Louvois, Louis XIV's Minister of War, and in the mid-nineteenth century, it reverted back into the ownership of the original family. The bedrooms with their paintings and murals are delightful, and the chapel, with its wood carvings and frescoes, was decorated by the Burgundian Ménassier. There are guided tours of the apartments and galleries and a small car and carriage museum in the grounds.

Anzy-le-Duc (2)

Situated 12 miles (19km) south of Paray-le-Monial. The Romanesque church with its three-tiered octagonal tower, is one of the most beautiful in southern Burgundy, and dominates the surrounding countryside. The church, inspired by Lombardy architecture, was built in two stages in the eleventh century, using local deep-ochre limestone. The projecting transept is capped by a cupola, and the nave, built last, spreads over five bays. The decorations of the capitals and brackets of the main doorway's cornices, are one of the finest and earliest examples of Burgundian Romanesque sculpture.

Arcy-sur-Cure (1)

The hump backed bridge across the river, which divides the town, makes a good photo opportunity. The two main sights are the Caves and the Château du Chastenay.

There is a path through the

massive limestone caves, which is suitable for the elderly and disabled. The guided tour lasts forty-five minutes. Although there are many caves and they stretch deep into the hills, most are not open to the public. Part of the Grande Grotte is open with its stalactites, stalagmites and other interesting formations. There is also a path along the river Cure which passes many other cliff caves, as yet not open to the public.

The small Château du Chastenay was built between 1549 and 1550 on the site of a fourteenth-century fortified manor house. It was used by the Templars as an alchemy, and has an interesting hexagonal tower which was a later addition. There is a small museum in the town hall with exhibits on the history of the area from the Stone Age to Roman times.

Arnay-le-Duc (2)

A charming old town with a lot of history. It saw action during the religious wars between the Protestants and Catholics, and it was here that the aunts of Louis XVI were arrested as they fled the Revolution. The fifteenth-century Church of St-Laurent has a domed vestibule, added in the eighteenth century. One chapel contains a fine Renaissance ceiling and a fifteenth-century wood gilt statue of St Michael, and the one opposite has a sixteenth-century pietà. Behind the church is Motte-Forte tower, all that remains of a castle destroyed during the religious wars.

The Maison Régionale des Arts de la Table, is a permanent exhibition about food, eating and cooking traditions in the area. It is in the former ancient Hospices St Pierre in rue St Jacques. About 8 miles (13km) to the west is Manlay Church, a well restored fourteenth-century forti-fied building with two towers and a square keep rising over the choir.

Arnay-sous-Vitteaux (2)

The zoo has more than 3,000 animals, as well as pleasure gardens. Locals come to buy the many species of young animals that have been bred in captivity, everything from bantams and white peacocks to Tibetan yaks. Open daily 10am to 7pm. ☎ 80 49 64 01.

Arleuf (2)

A Roman theatre dating from the first century AD has been discovered in the area known as Les Bardiaux. The semi-circular theatre is on a slope overlooking the surrounding countryside, and the excavation has revealed a number of interesting artefacts.

Autun (2)

Originally named *Augustodonum*, the second capital of the Eduens, and founded by the Romans under Augustus in 15BC as the 'sister and rival of Rome' to take the place of Bibracte (Mount Beuvray). It had many fine buildings and public monuments but it declined rapidly in the third century after repeated attacks. Today, one of the two original theatres remain, one of the largest in Gaul, plus impressive sections of the ramparts, the Arroux and St André gateways, the former which led to the Agrippa Way, and the Celtic-style Temple of Janus — although it was never dedicated to this god — with part of its 80ft (24m) tall tower intact. You can also visit the Pierre de Couhard, a Roman burial monument, pyramid-shaped, which is just outside town, close to the Cascade de Brisecou. Both the monument and waterfall can only be reached on foot, but there is a good path.

Autun prospered again during the Middle Ages, thanks to the patronage of Nicolas Rolin, who was born in the town in 1376. He became Chancellor to the Duke of Burgundy and John, one of his sons, became Bishop of Autun. It was John who added the belfry to the cathedral in 1462 after the previous structure had been struck by lightning. If you have the breath you can walk the 230 steps to the top.

The fifteenth century stone spire of the Cathedral of St Lazare (Lazarus) dominates the town, and the cathedral, largely built between 1120 and 1130 is regarded as one of the masterpieces of Cluniac art. The massive nave, flanked by side aisles, has seven large bays and there is a semi-circular apse, flanked by two chapels, beyond the two-bay choir. The nave is so large because it was built to accommodate the large numbers of pilgrims. The elevation is triple storey with broken arches, semi-circular windows and cruciform pillars rising to the base of the arch bands of the broken cradle vault

ceiling. On the Romanesque base of the apse, a Gothic vault has replaced the former barrel vault allowing the chancel to be raised. The magnificent sculptured biblical scenes, particularly on the capitals, are believed to be the work of Master sculptor Gislebertus. The most spectacular sculpture, however, is the Last Judgement which covers the tympanum and the lintel of the central doorway. Other Gislebertus carvings, such as Eve, can now be seen in the Rolin Museum. The Chapter House, built in the early sixteenth century, also has many fine biblical scenes carved in stone. Ingres's painting of the Martyrdom of St Symphorien is in a chapel to the north of the nave. To the north of the cathedral is the Fountain of St Lazare, built in the mid-sixteenth century by the Cathedral Chapter.

The Rolin Museum, in rue des Bancs, is housed in the fifteenth-century home of the Chancellor, which was substantially rebuilt in the nineteenth century. It contains many exhibits unearthed from the excavation of Bibracte, as well as displays about life in Autun in Roman, medieval and Gothic times. Exhibits include Gallo-Roman tombstones, bronzes, mosaics, the quite magnificent twelfth-century sculpture The Temptation of Eve, by Gislebertus, and the fifteenth-century painting of the Nativity by the Master of Moulons.

The St Nicolas lapidary museum, in rue St Nicolas, is partly installed in a Romanesque chapel whose apse is decorated in biblical murals. It contains Gallo-Roman and medieval lapidary collections.

The Natural History Museum, in rue St Antoine, concentrates on the Burgundy region with exhibits of minerals, fossils, birds, insects and animals.

Other places of interest include the Town Hall and its library which contains rare manuscripts and the Lycée Bonaparte, a former Jesuit College, with its very ornate wrought iron grille, dating from 1772. Napoleon studied here in 1179 when it was a military academy. About 4 miles (6km) south of the town, you can climb up to the granite Liberation Cross, erected in 1945 after the liberation of Autun. The path starts just beyond the entrance to Château Montjeu.

Tourist Information Office is at 3 ave Charles-de-Gaulle ☎ 85 52 20 34.

Auxerre (1)

This is a picture postcard town built on the hillside which slopes down to the Yonne, and the capital of Basse Bourgogne. There are many lovely old buildings in the narrow, winding streets which fan out from the Place de Cordeliers, the main square, an attractive harbour for pleasure boats and the surrounding vineyards of Chablis. It is the birthplace of poet Marie Noël, who died in 1967, and Paul Bert, physiologist and minister in the Third Republic, who died in 1886. Auxerre started as a small Roman settlement called *Autessiodurum*, established near the Gaul village of *Autricum*. By the middle of the third century it was already a thriving town because of its location on the main trade roads between north and south. Joan of Arc visited the town twice in 1429, the second time at the head of an army on its way to Reims for the coronation of Charles VII, and Napoleon stopped in Auxerre on his return from Elba and was welcomed by Marshall Ney.

The Chapel of the Vistandines has a number of Roman burial stones, a large stone horse, and the famous Gallo-Roman statue of Venus of Gyl'Evêque. It is open during the summer.

The Art and History Museum, open all year, has many exhibits found in the area, and these are now being combined as the Musée Saint-Germain. The Tour de l'Horloge, is the nearby fifteenth-century clock tower with a seventeenth-century two-faced timepiece, which was part of the city's defences close to the Gaillarde gate. There is a plaque to Cadet Roussel in the passage beside the tower.

St Germain Abbey has Carolingian crypts — the *Saintes Grottes* — and the oldest frescoes known in France, dating from the ninth century. Part of the crypt is believed to date from the early fifth century and two lateral naves are thought to have been added between AD493 and AD545 by Queen Clotilde. The chapels were added in the ninth century and these contain the frescoes, including the very rare fresco depicting the martyrdom by stoning of St Etienne (St Stephen). Demolitions during the nineteenth century have separated the twelfth-century church built on the crypt from the fine Romanesque bell tower surmounted by the tall eight-sided stone spire. Restoration work on the church continues to reveal many treasures from when it was a great seat of learning, attracting scholars and pilgrims from across Europe.

St Etienne Cathedral was started in the eleventh century, destroyed in the thirteenth century and then took 300 years to completely rebuild. The church is believed to have been built on the site of an even older sanctuary dating from AD400 but destroyed early in the eleventh century.

The Gothic church was built over the fine eleventh-century crypts with a triple central nave of six groin vaulted bays supported by huge pillars. It contains many treasures including the rare thirteenth-century Ogival art masterpiece, the Romanesque with its rare frescoes, including one depicting Christ riding a horse, on the arched ceiling.

Museum Lablanc-Duvernoy has an important collection of regional porcelain and Puisaye earthenware, housed in a fine eighteenth-century mansion. There are also tapestries, paintings and furniture. The Gallo-Roman site of Escolives-St-Camille is close by. There is a small natural history museum in the botanic gardens off boulevard Vauban.

The Church of St Eusebe, has a fine twelfth-century Romanesque tower surmounted by an octagonal stone spire built in the fifteenth century. In the heart of the pedestrian precinct and close to the clock tower are two statues sculptured by François Brochet. They are of Marie Noël, one of France's most important twentieth-century poets, and Cadet Roussel, an Auxerrois bailiff during the Revolution. The Church of St-Pierre-en-Vallée has a fine Romanesque façade and very ornate tower.

You can get a good photograph of the town from across the Paul-Bert bridge, and if you want to enjoy the many old half-timbered houses, take a walk around the place de l'Hôtel-de-Ville, and rues de l'Horlogue, de Paris, du Temple and Sous-Murs. Tourist Information Office 1-2 quai de la République, ☎ 86 52 06 19

Auxois Lakes (2)

This is a great outdoors area with more than 100 miles (161km) of well-marked trails around five reservoirs used to regulate water levels in the Burgundy Canal. The protected area is also rich in flora and fauna. You could easily spend a week, pleasantly strolling around the lakes and exploring the many picturesque villages en route, such as Mont-St-Jean, and the châteaux of Eguilly, Commarin and Châteauneuf.

Auxonne *(2)*

A former fortified garrison town on the Saône, where Napoleon Bonaparte served as a young artillery lieutenant between 1788 and 1791. Aged 18, he studied at the Royal Artillery School in Auxonne having completed his earlier training in Valence. He returned to Corisca in the late summer of 1789, and did not return to his post until early 1791. He left Auxonne in April 1791 having been promoted to lieutenant. The Bonaparte Museum is in the tower of the castle built by Louis XI, although it was altered and added to considerably between the eighteenth and nineteenth centuries. The museum has exhibits about Napoleon, the Gallo-Roman history of the region, and more recent local history. His statue stands in front of the Town Hall.

The Church of Notre-Dame dates from the thirteenth century but was added to over the next 300 years, and substantially redecorated in the nineteenth century, when many statues and gargoyles were added. The twelfth-century Romanesque tower is part of an earlier church. The church is noted for its sculptures, especially in the sixteenth-century porch and chapels.

Avallon *(2)*

This is a delightful old town with many pretty streets to explore and ramparts to visit. It was heavily fortified in the Middle Ages because of its important strategic position, and was the scene of several battles. The huge fortifications gave the citizens a false sense of security because in 1432 a band of mercenaries led by Jacques d'Espailly, managed to scale the ramparts and take the town by surprise. The Duke of Burgundy, Philip the Good, who had been campaigning in Flanders, raced back with his army, besieged the town and used huge catapults to fling great boulders against the ramparts. Although the walls were badly damaged, the Duke's troops could not dislodge the mercenaries and reinforcements were summoned. Before the Duke could attack again, however, d'Espailly slipped away at night abandoning his men, most of whom were killed when the town was retaken.

There are good views from walks along the ramparts with its many towers and bastions. The tree lined Promenade de la Petite-Porte follows the course of the old ramparts and is a delightful walk.

Points of interest include the eighteenth-century hospital, the sixteenth-century Auxerroise Gate with its neighbouring watch tower, the Vaudois, Beurdelaine and Escharguet Towers, Bastion of Côte-Gally, and Tour du Chapitre and Tour du Gaujard. The Beurdelaine is the oldest tower, built by John the Fearless in 1404 but strengthened over the next 200 years.

The ancient Collegiate Church of St Lazare was built in the twelfth century on the site of an earlier fourth-century crypt. Much of the church was destroyed when the tower collapsed and had to be rebuilt in the fifteenth century. Main points to note are the interesting elevations in the nave, the curious mixture of arches and groined vaulting, the two original magnificently decorated front doorways, and the many fine sculptures and carvings. The church got its name in the eleventh century, when Henry the Great, Duke of Burgundy, presented it with the head of St Lazare, a relic considered so sacred that it attracted thousands of pilgrims, and the church had to be substantially enlarged. Adjoining the church are the remains of the Church of St Pierre which was mostly destroyed during the Revolution. The nave which survived is now used for occasional exhibitions. The Tour de l'Horloge, with its turrets and belfry, sits astride the rue Aristide Briand and is one of the original fortified tower gates.

The Musée de l'Avallonais, open all year, has a remarkable and mixed collection of exhibits found during excavations by Professor A Leroi-Gourhan of the Cure valley between 1946 and 1963. Exhibits date back 50,000 years and include burial items, Gallo-Roman artefacts, the first-century AD lapidary collection of the Sanctuary of Montmarte discovered in 1822, and third-century mosaics, as well as paintings, jewellery, armour and religious sculptures. There is also a collection of fifty-eight prints by Georges Roualt depicting the horrors of war, and paintings by other artists including Toulouse-Lautrec and Callot.

The Costume Museum in rue Belgrand, is housed in a mansion dating from the seventeenth and eighteenth century, and the theme changes each year.

Azé (2)

The caves of Azé cover about 1 mile (2km) of galleries and two can be visited. Excavations have found remains from the Middle and late Stone Age and evidence that the caves were used by man until the Middle Ages. In the cave floor, a layer of much older clay has revealed bones of lions and bears. A river runs through the second cave.

The Cave Museum, open in the spring and summer, houses many of the exhibits found in the caves, including an impressive collection of minerals, silex, bones, weapons, tools, earthenware and coins — from the Acheulean period to the Middle Ages.

Bard-le-Régulier (2)

The town is 11 miles (18km) west of Arnay-le-Duc, with the twelfth-century Church of St Jean the Evangelist, formerly part of the Priory. The church was built on a slope which explains the rises in the floor. There are many stone statues, some dating back to the thirteenth century, an elegant octagonal tower dating from the end of the seventeenth century, and magnificent fourteenth century carved stalls. There is a nearby path to the Bard Signal Station offering good views.

Baubigny (2)

The remains of a medieval vineyard village have been found, mentioned in local records from 1285. Some of the houses were abandoned in 1348 during the plague and others were burnt down by mercenaries from

Opposite: The Hôtel-Dieu is a fifteenth-century masterpiece of Gothic art, with its paupers ward, chapel, apothecary's quarters, tapestries and fine furniture.

Chagny in 1360. Excavation by a Franco-Polish team started in 1965 and the extensive site can be visited by taking the path from the stone coloured washhouse of Baubigny which ascends the cliffs.

Béard (1)

Until recently this tiny twelfth-century cruciform church was used as a barn, but it has been painstakingly restored. It has a delightful steeple with two tiers of twin openings rising above the transept dome.

Beaumont-sur-Vingeanne (2)

This little village, north-east of Dijon, is noted for its pretty eighteenth-century château set in 16 acres (6 hectares) of parkland. It was built around the mid-1720s by Abbot Claude Jolyot, the chaplain to the king, as a refuge from the pressures of the Royal Court.

Beaune (2)

A charming ancient town unashamedly dominated by the wine trade, and surrounded by many of the world's most prestigious vineyards. There are countless opportunities to taste wine, and huge volumes are stored in the maze of cellars under the town. Beaune was originally a Gallic settlement, then a small Roman camp and then the seat of the Dukes of Burgundy until the fourteenth century, when they moved it to Dijon. The old town is still charming with its narrow cobbled streets nestling inside the massive ramparts that surround it. The huge fortifications date from the

fifteenth century and when the French King annexed Burgundy after the death of Charles the Bold in 1477 his army was unable to take Beaune. It was only after a lengthy siege that the starving citizens were forced to surrender. The ramparts are well preserved and you can walk almost all the way round the town on them, or drive round if you do not want the 1 mile (2km) plus walk. Many of the original towers and bastions survive including the impressive St Jean and Notre-Dame Bastions, and altered Filles and St Martion's Bastions.

The Hôtel-Dieu is a fifteenth-century masterpiece of Gothic art, with its huge paupers ward, chapel, apothecary's quarters, tapestries and fine furniture. It also has the polyptych *The Last Judgement* by Roger Van der Weyden. Founded as a charity hospice in 1443, the sombre, plain exterior belies the splendour inside, especially the magnificent Flemish-Burgundian courtyard. There is a fascinating fifteen-minute presentation depicting life in the kitchens during the fifteenth century. Throughout its life, the Hôtel-Dieu has served as a hospital and in 1971 became a hospital for the old and infirm of the area.

Before entering, note the interesting weather vanes bearing coats of arms, bell tower and elegant 100ft (30m) spire. The roof of the entrance porch is also charming, with its three slate gables and ornate pinnacles, and beautiful ornate iron work on the door.

The cobbled Cour d'Honneur has

to be one of the most magnificent courtyards anywhere, with its old stone well, and surrounded by the main building and wings with their magnificent patterned and multi-coloured glazed tiled roofs. Another charming feature of the roofs is the double row of alternating dormer windows and the many ornate turrets. At first floor level there is a gallery running the length of the building with elaborate wood-working and timber columns and supported by elegant stone pillars.

The Great Hall, more than 170ft (52m) long, almost 50ft (15m) wide and more than 50ft (15m) high, is equally impressive with its magni-ficent painted ceiling, and even more so when you appreciate that it was built as the poor ward. The ends of the massive beams are carved with grotesque heads. Originally it con-tained twenty-eight huge four-poster beds, all positioned in such a way that all the patients could see into the chapel. On Saints Days and other special occasions the beds were covered in splendid brightly coloured woven bedspreads, and some of these can be seen in the Polyptych Room. A life size painted wooden statue of the seated, bound Christ, dating from the fifteenth century, dominates one end of the hall, and note the skull peeping from underneath the tunic. The chapel's beautiful altar piece by Roger van der Weyden and commissioned by the Hospice's founder, Nicolas Rolin, can also now be seen in the Polyptych Room.

Other places of interest include the splendid collection of tapestries in the St Louis Room; the Pharmacy; Kitchens; St Nicholas Room with its exhibits telling the history of the hospice; St Hagues Room which has been authentically reconstructed to show how a ward would have looked three centuries ago and St Anne's Chamber, dedicated to the work of the nursing nuns.

The Museum of Burgundy Wine, in rue Nicolas-Rolin, in the former fifteenth-century home of the Dukes of Burgundy, has documents and tools concerned with the vineyards and the making of wine from ancient times to the present, and there are antique wine presses and vats in the cellar to the left of the entrance. There is also a scale model of the town's original fortifications.

The Musée des Beaux Arts, open during the summer, has a fine collection of Gallo-Roman sculpt-ures from the region, including carved burial stones and monu-ments, as well as other objects found during excavations, and a collection of fifteenth- and sixteenth-century paintings, mostly by Flemish, Dutch and French artists. Local artist Felix Ziem, who died in 1911, is also represented.

The ancient Collegiate Church of Notre-Dame was built at the be-ginning of the twelfth century, and is a fine example of the Cluny style, despite later additions. It has a six bay nave with broken barrel vaults, arch bands on pilasters, a three-storey elevation with wide arcades and side aisles. The higher sections of the apse, porch and unfinished towers date from the thirteenth and fourteenth centuries, and the side chapels from the fifteenth and sixteenth centuries.

The Church of St Nicolas, in the old wine merchants quarter, is a good example of transitional architecture between the Romanesque and Gothic styles. If you are interested in photography, visit the Musée Etienne-Jules-Marey in rue de l'Hôtel de Ville. Marey, who was born in Beaune, invented the *fusil photographique*, the first rapid-fire camera able to shoot twelve frames per second.

There are many opportunities for wine tasting in Beaune including: *Marché aux Vins*, rue Nicolas-Rolin *Halles aux Vins*, rue Sylvestre Chauvelot
Maison Calvert, blvd Perpreuil
Maison Patriarche et Fils, rue du Collè
Cave des Cordeliers, rue de l'Hôtel-Dieu
The Tourist Information Office is in the rue de l'Hôtel-Dieu. ☎ 80 22 24 51.

Just to the south of Beaune is the Château de Pommard, an elegant mansion built in the eighteenth century. It can be viewed from the entrance, and you can visit the caves and taste the wines.

Beaune-Tailly (2)

The town is 4 miles (6km) south of Beaune. From Beaune take the D18 to Tailly, then the D23 for Merceuil. From the A6 if heading south, exit at the Beaune-Tailly interchange, if driving north, take the Beaune-Merceuil exit. It is a great way to discover the history of the region from the Stone Age to the Romans. The Archéodrome of Burgundy museum, with indoor and outside exhibits, depicts life through the ages with reconstructed life-size neolithic huts and dwellings, a Gallo-Roman temple, fortifications, farms, craft workshops and so on. Open year round and explanatory leaflets in English.

Berzé-la-Ville (2)

The Priory Chapel of the Château des Moines has Romanesque paintings, and is considered a masterpiece of Clunisian art. The chapel was built by St Hugh alongside Berzé Priory, one of the residences of the Abbots of Cluny, and miraculously escaped being destroyed by fire at the beginning of the twelfth century. The magnificent paintings were not discovered until 1887 when layers of covering distemper were removed. The main painting, more than 13ft (4m) tall, decorates the semi-domed apse and depicts Christ in Majesty.

Berzé-le-Châtel (2)

The medieval castle was started in the thirteenth century and building, mostly on impressive fortifications, extended over the next 200 years. It has thirteen towers and two keeps, and there are guided visits of the walls.

Bèze (2)

A charming little market town on the banks of the river of the same name which is a tributary of the Saône. It has a number of very old buildings including the old seventeenth-century priory, and eighteenth-century church with fourteenth-century belfry and sundial. Also of interest nearby are the Source of the Bèze with its fast flowing spring, and the Grottes de Bèze, a series of water etched caverns offering a short underground boat ride.

Bibracte (2)

The museum houses many of the exhibits found during the excavations of this Gallic town on the top of Mont Beuvray. There are guided tours of the remains. See also Mont Beuvray.

Bissy-la-Mâconnaise (2)

The late Romanesque church has a rustic porch leading to a single nave with fine timber work above, and there is a turreted staircase built against the tower. It is surrounded by typical houses of the Mâconnais.

Blanot (2)

This small village at the foot of Mont-St-Romain, is noted for the three well preserved Merovingian tombs which can be seen at the priory near the church. These are part of a sixth- and seventh-century necropolis, which has still only been partially explored. Little of the fourteenth-century priory remains, but parts of the living quarters and cloisters can be seen, along with two towers (one fourteenth century), and the round tower which dates from the fifteenth century. The stone covered eleventh-century church has a beautiful Romanesque bell tower

with a festoon of Lombardian arcatures, and the apse is decorated by an intricate frieze beneath the eaves. Just outside the neighbouring hamlet of Fougnières, you can explore a series of caves although the half mile (1km) path is steep in places and head room is restricted. There is a small exhibition of implements and bones found in the caves, which indicate the presence of man up to 100,000 years ago.

Bligny-sur-Ouche (2)

The early Gothic church was formerly the castle chapel. Only the spire with its Lombardian architectural features is Romanesque.

Bois-Ste-Marie (2)

The church was built between 1000 and 1125, and has been beautifully restored. The ambulatory is the oldest part, and unusual in that it is covered with rising groined vaults falling back to the choir.

Bourbon-Lancy (2)

A quaint hill town and health resort overlooking the Loire Valley and noted for its spas, which are said to ease rheumatic and circulatory problems. There are five springs and a new spa house has been built by the park.

The archaeological museum concentrates on local prehistoric and Gallo-Roman exhibits, and is in the eleventh century Romanesque priory of St Nazaire, founded by Ancel of Bourbon, and thus the town's name. The church was never vaulted and has a plastered ceiling.

✳ The massive tower was added in the seventeenth century. Exhibits include a sarcophagus containing the remains of a pilgrim from Compostello in Spain. It also has an exhibition of nineteenth-century paintings and sculptures and art shows are held during the summer. Enquire at the town hall for visits.

✳ 🏛 Other places of interest include the fountain and clock tower, formerly the belfry; the Military Museum with an impressive collection of French army uniforms; and the Bourbon Expo which displays old agricultural machinery and equipment. The Hospice
✳ d'Aligre is noted for the pulpit in the chapel which was given by Louis XIV to Elisabeth d'Aligre, Abbess of St Cyr.

🏛 To the south of town is the near perfectly proportioned Château of St-Aubin-sur Loire, built in the late eighteenth century, and noted for its furnishings, including the tapestries adorning the main staircase. About 4 miles (6km) north-east of the town is another of the signal posts built on top of hills to send messages around the country. There are fine views from the 1,540ft (469m) summit.

Bourg-en-Bresse (2)

This is a market town in the centre of a rich agricultural area. It is especially famed for its poultry, considered so good that it has its own appellation, the only animal product granted that privilege. The town is also noted for its timber furniture, often made from the wood of fruit trees, pottery and enamel work. It has many fine old buildings, including half timbered houses dating back to the fifteenth century. Bourg was a sleepy village until the thirteenth century when it was annexed by the Dukes of Savoy. They created the province of Bresse and made Bourg its capital. In 1536 they briefly reverted to France when the Duke of Savoy refused the French army permission to cross his territory. The French went ahead anyhow, and claimed Bresse and Savoy. The lands were returned to Savoy in 1559, but Bourg became part of France again in 1601 by the Treaty of Lyon following the French king's successful invasion of the region.

The main sight is the church of Brou, on the outskirts of the town. It was commissioned in 1506 and completed in 1532 as a memorial to the husband of Archduchess Marguerite of Savoy who died in 1504 aged only twenty-four after having caught a cold when hunting. Tragically, Margaret died two years before the church was completed. It is a beautiful showy Gothic building with a fine interior and rare triple-arched rood screen. There are many fine marble statues, the three ornate Royal tombs of Margaret, Philibert and Margaret of Bourbon, and seventy-four individual monks' stalls carved in oak in front of the choir, and the original stained glass windows made by Lyon craftsmen. Margaret and her husband, Philibert the Handsome are depicted on the tympanum. The church is the setting for a *son-et-lumière* held on Thursday and weekends from May to September.

The nearby cloisters house an art museum with many works by Dutch, Flemish, French and Italian Masters from the sixteenth to nineteenth centuries.

Other sights include the Church of Notre Dame, started in the early sixteenth century but not completed until more than 100 years later, which accounts for its many styles from flamboyant Gothic to Renaissance. It has fine carved stalls, eighteenth century carved wood pulpit and organ loft, and a thirteenth-century carved black Virgin in a chapel near the choir.

Brancion *(2)*

An ancient market town in the Mâconnais, with imposing fourteenth-century ramparts surrounding the castle, narrow streets and centuries old houses.

The picturesque medieval castle dates back to the tenth century and parts of the original building remain. Most, however, dates from the fourteenth century when it was enlarged by Philip the Bold. There are fine views over the town from the keep. An explanatory leaflet in English is available.

Nearby is the twelfth-century Romanesque church of St Pierre at the far end of the promontory and overlooking the wide Grosne valley. It has a five bay blind nave with broken, barrel vaults buttressed by side aisles. It contains thirteenth-century paintings, and the tomb of Jocerand, the last Lord of Brancion.

Breugnon *(1)*

Site of the Menhir of Pierre Fiche, one of the rare megaliths of the Nièvre region. It is located at the end of the woods, on the left, about 2 miles (3km) out of Clamecy on the N151.

Brèves *(1)*

The town has a display of objects found during the excavation of a massive Merovingian necropolis found recently. More than 200 tombs have been discovered which included fascinating burial objects, jewellery, ceramics, glassware and weapons. Open during the summer for six weeks.

Briare *(1)*

A small town on the Loire noted for its historic canal and ceramics industry. During the early part of the twentieth century Briare was a leading producer of buttons, made from Norwegian felspar.

The Briare Canal, linking the Loire and Loing Canals was started in 1604 and took thirty-eight years to complete its 35 miles (56km). It was the first canal in Europe built to link two others, and the impressive metal 2,170ft (661m) long canal bridge was built by Eiffel. It carries the Loire Canal over the river to connect with the Briare Canal.

South of Briare are two museums housed in a sixteenth-century lime kiln. One contains more than 120 old and vintage cars, and the other deals with history of lime making over the past 400 years.

Above: Roses are often planted beside vines to attract insects in an effort to aid pollination.
Below: Attractive bar in village centre of Chablis.

Above: The Abbaye de la Bussière sur Ouche, near Chateauneuf, south-west of Dijon.
Below: Château des Nobles near Brancion, north of Macon.

Brionnais (2)

This small agricultural region is noted for its many fine Romanesque churches, in particular, Anzy-le-Duc, Berzé-la-Ville, St-Julien-de-Jonzy, Semur-en-Brionnais and Varenne-l'Arconce. There are other interesting churches at Chapaize and Perrecy-les-Forges.

Buffon (1)

A thriving industrial town in the eighteenth century. There is an exhibition about traditional iron working in northern Burgundy.

La Bussière-sur-Ouche (2)

The ancient abbey Church of Notre Dame was consecrated in 1172 and has a Cistercian simplicity. There is also the moated Château of Les Pêcheurs, built by Louis XIII on the site of an earlier castle. It contains a collection of engravings, and there is a small museum about fresh water fishing. Several buildings remain of the thirteenth-century abbey. There are peaceful gardens and an old thirteenth-century wine cellar and press plus dovecote.

Bussières (1)

The hill of Monsard dominates the village and its summit is the site of a neolithic camp and Gallo-Roman settlement. The camp was protected by ditches and earth ramparts. The ditches have long since been filled in, but the earth rampart can still be clearly seen. The views from the summit show why the site had so strategic importance.

Bussy-le-Grand (1)

The twelfth-century church has fifteenth- and seventeenth-century additions. The wooden tie beams over the nave are an usual feature, and the tower is topped by a modern spire. The nineteenth-century chapel used eighteenth-century stalls and wood panelling.

Bussy-Rabutin (1)

The Château of the Count Roger de Bussy-Rabutin, who was Madame de Sévigné's cousin, is well worth visiting. The Count led a troubled life and his satirical writings got him exiled from the Royal Court to Burgundy, and for one, imprisoned in the Bastille. The moated château has a main block, rebuilt in the mid-seventeenth century, and two Renaissance side wings. The highly decorated interior was designed by the Count, presumably to remind him of the splendour of the Royal Court from which he had been banned. Of particular interest are the carved wood panels in the dining room, the painted room in the west tower where he worked, and the two collection of paintings, one showing famous French soldiers through the ages, including the Count, and the other, in his bedroom, of portraits of ladies from the Royal Court.

Cervon (1)

A former Collegiate church built in the second half of the twelfth century and extensively restored. The sculptures in particular, are worthy of note, with the west door, tympanum and covings representing Christ in Majesty.

Chablis (1)

Famous as the home of one of the world's finest white wines, and an attractive little village on the banks of the River Serein. The huge turreted Porte Noel gateway is all that remains of the town's old fortifications. The Maison de la Vigne and Vine de Chablis, part of the tourist office, in rue de Chichée, offers information on wine tasting, wine tours and the wines of the area. There is an English video presentation about the vineyards.

The Church of St Martin, was built in the twelfth century, and housed the relics of St-Martin-de-Tour. There is a finely decorated thirteenth-century Romanesque doorway. Little remains of the Church of St Pierre which was the parish church until the late eighteenth century.

Chalon-sur-Saône (2)

This is a bustling industrial town which has developed largely because of its position on both the navigable river and the Central Canal, built around the turn of the eighteenth century. Because of its location, Caesar made it one of his main supply bases during his invasion of Gaul, and during the Middle Ages it was famous for its huge fur sales, which attracted buyers from throughout Europe, and these still take place each year.

The Cathedral of St Vincent has been rebuilt many times, and all that remains of the original twelfth-century church are the cruciform pillars, nave arcades and groin vaulted side aisles. The sculptured capitals are exceptional, and the neo-Gothic façade, built in the early nineteenth century, is the oldest example of this style in France. The Church of St Pierre, built around the turn of the seventeenth century, was originally the chapel of the Benedictine Abbey. It has many fine statues, carved choir stalls and Regency organ. The Deanery Tower, built in the fifteenth century, was originally close to the cathedral. It was dismantled and rebuilt on its current site in 1907.

The Denon Museum, open all year, and housed in the former Ursuline convent, has a wide range of archaeological exhibits from mammoth bones to Stone Age flints and Gallo-Roman artefacts. It is named after the exceptionally gifted Denon who lived in the town. He was a diplomat, engraver, pioneer lithographer and Egyptologist who eventually became Director of Museums in France under Emperor Napoleon. There is also an important collection of bronze and iron weapons and armour, including a remarkable crested helmet from the late Bronze Age dredged up from the Saône, and the Merovingian period is represented by objects from the excavation of the necropolis at Curtil-sous-Burnand. It is also noted for its collection of seventeenth- and eighteenth-century paintings, and southern Burgundian arts and crafts.

The Nicéphore Niepce Museum, overlooking the river in an eighteenth- century house in rue des Messageries, is the most important photography museum in Europe, tracing the history of photography from its earliest days to the present with photographs taken on the moon. Joseph Nicéphore Niepce (1765-1833) was born and died in Chalon and is regarded as the father of photography. Exhibits include the first camera ever used to take a photograph. In 1816 he succeeded in taking a photograph in a darkroom, and six years later succeeded in taking the first 'real' photograph. There are guided visits of the old town, and many old half-timbered buildings to see, especially around the cathedral. Other sights include the hospice, built in the sixteenth century, with many of its original furnishings and superb carved wood panels, and the Roseraie St Nicolas, 2 miles (3km) north-east of town, with walks through the thousands of rose bushes, gardens and orchards. Tourist Information Office, square Chabas, boulevard de la République, ☎ 85 48 63 55.

Champallement (1)

The woods along the St Révérien road contain the ruins of a large Gallo-Roman village which developed along a Roman road. The site is open to the public and contains many ruins which have been unearthed during the excavations which began more than a century ago. Remains include a rare Gallic octagonal temple surrounded by shops and workshops, a butchers shop, and a theatre. Artefacts found at the site are displayed in the presbytery of Champallement which is open during the summer.

Champvoux (1)

Only parts of the original eleventh-century church remains. The church is noted for its very high choir, the capitals of the monolithic pillars, carved with three rows of stylised foliage and human heads, and outside, the chevet with triple apse.

Chapaize (2)

The spectacular eleventh-century tower of St Martin's church can be seen over a wide area, and is an example of the early marriage of Romanesque architecture and Lombardian art. There are massive round pillars supporting the arches and arch bands which in turn support the groined vaulting above the nave. The church was started in the early eleventh century and built of local limestone, and the tower is 115ft (35m) high.

Charlieu (2)

Little of the original eleventh-century church of St Fortunat remains except the three single bay naves with their richly decorated sculptures. The northern doorway is decorated by carvings of Christ in Majesty, surrounded by the symbols of the Gospel writers, and there are very fine sculptures on the original capitals and piers. The west door has a scene of the Ascension, a common sacred decoration in the Brionnais

Above: The castle of Chateaurenard which overlooks the town, north-west of Auxerre.
Below: The town of Chatillon-Coligny on the Loing and Briare Canal.

region. The church was largely destroyed during the French Revolution.

Charney-les-Macon *(2)*

The Church of St Pierre was built in the twelfth century and has been modified several times, although it still retains much of its Romanesque charm.

Charolles *(2)*

The Maison du Charolais is an information and exhibition centre showing local products, pottery, china, arts and crafts, and the tourist section is in the former Convent of Clarisses. The Charolais region is famous for its meat production and the eccentricity of its spelling. The region and famous white cattle are Charolais, while the sheep, bred in the grasslands of Morvan, Auxois, Charolais and Nivernais are Charollais — with a double 'l'. The sheep are noted for their savoury, almost perfumed meat which is highly regarded by connoisseurs. It is believed that Charolais beef gets its special characteristics — tenderness, flavour and leanness — because the cattle are reared mostly on grass in the open, spending only two or three months in doors over winter. The county of Charolais is one huge pastureland which was initially Burgundian, then Spanish, French and then Burgundian again. This accounts for its wealth and diversity of architecture.

There are the châteaux of Mont-St-Vincent, Digoine and Chaumont at St-Bonnet-de-Joux which is famous for its massive stables. The King decreed that only the Royal Stables could have 100 horses, so the Chaumon stables have ninety-nine magnificent stalls. There are the Romanesque churches of Pulay, Gourdon, La Giche, Mornay and Viry, and if you are a church spotter, you can climb to the summit of Mont Suin, from the top of which it is said you can spot fifty spires and towers. The Route du Charolais is well signposted and allows you to discover the Romanesque heritage, châteaux, landscapes and specialist local produce of the Charolais.

Chassey-le-Camp *(2)*

This is the site of the camp of Chassey which is on a narrow plateau bordered by sheer cliffs and protected at each end by earthen ramparts. Originally thought to have been a Roman camp, excavations have shown evidence of Stone Age culture. The site was then occupied through to Gallo-Roman times.

Château-Chinon *(2)*

The city is the capital of the Morvan and François Mitterand was mayor for many years before becoming President of France, and he was responsible for the unusual fountain in front of the town hall. The Museum of Septennat, on top of the hill as you leave town, houses a collection of official presents and gifts received since 1981 by Mitterand, who was President until 1994. The Costume Museum has an exhibition of French costumes from the eighteenth to beginning of the twentieth century.

Ask at the town hall if you want to visit the permanent exhibition of objects from Stone Age to the Gallo-Roman period found at several sites in the Haut-Morvan, especially the island in Lake Settons, Fou de Verdun, Huis l'Abbé, and Les Bardiaux. There is a viewing table from the summit of the Calvary and good panoramic views.

Châteauneuf-en-Auxois (2)

The fifteenth-century castle is noted for its military architecture — massive thick walls, towers and moat — and was built on the site of an earlier one dating from the twelfth century built by the Lord of Chaudenay. It was presented to the state in 1936. There are guided visits lasting thirty-five minutes, and explanatory leaflets in English. The Church of St Paul has a tripartite façade and the square two-storey tower topped by pyramid masonry, dominates the Sornin valley. The interior has a three bay nave, and very narrow side aisles separated by broken arcades. The village has many old houses, some dating back to the fourteenth century.

Châteaurenard (1)

The village is named after the château, now in ruins apart from some towers, which stood on top of the hill. There are some attractive old houses, and the church, dating from the eleventh century, stands in the grounds of the ruined castle. A seventeenth century château,

privately owned, stands in its own parkland on the left bank of the Ouanne.

Châtel-Censoir (1)

The eleventh-century chancel with triple apse is on a different level from the nave, which like the rest of the church dates from the fifteenth century. The chancel is noted for its capital carvings of strange beasts.

Châtel-Gérard (1)

The Priory of Vausse was founded at the end of the twelfth century by Anséric of Montreal. Although now privately owned, the priory is open during the summer and the surrounding park and countryside offers good walking. The thirteenth-century church and fourteenth-century chapel are Gothic, but the cloister is Romanesque.

Châtillon-Coligny (1)

A delightful town on the Loing and Briare Canal. Admiral Gaspard de Coligny who was murdered on St Bartholomew's Day in 1572, was born here. His daughter married William, Prince of Orange, and the statue in his memory was erected by the Dutch. The writer Colette married in the town and lived there for many years.

The château was rebuilt in the sixteenth century but incorporated many of the original twelfth-century features, including the keep with its secret underground passages. Much of the château was destroyed after the Revolution. The museum, in a former fifteenth-century work-

45

Above: The Clos de Vougeot which dates back to the sixteenth century.
Below (*left*): Paray-le-Monial near Digoin, (*right*): The abbey at Cluny.
Opposite: The Church of St. Martin in Clamency.

house, concentrated on the history of the town and the great families associated with it. Of interest nearby are the series of seven locks on the Briare Canal, built on the orders of Henri IV, during the early seventeenth century, and in permanent use until 1887, when they were made redundant by six new locks.

Châtillon-en-Bazois (2)

Situated on both the charming River Aron and the Nivernais Canal, this is an important boating centre, both for cruising and boat building with a number of yards. There is a sixteenth- century château with much older tower, and the church has some interesting objects, including the fourteenth-century tomb of Jehan de Châtillon, and a carved stone altarpiece.

Châtillon-sur-Seine (1)

At the confluence of the Seine and Douix, this is an important market town and the centre of a thriving wool industry for centuries. Châtillon was the scene of a congress in 1814 between Emperor Napoleon and the armies set against him which were about to march on Paris. Napoleon would not agree peace terms and vowed to fight on, but the armies of Austria, Prussia, England and Russia were too powerful and the Emperor was quickly beaten and toppled. Ironically, it was exactly 100 years later in Châtillon, where the French army took up last ditch positions against a crushing German onslaught. Under General Joffre, the German attack was halted and

allowed the French to counter attack at Marne.

The Archaeological Museum in rue du Bourg is open all year and housed in a fine sixteenth-century Renaissance building. It contains many important proto-historic exhibits from the region, as well as fifth-century ceramics from Mont Lassois, and the fabulous Vix treasure, the highlight of which is a very ornate bronze vase on an iron tripod. It was found in the Royal chariot tomb of a 500BC princess at St Colombe. The vase was fashioned by Greek craftsmen about 1,000BC, and the tomb also contained the burial furnishings of the princess, who was buried in her chariot with her finest gold, silver and bronze jewellery, including a golden diadem. There are also lapidary sculptures found at the sanctuary of Essarois, and exhibits of everyday Gallo-Roman life found at *Vertillum* (Vertault). The town lies on what used to the 'Tin Route' which ran from the Cornish tin mines in England through to the Mediterranean.

The Church of St Vorles sits on a terrace overlooking the town. It was built in the eleventh century and is one of the oldest Romanesque buildings in Burgundy, although it has been greatly altered over the centuries. The first transept before the nave has Carolingian influences, with massive structures and almost a complete absence of interior decoration.

The Source of the Douix is charming, and the spring pours out huge volumes of water, especially after heavy rains. The spring is so prolific because it is fed by many others in the area.

Chevenon (1)

The Church of St Etienne, the oldest parts of which date from the second half of the twelfth century, was secularised during the French Revolution, and is now being extensively restored. Of particular interest is the southern doorway whose arches are decorated with chevrons.

Ciel (2)

This ancient church, which has been partly rebuilt, dates from the latter part of the twelfth century. The church was badly damaged in the seventeenth century when the vault collapsed, bringing down much of the nave. It has an unusual tower with a square base surmounted by a belfry amid high octagonal multi-coloured brick spire.

Cîteaux Abbey (2)

The magnificent birthplace of the Cistercian order, founded by Abbot Robert of Molesme in 1098, and a hugely important religious centre for centuries.

St Bernard joined the abbey in 1112, and after becoming abbot was largely responsible for establishing its power and influence. Cîteaux suffered during the Revolution, the monks were banished and many of the buildings destroyed. The later buildings that survive and other remains, however, make it an atmospheric place to visit.

Clamecy (1)

A lovely old town on the Yonne, a little off the main tourist path, but worth visiting for its old houses, fine collegiate church of St Martin with its imposing tower, and the unusual tale of the Bishops of Bethlehem. William IV of Nevers who died in Acre in 1168 during the Crusades, bequeathed a hospice in Clamecy as a refuge for the Bishops of Bethlehem, in case the Holy Lands fell to the Saracens.

When Jerusalem did fall, the Bethlehem Bishops took up the bequest and were granted their own diocese, which survived until the Revolution. It does explain, however, why such a small town had its own Bishop.

The Church of St Martin dates from the twelfth century, and the museum, open all year, contains many burial furnishings from a proto-historic tumulus, about 100,000 years old, and objects from the Gallo-Roman excavations at Entrains and Compierre, including bronzes, lapidary sculptures, ceramics and coins. It also tells the story of the region, especially the timber industry and how the trees felled in the Morvan forests where floated down the Yonne to Paris as far back as the sixteenth century. The timber was floated down the many tributaries to the town, where it was gathered until the heavy spring rains, when the flood waters carried it down river to Paris. This practice continued until the 1920s when barges were used year round.

Clayette (2)

The town is known for its annual horse racing and has a fourteenth-century moated château, which was modernised in the nineteenth century, and orangery.

Clos de Vougeot (2)

The château is about 10 miles (16km) south of Dijon, dates from the mid-sixteenth century and stands surrounded by vineyards. It is owned by the Confrerie des Chevaliers du Tastevin (Brotherhood of the Knights of the Tastevin), founded in 1934 to promote sales of Burgundy wines. There are now more than 12,000 knights from around the world, and regular meetings and inductions are held at the château. These formal ceremonies with robes and processions are often in front of 500 guests, who then enjoy a sumptuous banquet. There are tours of the château and video presentations about the work of the Confrerie.

Cluny (2)

The old town has changed little over the centuries and is most noted for its beautiful abbey, although this has suffered greatly. The Abbey of St Peter and St Paul was founded in AD910 by William the Pious and dedicated as a centre for teaching and prayer. Within a century it was exerting a tremendous and powerful influence over Christian Europe. For almost 500 years it was the largest church in Europe until St Peter's was built in Rome. It was said at the time that wherever the wind blows, the Abbot of Cluny owns. At the height of its influence, the abbey had more than 10,000 monks and 1,500 establishments dependent on it. The great abbey reflected this power and prestige. Between 1088 and 1109 Abbot St Hugh oversaw the abbey's enlargement which included an eleven bay nave with double side-aisles, two transepts, and apse and ambulatory and five radiating chapels. Although planned to be 450ft (137m) long, the building was extended to just over 606ft (185m) by the addition of a narthex, of three naves and five bays. The building was 96ft (29m) from floor to the top of the vault, and 107ft (33m) to the domes under the tower. In 1760 the abbey closed, and in 1798 the State declared the church public property, and much was dismantled or destroyed over the next twenty-five years. Still standing is the southern arm of the massive transept but it is more than enough to get an impression of how vast the abbey was. The 205ft (63m) high octagonal tower of the Holy Water, is the only one of the original two towers and six steeples. Many of the fine sculptured capitals remain, and some of these and other carved ornaments are on display in the Farinier Museum, formerly a thirteenth-century granary, with a beautiful high, vaulted wooden roof.

The beautiful Romanesque Parish Church of St Marcel was built in 1159 and has three storeys and an octagonal belfry under the pointed brick spire. The frescoed ceiling of the chapel is exceptional.

The Church of Notre Dame was built in the early twelfth century and has some interesting Gothic additions.

The Ochier Museum, in the former fifteenth-century Abbot's Palace with stone floors and giant fireplaces, concentrates on medieval art and archaeology, and has many fine sacred sculptures. The exhibits show the opulence and wealth of Cluny at its height. Guided visits of the abbey start here. You can also visit the Cluny National Stud Farm, founded in 1806, and one of twenty-three in France. It was founded by Napoleon. Cluny has many fine old buildings, such as the twelfth-century house at 25 rue de la République, and the former thirteenth-century mint at 6 rue d'Avril.

Commagny (2)

The church built early in the twelfth century is intact and well preserved. The semi domed apse is noted for its unusual decoration and interesting capitals.

Commarin (2)

The château dates from the fifteenth century but most of the building dates from the seventeenth and eighteenth centuries. The public rooms are mostly furnished in mid-eighteenth-century style, although there are some fine sixteenth-century tapestries.

Cormatin (2)

The château was built around 1620 and later belonged to the Marquess Jacques de Blé, who was influential in the court of Louis XIII. He luxuriously refurbished the building and some of the magnificent rooms from this period, with their original seventeenth-century paintings, can be seen, including the splendid baroque St Cecilia's room. The building is also noted for its huge façades, grand staircase, moats, and grounds with lakes and mazes.

Corvol-l'Orgueilleux (1)

Four sarcophagi, three of them decorated, are on display in the Church of St Vincent de Corvol. They date from the sixth and seventh centuries, and come from the old cemetery of St Maurice at Corvol.

Cosne-sur-Loire (1)

A quiet industrial town on the Loire which was famous in the eighteenth century for its munitions industry with many forges producing cannon, muskets and huge sea anchors, using coal shipped in by river from the Nivernais.

The Church of St Agnan, was built in the eleventh century by Hugh, Abbot of Cluny, and the capitals are decorated with many fine carvings. In the main doorway there are also fine carvings of mythical beasts. There is an exhibition of prehistoric stone tools in the Maison des Chapelains. These and the many Gallo-Roman domestic objects were all found locally. There are also pottery and metal implements from the Merovingian, Carolingian and medieval periods, including the remains of a pottery kiln, and sculptures and carved wooden beams from the Romanesque era.

The Municipal Museum tells the story of the River Loire, and also has many fine paintings. There is a farm machinery museum at nearby St Loup with traditional harvesting machines, and during the season, there are demonstrations of old time harvesting and hay-making, threshing and ploughing.

Couches (2)

Château de Marguerite de Bourgogne still has its keep, towers and high defensive walls, as well as glazed tiles and Gothic chapel. Guided tours are available.

Couches is also the site of the six menhirs, which have been regrouped at the crossroads of the D225 and CV4. The biggest of the menhirs, the tallest in eastern France, stands 23ft (7m), and dates from the late neolithic period. A seventh menhir, which completed the group, has not been found.

Curgy (2)

The granite church has a narrow four bay nave, but three semi-circular apses give it an almost rectangular appearance. The square tower is built above the first bay.

Curtil-sous-Burnand (2)

A Merovingian cemetery has been excavated in the area known as 'Munot', and so far, more than 400 tombs from the sixth and seventh centuries have been found, some of which are on display. These include sarcophagi, stone slab tombs and a scale model which shows just how extensive the original site was. Objects discovered during the excavation are displayed at the Denon Museum in Chalon-sur-Saône.

Decize (1)

The town was built on an island of the Loire and is at the junction of a number of waterways including the Nivernais Canal. The Church of St Aré is in the centre of town and dates from the eleventh century, and is unusual in that it has a Merovingian double crypt built in the seventh century to house the tomb of St Aré of Nevers. He ordered that on his death, his body be put in a boat and floated down river and that he be buried wherever the boat came to rest.

Dicy (1)

La Fabuloserie houses a weird collection of more than 1,000 strange and unusual works of 'art brut'.

Digoin (2)

The town has long been an important pottery centre and prospered after canals were built connecting the Loire and Saône. The museum, open during the summer, has an exhibition of ceramics from the Gallo-Roman workshops in Gueugnon and Coullanges (Allier), as well as moulds and ovens, and the eighteenth-century ceramics industry of Digoin and Paray-le-Monial. The nineteenth-century Church of Notre Dame is a mix of Romanesque and Byzantine styles with a modern tympanum carved in the late 1970s.

Dijon *(2)*

The city grew up around the ancient site of *Castrum* and was the seat of the Dukes of Burgundy, which accounts for its many splendid old buildings, including palaces, churches and monuments. In the fourteenth and fifteenth centuries, Dijon was an international centre for the arts, in the sixteenth and seventeenth centuries it thrived with the Ducal Palace serving as Burgundy's Parliament, and industry has flourished since the eighteenth century. During the Age of Enlightenment and the reign of Louis XIV, Dijon was home to Bossuet, Buffon and St Jeanne de Chantal. Today it is a charming, bustling university city with a number of industries, and much to see and do, a finely restored old town, many fine museums, wonderful restaurants and great wines to enjoy. It also boasts more than 1,500 acres (600 hectares) of parks and open spaces, including the charming Jardin de l'Arqueloise in ave Albert, with more than 3,500 species of plants and trees on display. One of Dijon's greatest achievements is that it has remained remarkably unscathed over the last 1,000 years despite wars and Revolution, and a tour of the city is literally a review of 1,000 years of history, traditions, and architecture both secular and religious. It is also a very busy city with something happening at most times of the year, especially the large antiques fair in May, the street shows in July and August, the international wine and folklore festival in September and the international gastronomic fair at the end of October and beginning of November, which started in 1921 and now attracts more than 200,000 visitors each year. Restaurants compete with each other to put on the finest shows using the best local wines and produce.

There is a city bus service which is convenient and cheap to use, and most of the bus stops have maps of the area, which are very convenient if you want to get your bearings.

The **Cathedral** is built over the tomb of the third-century evangelist St Bénigne, who gives it its name. A basilica was built over the tomb and consecrated in AD535 but it was almost a ruin when, in 1002, a young Lombard monk Guillaume de Volpiano, was sent by the Abbot of Cluny to restore it. The new church took sixteen years to build but all that remains today, after centuries of fires and devastation, is the eleventh-century crypt. The rest of the church dates mostly from the fourteenth century. The carvings are amongst the first known in Romanesque art to use human figures.

The Gothic Church of St Philibert was built in the mid-twelfth century and greatly altered in the fifteenth century. It is now used as an exhibition hall.

The **Archaeological Museum**, in rue Docteur Maret, has a wonderful collection of exhibits dating from prehistoric times to the Merovingian period, including the famous gold bracelet from La Rochepot, weighing almost fifty ounces, and sacrificial figurine offerings carved in stone, bronze and wood found at the Sources of the Seine. It was thought that the springs had healing powers, and if people had aches or pain, they would leave a carving of that part of the body as an offering. That explains why many of the sacrifices appear to be arms and legs. There is also a lapidary collection and a display of religious sculpture on grave stones and other objects.

The **Fine Arts Museum**, in the place de la St-Chapelle, is in the former semi-circular Palais des Etats de Bourgogne, and contains the tombs of Philip the Bold and John the Fearless. Exhibits include furniture, ceramics, weapons, and paintings and sculpture from the Middle Ages to the twentieth century, including works by Rubens, Brughel, Rodin, Monet and Manet. There is also the Granville collection of modern and contemporary art. The ducal kitchens on the ground floor, dating from around 1435, the fourteenth-century Chapter House and fifteenth-century guard room can also be visited.

Philip the Good's Tower in the main courtyard of the Duke's Palace, was built in the fifteenth century, and offers great views over the town and surrounding countryside.

The **Espace Grevin** (Burgundy Wax Museum) in ave Albert 1-er has tableaux depicting scenes from Burgundian history from the sixth century BC to the present. Wine tasting sessions are also held in the ancient cellars.

There are many fine old half-timbered buildings in the Notre-Dame quarter, and Les Halles, is one of the region's finest and busiest covered markets.

The best way to see Dijon is on foot and a good place to start is at the **Tourist Office** in Place Darcy, a short way from the railway station. Also in the square is the *Polar Bear*, sculptured by Pompon, and you can relax and watch the swans on the small lake. At the other end of the square is the **Porte Guillaume**, which opens on to the rue de la Liberté, the town's main shopping area. Turn right, however, into rue Docteur Maret for the Archaeological Museum, and then continue to place St Benigne and the **Gothic cathedral**. Continue on to **Church of St Philibert**, topped by its sixteenth-century spire, and then walk along rue Danton to the former **Church of St Jean** dating from the fifteenth century, and now home to the theatre of the Parvis St Jean. At the chevet of the church there is a **statue of Bossuet** by Paul Gasq. The great seventeenth century prelate was born in this quarter. Walk up place Bossuet with its many fine mansions, into Rue Bossuet for the area known as **Le Coin du Miroir**, with its Renaissance watchtower and half-timbered houses. Turn right into rue de la Liberté for a short distance and you come to the place François Rude, with its fountain topped by the famous statue of Bareuzai, trampling grapes with his feet. There are several delightful cafés in the square where you can sit

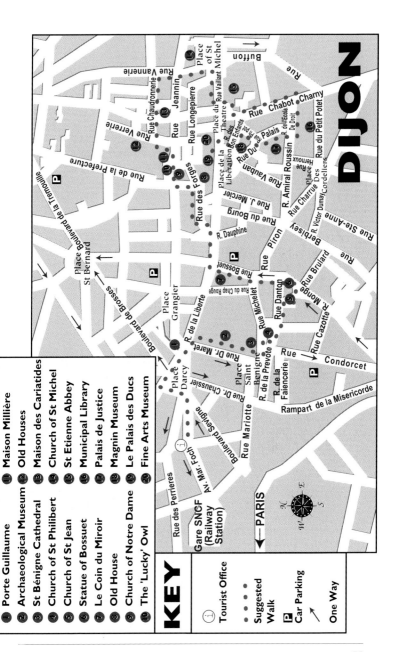

DIJON

KEY

- (i) Tourist Office
- •••• Suggested Walk
- P Car Parking
- → One Way

1. Porte Guillaume
2. Archaeological Museum
3. St Bénigne Cathedral
4. Church of St Philibert
5. Church of St Jean
6. Statue of Bossuet
7. Le Coin du Miroir
8. Old House
9. Church of Notre Dame
10. The 'Lucky' Owl
11. Maison Millière
12. Old Houses
13. Maison des Cariatides
14. Church of St Michel
15. St Etienne Abbey
16. Municipal Library
17. Palais de Justice
18. Magnin Museum
19. Le Palais des Ducs
20. Fine Arts Museum

Gare SNCF (Railway Station)

← PARIS

and enjoy the atmosphere. Cross the square and take the rue des Forges, until the eighteenth century, the city's main street, and admire the many medieval and Renaissance façades. The main tourist offices are in the Hotel Chambellan which has an exceptionally flamboyant Gothic frontage, and an inner courtyard with galleries and spiral staircase.

The thirteenth-century Gothic **Church of Notre-Dame** has an extraordinary frontage with false gargoyles, topped by the Horloge à Jacquemart, a mechanical clock built in 1383, having been commissioned by Philip the Bold. The original clock had a single male figure which struck the hour, in 1610 a female figure was added, and then over the years, more figures. The church's stone owl, the bird symbol of Dijon, has been rubbed smooth by the numbers of people rubbing it for good luck. Inside in a chapel to the right of the choir, is the eleventh-century Black Virgin, which has long been revered. It has been attributed over the years from saving Dijon from disaster, particularly in 1513 when a siege by Swiss soldiers was suddenly lifted, and again in 1944 when it was liberated by the Allies. Legend has it that the siege by the 30,000 strong Swiss army was lifted after the Dijonnais supplied them with barrels of wine. Why they lifted the siege is still a mystery, but perhaps after drinking the wine, they got homesick and thought it was time to leave. A tapestry in the chapel celebrates these two deliveries from disaster.

Continue past the church into the rue de la Chouette, named after the **church's owl** sculpted on a pillar. ✻ Legend tells that those who stroke the bird will gain wisdom and happiness. Further along is the fifteenth-century **Maison Millière**, 🏛 with its rooftop animal decorations, and next door to the **Hôtel de Vogüé**, 🏛 an elegant seventeenth-century mansion, with sculptures by Sambin in the inner courtyard, and multi-coloured tiled roof. Cross into the rue Verrerie, which also has many fine old buildings and decorative sculptures, and houses the antique dealers quarter. Turn right into rue Chaudronnerie for the seventeenth-century **Maison des Cariatides**, 🏛 with its very unusual façade, and then south on rue Vannerie, lined with beautiful eighteenth-century residences and Le Compasseur 🏛 watchtower, into place St Michel, and the Renaissance **Church of St** 🛆 **Michel** built in the fifteenth and seventeenth centuries. There are some remarkable carvings over the central doorway. Take rue Vaillant for the Rude Museum, and the other remaining buildings that formed the former **St Etienne Abbey**. The 🏛 former fifteenth-century abbey church is now the Chamber of Commerce. Turn left into the place du Theatre and then take the rue Chabot Charny south, and then turn right into rue de l'Ecole de Droit for the **Municipal Library** and the 🏛 **Palais de Justice** in the rue de Palais. 🏛 The door to the sixteenth-century palace was sculptured by Sambin. You can also visit the Salle des pas

Perdus and the rich Chambre Dorée.

Take the rue Philippe Pot and admire the sculptures of the Hôtel de Vesrotte, and then cross over into the rue des Bons Enfants for the **Magnin Museum** in the seventeenth-century Hôtel Lantin. The mansion has luxurious furnishings and the exhibits are attractively displayed.

It is then only a few steps into the place de la Libération and the magnificent buildings of **Le Palais des Ducs et des Etats de Bourgogne**. The palace, designed by J Hardouin Mansart, has a magnificent façade dating from the seventeenth and eighteenth centuries, topped by the Philippe Le Bon Tower. Today, it houses City Hall and the **Fine Arts Museum**. For further information: Tourist Information Office, place Darcy ☎ 80 43 42 12

Donzy (1)

The Priory of Donzy-le-Pré was attached to Cluny in 1109. Much of the church is now in ruins but it is still noted for the magnificent tympanum with its carvings depicting the Crowned Virgin holding the baby Jesus. The Mill of Maupertois is now a milling museum open daily from June to October.

Druyes-les-Belles-Fontaines (1)

The twelfth-century Romanesque Church stands close to the springs which give the village its name, and near the foot of the cliffs on which the Counts of Nevers built their castle, now in ruins. The church has a fine semi-circular main doorway, barrel vaulted nave and chapel.

Égreville (1)

A small town with a sixteenth-century covered market and twelfth-century château, rebuilt in the sixteenth century, and remodelled again 100 years later by Maréchal de la Châtre, of the Catholic League. The composer Massenet spent the last thirteen years of his life living and working in the house before his death in 1912. The church dates from the thirteenth century.

Entrains-sur-Nohains (1)

Entrains was formerly a small but prosperous Gallo-Roman town, and excavations have revealed great treasures, including the largest Gallo-Roman sculpture in the Museum of National Antiquities, a seated Apollo with lyre, 8ft (2m) high.

Other finds include a huge theatre, artisans district and blacksmiths, houses, cellars, courtyards, wells and cobbled streets. The exhibition, open during the summer, also contains exhibits from the excavations of the fifth century BC Oisy tumulus, from the Gallo-Roman town of *Intaranum*, and the Merovingian necropolis of Corvol.

Époisses (1)

The village is noted for its cheese matured in Burgundy *marc* (brandy), and its charming medieval château, acquired by the Guitaut family more than 300 years ago and still their home, although they have taken great efforts to ensure the original character and splendour of the house, its outbuildings, moat and fine grounds is preserved. The château has played host to many famous people over the centuries, including Madame de Sévigné and Britain's Queen Elizabeth II. The huge dovecote used to house 1,000 pigeons. The château grounds are open year round and there are guided tours during the summer.

Escolives-St-Camille (1)

There have been settlements here since neolithic times and a thermal baths, built at the end of the third century AD, has recently been excavated. The site includes covered pool, and small separate baths. Part of the baths was built from a large monument with arches, destroyed during an invasion of AD253. The Merovingians converted the baths to a necropolis.

Hundreds of objects from neolithic to Merovingian times are displayed in the exhibition which is open during the summer.

The small twelfth-century church has an octagonal brick built tower and open porch formed by a number of semi circular arcades built over two crypts, one containing the body of St Camile, one of the women who brought the body of St Germain from Ravenna to Auxerre in AD448.

Étaules (2)

North of Dijon is the site of the fortified Chatelet d'Étaules located on a steep rock promontory which provided protection to settlements from the neolithic to the Bronze Age. You can reach the site by a path which starts at the parking area off the RN71 and descends into the Val-Suzon. There is an exhibition of objects found at the site in the village community centre.

Farges-les-Mâcon (2)

A small early eleventh-century church, and an example of Mediterranean Romanesque art, with a blind central nave flanked by side aisles, and a two storey square tower can be visited here.

Ferrières (1)

A small town with winding streets and dominated by the former Benedictine Abbey of St Pierre et St Paul. Its twelfth-century Gothic churchis believed to be on the site of an eighth-century sanctuary. It has fine stained glass windows and statues.

Ferté-Loupière, La (1)

An old fortified market town with twelfth-century church extended in the fourteenth and fifteenth centuries with large biblical murals, discovered at the beginning of this century when layers of distemper were removed. The murals include a 50ft (15m) *Dance of the Macabre* dating from 1480. An English translation of the meaning is available.

Fixin (2)

A village famous for its wines and the monument to Napoleon in the park in the centre of the village, and erected in 1847 by Noisot, who instructed that on his death, he be buried upright, sword in hand beneath the statue so that he could continue to serve the emperor in death. The tiny Church of St Antoine is in the nearby hamlet of Fixey close to the vineyards. The earliest parts date from the Romanesque period and pillars in the nave support the flat stone roof and ease the pressure on the walls.

Flavigny-sur-Ozerain (1)

This was a fortified town in the Middle Ages and parts of the ramparts and gateways can be seen. There are a number of important pre-Romanesque remains within the ruins of church of the ancient Abbey of St Pierre founded in the seventh century. The crypt is all that remains of the two tier apse built around AD758. It is built with small stones and thick barrel-vaults resting on four columns of Roman origin.

The recently excavated Chapel of Our Lady of the Pillars appears to date from the same period.

Fleurigny Château (1)

The thirteenth-century moated château has a charming inner court-yard with views of fine Renaissance façades, and the chapel is of note because of its sixteenth-century stained glass by Jean Cousin.

Fontaine-Française (2)

The scene of a battle in 1595 when Henry IV, although massively out-numbered, defeated the combined armies of Spain and the Catholic Holy League. A monument com-memorates the event.

Fontaines-près-Vézelay (1)

The site of an important Gallo-Roman ironworks, in the public forest of 'des Ferrières' (the iron-workers). Some of the excavated sites can be visited, including the remains of a villa and small temple dedicated to Mercury. Access is signposted from the Vézelay to Clamecy road.

Fontenay (1)

This is the best preserved Cistercian abbey found anywhere and noted for its perfect Romanesque style. It was founded by St Bernard in 1118, took almost eighty years to com-plete, and prospered until the religious wars of the sixteenth century. It is now a UNESCO registered World Heritage site. It was sold as a national asset during the Revolution, and for many years was used as a paper mill. It was bought in 1820 by Elie de Montgolfier, descendents of the pioneers of flying, and has been in the same family ever since. The paper mill closed in 1906 when the abbey passed to Edouard Aynard, Raymond de Montgolfier's son-in-law. He was responsible for the superb restoration and the family continue to maintain and preserve this architectural treasure, which offers a wonderful insight into what life in a large medieval abbey must have been like. You can visit the church, cloisters, chapter room, dormitory, heated rest room, lodge, bakery, infirmary, workshops, gardens, fish breeding ponds and even the abbey's prison. The abbey is set in lovely gardens with many fountains, that gave it its name. The main buildings to survive are the old Minster of Notre Dame and the cloisters. The church is sober and lacks unnecessary decorations. There is staircase in the south transept leading to a small dormitory. Just to the south is the cloister, also simple but less austere than the church, and the chapter house, arcade and scriptorium, where the monks worked on the manuscripts.

Garchizy (1)

The Church of St Martin has a fine octagonal tower, and the first storey is decorated on four sides by a multifoil arcade.

Gevrey-Chambertin (2)

A visit to the Château de Gevrey-Chambertin is well worth it, not only to visit the house and learn about its history, but also to taste the fabulous wines. The original house was built in the tenth century and the wooden floors have been worn so smooth over the centuries that you skate, rather than walk across them. There is much fine wrought iron work and heavy wood furnishings and the sense of history adds the pleasure of drinking the wine, a favourite of Napoleon I. The oldest parts of the church date from thirteenth century and it has a handsome Romanesque doorway.

Gouloux (2)

You can watch clogs being made at the Clogmaker's workshop, open daily from 9am to 12noon and 2pm to 6pm. There are tours every hour.

Gourdon (2)

This small granite church looking out to Mont St Vincent is a merger of Cluniac and Brionnais styles.

Guérigny (1)

There is a permanent exhibition built around a potter's kiln. The pottery was established by a group of artisans whose products were sold throughout the region. Ask at the town hall if you want to visit the exhibition, which is housed next to the school of the Vieux Frêne. The Royal Forges of La Chaussade are now an industrial archaeology museum featuring blacksmiths, steam engines, power hammers, as well as model boats and other exhibits.

Hauteville (2)

The fish bone construction of the façade and north wall of this ancient church dates it to around 1000.

Issy-l'Évêque (2)

Mont Dardon, near the village of Uxeau, was occupied from neolithic times until the Middle Ages. The summit was surrounded by an earth rampart, part of which can still be seen. Recent excavations, not open to the public, have found the ruins of a medieval church. There is a landmark indicator on the summit which points out the various sights that can be seen from the top. There is an exhibition of objects found at the site, in the market town of Issy. It is housed in the old fortified tower known as Luzy.

The Issy Church dates from the eleventh century and combines both Cluniac and Brionnais styles.

Jailly *(1)*

The choir and transept are all that remain of the twelfth-century priory. The later west doorway is noted for its fine decorations.

Joigny *(1)*

A small town nestling in a bend of the Yonne with many fine old buildings and surrounded by vineyards which can trace their history back to the Middle Ages. The inhabitants of Joigny and area were known as the Maillotins, which explains the golden mallet on the town's coat of arms. Marcel Aymé was born here, and worth visiting are the Maison de l'Arbre de Jessé, twelfth-century Porte de Bois and the St Jean and St Thibault churches, both dating from the fifteenth centuries, and both with many fine statues and carvings.

La Celle-sur-Loire *(1)*

Home of the Western Burgundy Folk Museum with exhibits of agricultural and rural life.

La Charité-sur-Loire *(1)*

A charming small town on the Loire with its red tiled rooftops and ramparts, and sixteenth-century stone bridge. The town was founded in the eighth century, on the site of an ancient settlement, when a religious order established itself. The town was frequently attacked by Arab raiders, and little remains from that time. When the Church of Notre-Dame was completed in the twelfth century, it was, after Cluny, the largest in all Christendom and was consecrated by Pope Pascal II in 1107. It was modelled on Cluny and was a major assembly point for pilgrims bound for Santiago de Compostela, being able to accommodate 5,000 people. It has suffered greatly over the centuries, and was badly damaged by fire in 1559, but is nevertheless a remarkable example of both Cluny and Romanesque architecture. The Holy Cross Tower is decorated with blind arcatures, and a strange frieze lightened by two storeys of openings. There are many elegant carvings and sculptures, particularly on the capitals, tympanum of one of the walled up doorways, and the lintel. The fifteenth-century door leads out to the Place St Croix, where the ten bay nave once stood, and the sixteenth-century passage de la Madeleine leads to the Grande Rue.

The town museum, which is open during the summer, has exhibits from the recent excavations of the first Cluniac church, and the archaeological section depicts everyday life in a medieval monastery.

Clayette, La *(2)*

The Motor Museum features about 100 old vehicles in the grounds of the castle.

Laduz *(1)*

The Museum of Rural Arts and Crafts has exhibits of local crafts and

Above: The small town of Joigny nestles on a bend of the River Yonne
has many fine old buildings and is surrounded by vineyards.
Below:The church at La Ferté Loupière is noted for its murals.

Above: Le Rochepot is noted for its turreted Château de Rochepot, with its glazed tile roof and wooden drawbridge.
Below: Le Château du la Verriere and glass furnaces at Le Creusot.

a display of thousands of tools. There is an annual exhibition on local folklore and culture.

Laives (2)

The Church of St Martin stands alone on the hill. It was built in the eleventh century and restored in the fifteenth. It is noted for its large square tower with unusual openings.

La Machine (1)

The Miners Museum is at 1 ave de la République and depicts the life and work of miners over the centuries. There are mine reconstructions with galleries, engine rooms, and shafts, which can be visited by following the signs opposite the museum.

La Rochepot (2)

The twelfth-century church is roofed with lava-stone, and the door is flanked by columns crowned with exceptional capitals, but the village is most noted for the fairy tale many turreted Château de Rochepot, with its glazed tile roof and even a wooden drawbridge.

Régnier Pot was a knight captured by a Sultan during the Crusades. When he refused to marry the sultan's daughter, he was thrown to the lions, but by a miracle, he emerged the winner, and because of his valour was given his freedom. He returned to France and bought the château that now bears his name. The house was built in the twelfth century, was refurbished by Rochepot, and later fell into some disrepair, but it was beautifully restored in the nineteenth century to its full former glory. You can see the ancient kitchens, dining room, chapel and guard room, and enjoy a tasting at the end of the visit. You can also see the 230ft (70m) well which cost a fortune to sink through the hard rock. Rochepot ordered the well to be dug, determined after his experiences in the dry desert, never to be short of water again.

Laroche-St-Cydroine (1)

The ancient priory church was built at the end of the eleventh century under the jurisdiction of the Benedictine Abbey of La Charité-sur-Loire. An octagonal two tier tower is typical Cluniac style.

Le Creusot (2)

The Museum of Man, Metal and Industry, open all year, is in the Château du la Verrerie, at the side of the main town square. A considerable number of ancient cannon surround the château. Two cone-shaped buildings by the château are old glass furnaces. One houses an exhibition and the other a theatre, where Sarah Bernhardt sang.

Ligny-le-Chatel (1)

The church is unusual in that the timbered nave and aisles, transept, tower and main doorway are Romanesque and dwarfed by the massive Renaissance choir built between 1554 and 1574.

Lormes (2)

The town has one foot in the Morvan and the other in the Nivernais. It is very popular during the summer and makes a good touring base. There are several pleasant walks in the area and fine views from the modern church built in Romanesque style on top of the hill, and from the summit of the Mont de la Justice, 1,540ft (469m) high, and 1 mile (2km) north of town.

Louhans (2)

This is a flourishing market town, noted for its poultry and the pig and cattle markets. Things to see include the Hôtel Dieu and apothecary. The ancient hospital dates from the seventeenth century and the apothecary's quarter from the fifteenth and sixteenth centuries. One of its main features is the beautiful long archway in the Grande-Rue. The *Independent*, the region's newspaper, closed down in 1984 and the printing room and offices are preserved as they were left, as a museum.

Luzy (2)

The medieval town is still dominated by the fourteenth-century tower on top of the hill, and the Town Hall houses a fine collection of seventeenth-century tapestries. There is a Tibetan monastery in the Château de Plaige, just over 10 miles (16km) to the west on the D114. It was founded in 1974 as a education centre. The pagoda temple is in the grounds.

Mâcon (2)

The town sprawls along the banks of the Saône and is surrounded by vineyards. The river is increasingly popular with boaters and there is a bustling marina in the town. The town has always been important as a trading centre because it is at the crossroads of the main commercial routes between Paris and the Mediterranean, and Switzerland and Germany and the Atlantic.

The Cathedral of St Vincent was built in the eleventh century, but all that remains is the narthex with its strange tympanum and sculptures.

The Municipal Museum is located in the former seventeenth-century Ursuline Convent and tells the history of the region from the earliest presence of man. It has exhibits from the palaeolithic and neolithic periods and the excavations at Solutré, Charbonnières, Verchizeuil and La Senétrière. One display features a reconstruction of the late Bronze Age necropolis at La Bergère, with funeral urns and other burial furnishings. There are ceramics and a potter's kiln from the Gallo-Roman period found by the Saône at Varennes, and an exhibition of weapons and armour from the Middle Ages. The museum is open all year.

The Lamartine Museum in the Hôtel Sennecé, houses a collection of documents about the statesman and poet Lamartine who was born in the town in 1790, as well as furniture, tapestries, paintings and objets d'art. There are good views of the town from the Pont St Laurent, built across the Saône in the fourteenth century and restored in the nineteenth century. Tourist Information Office, 187 rue Carnot ☎ 85 39 71 37.

Mailly-le-Château *(1)*

This is an old fortified town overlooking the Yonne with its fifteenth century bridge and beyond to the Morvan. The fortified Church of St Adrian dates from the thirteenth century, and the charming little twelfth-century cemetery chapel has been well restored.

Mâlain *(2)*

Situated to the west of Dijon, used to be called *Mediolanum*, and was a prosperous Gallo-Roman town between the first century BC and the third century AD. Excavations have so far uncovered a whole urban quarter with main street, square, shops, artisans workshops, warehouses, houses with cellars and complete with underfloor heating systems. Some of the items found are now on display in Dijon, but there is an exhibition on site of many articles used in daily life, both for work and play. The museum and site are open during the summer.

Marcenay *(1)*

Parts of the church date from the eleventh century. The sarcophagus of St Vorles, once curate of Marsannay, lies in the crypt.

Marcigny *(1)*

There is a fine ceramic collection on display at the Musée de la Tour du Moulin, in the fifteenth-century mill tower which is open from 1 March to 1 November. The tower was owned by the Benedictine priory and is now devoted to local history as well as its pottery and ceramic exhibits. The town also boats many fine old half-timbered houses.

Mars-sur-Aller *(1)*

The attractive Church of St Julien, built in the eleventh and twelfth centuries, has a very unusual transept with a huge apse surrounded by three naves. There are many fine capital carvings.

Massay *(2)*

The small eleventh-century church is typical of early Romanesque art with single-timbered nave. The fine two tier bell tower has Lombardian features, and the base of the eleventh-century font is believed to be Roman.

Mazille *(2)*

This early twelfth-century church has changed little over the centuries. It is noted for its decorated columns and elegant square tower, topped by a pyramid stone tower.

Metz-le-Comte *(1)*

This small church was built in the twelfth century within the walls of the castle birthplace of the Counts of Nevers. The original nave pillars and their capitals remain. There is a half buried sanctuary under a roof of large flat stones.

Milly-Lamartine *(2)*

The Manor of Lamartine was built in 1705 and the nineteenth-century poet Lamartine spent his childhood here, returning each autumn to oversee the grape harvest.

Mirebeau-sur-Bèze (2)

Aerial photographs in the 1960s revealed the outlines of a Roman fortress on the left banks of the river, complete with ramparts, barracks and streets, and outside the walls, baths and civilian buildings. Excavations, which started in 1968, have unearthed the command headquarters and baths, and on the right bank of the river, a Gallo-Roman sanctuary with two temples and wells, and a wealth of objects have been found. Ask at the town hall for permission to visit.

Montargis (1)

In the middle of an area noted for hunting and fishing and the town, the capital of the Gâtinais, stands at the junction of three canals, the Loing, Orléand and Briare, which adds considerably to its charm. Many of the houses are on the canals, and flowering bushes and hanging baskets over the water make for very good photographs. Other places to see are the Girodet Museum in the Hotel Durzy, dedicated to the painter Anne-Louis Girodet (1767-1824), who was born in the town, although there are works by many other artists and sculptors; and the Gâtinaus Museum, in a fifteenth century tannery, and devoted to local archaeological finds.

Montbard (1)

An industrial town specialising in steel, on the River Brenne, and birthplace of the great scientist and naturalist Buffon in 1707. His greatest achievement was the massive *History of Nature* published in thirty-six volumes over forty years. Although Keeper of the King's Garden and Museum (now the Jardin du Roi) in Paris, he spent much time in Montbard laying out the gardens of his château, and doing much of his writing there. The château, originally built around the tenth century, was mostly rebuilt by Buffon, and the gardens now form the Parc Buffon. The Tour de l'Aubespin was used by Buffon for wind experiments, and now offers fine views of the town, and the Tour St Louis, built in the tenth century and the birthplace of the mother of St Bernard, was Buffon's study. Buffon's Forge, which can be visited, was built in 1748 about 4 miles (6km) north-west of town, both to conduct experiments and to put into commercial use, many of his ideas about the use of iron and other metals. Buffon is buried in the small chapel next to the church. The museum is open all year although you may have to ask at the Town Hall for it to be opened. Most of the exhibits were found locally and include objects from burial mounds, mosaics from Nan-sous-Thil, iron and bronze work, worked bone, ceramics, glassware and coins from Perrigny-sur-Armançon.

Mont Beuvray (2)

The site of the Gallo-Roman town of Bibracte, capital of the Eduens. Here, in 52BC Vercingetorix was made commander of the armies of Gaul with the task of repelling Caesar's

Legions. The area is now largely covered by forest, although parts of the town and ramparts were uncovered in excavations at the end of the nineteenth century. A complete restoration of the site is now under way and many of the objects found are on display in the Rolin Museum. Others, together with photographs and maps of the site, can be seen in the town hall at St-Léger-sous-Beuvray.

Montceaux-l'Etoile (2)

The main doorway of this small twelfth-century church is regarded as one of the best examples of Brionnais sculpture. The tympanum and lintel are carved from the same block and have outstanding carvings.

Montceau-les-Mines (2)

The town expanded rapidly following the discovery of coal nearby and many industries were established to take advantage of this cheap fuel. The fossil museum has exhibits dating back 300 million years, and most were discovered during mining operations. Two miles (3km) from town is Blanzy, which also thrived because of the coal, and it has a fascinating mining museum.

Montenoison (1)

The ruins of a thirteenth-century castle built by the Countess of Nevers, are on the summit of this hill, which at 1,368ft (417m), is one of the highest in the Nivernais. There is a path from the chapel to the Calvary which offers panoramic views.

Montréal (1)

A medieval town with ramparts, narrow, twisting streets, and many fine old half-timbered houses. The Porte d'En Bas, the town's lower gateway, has some thirteenth-century features, and the twelfth-century Gothic church is noted for magnificent carved oak choir stalls and alabaster altar piece. The town's upper gateway, beside the church, acts as the belfry.

Mont-St-Jean (2)

Some of the eleventh- and twelfth-century features of this church, built within the castle walls, remain. The Romanesque crypt contains the remains of St Pélagie.

Mont-St-Vincent (2)

The granite church, built in the eleventh century, sits on one of the highest spots in the Saône-et-Loire. It lost its tower in 1743.

The Régnier Museum, housed in the restored fifteenth-century salt warehouse, contains mostly exhibits from the region. There are Stone Age tools from the camp at Chassey, Gallo-Roman objects from the small craftsmen's town of Portus, and Merovingian artefacts from the necropolis at St-Clément-sur-Guye.

Morvan (2)

This is an area of ancient granite hills, forests, lakes and streams, and meadows full of wild flowers in the spring and summer. The name comes from the Celtic for 'Black Mountain' and there are many

Druidic remains, such as standing stones, in the area. It is still very much Gallic in spirit. The local dance is *la bourrée*, very similar to a Scottish jig, and bagpipes are played at any celebration.

Today the region covers 500,000 acres (200,000 hectares) and straddles four departments. Entry points to the Morvan area are through Avallon, Saulieu, Arnay-le-Duc, Autun, Luzy and Corbigny. The region includes the Haut-Folin which rises to 2,962ft (903m), Mont Beauvray, with its special place in Gallic history and Bibracte, the camp on the summit, which is considered the most important archaeological site in France, and was once the richest town in Burgundy with iron forges and acclaimed jewellers. Mont Beauvray is also the closest mountain to Paris.

The Morvan National Park, designated in 1970, makes a worthwhile detour with its pretty lake, hill and forest walks and drives. It is also rich in wildlife, with deer and wild boar, and many rare wild flowers and butterflies.

Moulins-Engilbert (2)

Moulins-Engilbert nestles beneath the old castle and is famous for its busy weekly Charolais cattle market, held each Tuesday. The former Benedictine priory is just south of town on top of the hill at Commagny. There is a small Romanesque church and the well-preserved façade of the fifteenth-century lodge, which housed guests, tower and belfry.

Nevers (1)

On the banks of the Loire, Nevers is on the western borders of Burgundy, and famous for its earthenware and ceramics which have been produced since the sixteenth century. It used to have strong ties with the north Italian city of Mantua and many famous Italian craftsmen worked in Nevers in the ceramics industry. There are many fine examples of this work in the Frédéric Blandin Municipal Museum, reached via the Promenade des Ramparts in the abbey gardens. It also houses many of the objects discovered during excavations in the area over the past 200 years. There are many sculptures, tomb stones, glassware, figurines in earthenware and pottery, and mosaics from Villars. Parts of the old medieval wall and the massive Porte du Croux, built in 1393, can be seen behind the museum.

Other places of interest include: the Cathedral of St Cyr-Ste Juliette, built during the Middle Ages, with a 160ft (49m) high square tower, on a site that has seen five churches since the beginning of the sixth century. The church is unusual in that it has two apses, one Romanesque and the other Gothic. The Palais des Ducs opposite the cathedral has a strong Italian influence because of the Clèves and Gonzagues families, while the Church of St Etienne, built in the eleventh century, is noted for the symmetry of its design, and soberness of its interior. St Gildard's Convent was where St Bernadette Soubirous of Lourdes spent the last thirteen years of her life. She died in 1879 and is buried here. There is a small museum dedicated to her life. The Ducal Palace has a rich Renaissance façade although there is no public access inside.

Nivernais, is the province of Nevers and Burgundian by adoption. It gave the River Loire its first great castle, the Château du Nevers, and its first vineyards at Pouilly and Sancerre. Today it has many beautiful towns and villages such as Nevers and La Charité-sur-Loire, with are steeped in history, as well as more modern attractions, such as the motor racing circuit at Magny-Cours.

Nolay (2)

The birthplace of the politician Carnot, whose statue stands in front of the house where he was brought up. There is a fourteenth-century covered market, and the fifteenth-century church, largely rebuilt in the seventeenth century after a fire, has an unusual stone belfry.

Noyers (1)

A pleasant old wine town with many well preserved old buildings, especially around the main square, Cornmarket and rue du Poids-du-Roy, and surrounded by ramparts and towers.

The small municipal museum has exhibits discovered locally, and the exhibition changes each summer. The Museum of Art Naïf, in an eighteenth century mansion, has a remarkable collection of old and modern naive paintings, notably by

Bombois, Bauchant and Bois-Vive. The huge Church of Notre Dame, built in the fifteenth century, has a mixture of Renaissance and Gothic styles.

Nuits-St-Georges (2)

A pretty little town long noted for its fine wines. The reputation of the wines was greatly enhanced when Louis XIV's physician ordered the king to drink it with each meal as a tonic.

The museum contains a wealth of objects found during the excavations of the Gallo-Roman town of Bolards, illustrating the craftwork and religious activities of the town and including a rich collection of funerary sculptures. There are also objects from the excavation of the Merovingian ruins at Argilly.

The 50 acre (20 hectare) Bolards site can be visited although only part has been excavated. You can see some houses with cellars and sanctuaries, including a large temple to Apollo and the sanctuary of Mithra. There is a small military museum with exhibits from the Battle of Nuits-St-Georges on 18 December 1870 when the French defeated the Prussins. The thirteenth-century Romanesque Church of St Symphorien has many examples of fine wood carving.

Pannesière Chaumard Dam (2)

The massive dam, north of Château Chinon, is more than 1,100ft (335m) long and holds back a 5 mile (8km) long reservoir. Further downstream is a large hydro electric station.

Above The fabulous Château Corton-André at Aloxe Corton.
Below: (*left*): Nuits St. Georges, (*right*): Château de Savigny, near Beaune.

Paray-le-Monial (2)

The town is dominated by the magnificent Basilica of the Sacred Heart, built at the end of the eleventh century, and fully restored over the last 150 years. It is a miniature version of the abbey church of Cluny. The nave rises on three storeys, and the many semi circular bays and three tiers of openings allow the light to flood in. The north doorway is famous for its carvings based on Arab art.

The Relics Chamber, behind the basilica, has a twice-daily slide show (10am and 3pm) about the life of St Marguerite Marie, who had her numerous visions of Jesus in the late seventeenth century, after taking her vows at the convent at Paray-le-Monial. She was made a saint in 1864 and more than 30,000 people attended pilgrimage to Paray-le-Monial. The church and the saint's relics, still draw pilgrims from around the world. She is buried in the Chapel of the Visitation.

The diorama is staged in the park behind the Basilica. Painted statues represent the life of the saint and the history of the city in twenty-one tableaux.

The Museum of Charolles Porcelain, in the Benedictine priory in ave Jean-Paul II, contains more than 2,000 pieces collected since 1836, and the Musée Hiéron, is devoted to sacred art from the twelfth century, with paintings, sculptures, carvings and vestments.

Parc du Morvan (2) see Morvan

Parigny-les-Vaux (1)

The Church of St Jean Baptiste is unusual in that has two naves side by side, the smaller, northern nave dates from the eleventh century and has a remarkable steeple, the other built post twelfth century, is also Romanesque.

Parly (1)

The Church of St Sebastien was built in the twelfth century on an old feudal mound. It has a fine steeple and decorated door, although the latter is in bad condition.

Perrecy-les-Forges (2)

The Romanesque church dates from 1130, has a fine Brionnnais two-storey bell tower, and is noted for its tympanum carvings and capitals.

Pierreclos (2)

The castle was built in the twelfth century and was not added to until the seventeenth century, so contains many styles of architecture. It is noted for its terraced gardens and fine panoramic views, the guard-room, vaulted cellar, Romanesque chapel, medieval kitchen and spiral staircase. A former lady of the castle was the inspiration for one of Lamartine's works.

Pierre-de-Bresse (2)

The moated castle and Burgundy Bresse museum, set in parkland, has a permanent exhibition about the archaeology, natural history and way of life of the area. The château was built in the seventeenth century from local limestone with a slate roof, and the main block and wings ending in round tours, have classic proportions. It has very ornate stonework, especially in the arching over the main doorway, and a spectacular staircase in the left wing which houses the museum.

Pierre-qui-Vire-Abbey *(2)*

The monastery was established in the mid-nineteenth century by Father Muard, who was born in Sens in 1809. The foundation stones were laid in 1850 on land overlooking the River Cousin, donated by the Chastellux family. It is named after the nearby Druidic rocking stone. Father Muard died in 1854 but the community thrived, and in 1859 joined the Benedictine Order. There is an exhibition room which explains the lives of the monks and their work.

Pontaubert *(1)*

This ancient church was used by the Order of the Knight Hospitallers, and is a fine example of twelfth-century Romanesque Burgundian architecture. The two upper tiers of the tower and the doorway are Gothic.

Pontigny *(1)*

The abbey, the second 'daughter' of Cîteaux, was founded in 1114, and the abbey church was built between 1150 and 1212, at the transition between Romanesque and Gothic architecture. The twelfth- and thirteenth-century buildings that remain are considered one of the finest examples of Cistercian archi-tecture in France, relying on the purity of line rather than decor-ations. The stalls and baroque choir screen were added in the sixteenth and seventeenth centuries. Thomas à Becket was sheltered in the abbey in 1164 having fled Canterbury to escape the wrath of Henry II. He spent six years in France and was murdered in 1172, two years after returning to England.

Pouges-les-Eaux *(1)*

A small spa town close to the Loire with a very peaceful air, good views, and opportunities for a range of sporting activities.

Pouilly-en-Auxois *(2)*

A small town, mostly noted because it stands at one end of the 10,900ft (3,323m) tunnel that carries the Burgundy Canal. The fourteenth-century Church of Notre-Dame Trouvée is named after a long lost statue of the Virgin which was miraculously rediscovered.

Précy-sous-Thil (detour from 1 or 2)

About 10 miles (16km) north of Saulieu, can be visited as a small detour from either tours one or two. It used to be the centre of an important iron industry. At Thil, 11/2 miles (2km) east, is the former fourteenth-century collegiate church with remarkable vaulting and frieze. The castle, built on a Roman camp, dates from the ninth and twelfth centuries, although the keep was added in the fourteenth century.

Above: The abbey at Pontigny was founded in 1114, and the church was built between 1150 and 1212.
Below: St. Amand-en-Puisaye, on the D955, south-west of Auxerre..

Prémery *(1)*

The small town has a thirteenth-century church with an oversize belfry, and the remains of a château started in the fourteenth century with a fortified gateway, and owned by the Bishops of Nevers.

Quarré-les-Tombes *(2)*

The town is named after the many well-preserved sarcophagi from the Middle Ages around the church, which originally came from a large necropolis. More than one hundred stone coffins have been found and it is believed that the necropolis, built around the seventh century, may have contained more than 1,000 tombs. Why such a large necropolis was built is still a mystery.

Ratilly *(1)*

The splendid thirteenth-century château with its huge towers and high walls, is surrounded by a dry moat and set in lovely parkland. There is a pottery, showroom and an exhibition about the potters art. Open daily 10am to 5pm mid-June to end of September. Rest of year Monday to Saturday 3-6pm.

Reulle-Vergy *(2)*

The museum, open during the summer, displays the history, arts and craft traditions of the Hautes-Côtes. There are Stone Age artefacts found at Roche-Morand, neolithic finds from around Vergy, and grave stones fund during the excavation of the Gallo-Roman necropolis at Meuilley-Messanges.

Romenay *(2)*

The museum of Bresse has an exhibition put together by the Friends of Old Romenay, which traces the history of the area from around 6500BC with objects found at Sermoyer, to Gallo-Roman remains and items from the Middle Ages, carved from antlers found in the excavations of a defensive moat at Loisy.

Sacy *(1)*

Restif de la Bretonne was born in Sacy in 1734 under the shade of the church with its eight-sided Romanesque tower.

St André-de-Bage *(2)*

The Church of St André was built at the end of the eleventh century by the Abbots of Tournus. It has a fine octagonal tower, and an elegant masonry spire.

St Amand-en-Puisaye *(1)*

Guided tours of the potters' workshops are available where handmade and industrial pottery is produced.

St Brisson *(2)*

The headquarters of the Maison du Parc Naturel Régional du Morvan, with information about the area and a summer exhibition. The Museum of the Resistance in the Morvan, is in memory of the Maquis, and is open during the summer. There is year-round free access to the Herbularium, which contains more than 160 types of herbs, each labelled for identification.

St Christophe-en-Brionnais (2)

Every Thursday one of France's biggest cattle markets takes place here with up to 4,000 animals being sold. There are all the usual stalls associated with such a large market, and it is a good opportunity to mingle with the locals and try the many regional specialities served. The market is held on Wednesday if the Thursday is a public holiday.

St Éloi (1)

The Church of St Symphorien was built in the twelfth century but secularised during the Revolution and used as a farm building until recently when it was rescued by a society, and is now being restored.

St Fargeau (1)

This is the main town of the Puisaye and developed rapidly after the building of the smelting works. The Renaissance château is a huge pink brick pentagon with six towers crowned with bell towers, built on the site of a tenth-century castle. The largest tower was built in the mid-fifteenth century by Jacques Coeur, the Royal Treasurer and Lord of St Fargeau. Later it was owned by Louis XIV's cousin, Anne-Marie-Louise d'Orléans — La Grande Mademoiselle. She was exiled to St Fargeau after supporting an unsuccessful rebellion by nobles, but the house was in a state of disrepair so she called in Le Vau, the architect of Versailles, to smarten things up. He built the magnificent inner courtyards and refurbished the interior. Louis-Michel Le Pelletier, another owner, is buried in the chapel. As a Deputy in the National Convention, he voted in favour of Louis XVI's execution, but was assassinated the night before the king died, and because of this, he was considered the first martyr of the Revolution. Guided tours of part of the house are available. The château is set in beautiful parkland, and is used for historical pageants. The château farm also makes an interesting visit, as it depicts rural life at the turn of the century.

St Florentin (1)

This is a small industrial town, still with some fortifications and towers, and famous for its cheeses, its excellent nearby freshwater fishing and open-air theatre. During the Revolution, the town was known as Mount Armance. The church on top of the hill took almost 250 years to build. Work started at the end of the fourteenth century but was then disrupted by the Hundred Years War, which is why it started out as Gothic and finished with Renaissance touches. The sixteenth-century stained glass windows are particularly noteworthy for their design and intensity of colour. The fountain was erected in 1979 as a replica of the fifteenth-century original. The water spouting bronze griffins are the originals.

St Germain-en-Brionnais (2)

The church was built in sandstone at the end of the eleventh century, and has many fine carvings.

St Honoré-les-Bains *(2)*

The town has been a spa since Roman times and was very popular in the nineteenth century. The highly sulphured waters are said to be particularly good for respiratory complaint.

St Julien-de-Jonzy *(2)*

The twelfth century Romanesque church is noted for its beautifully carved tympanum, from single sandstone block, and lintel carvings, and the little Brionnais bell tower.

St Julien-du-Sault *(1)*

This small town on the Yonne has a thirteenth-century church with an impressive Renaissance choir, and stained glass windows, some of which date back to the thirteenth century. Other sights include the sixteenth-century timbered Maison de Bois, and the hill top chapel and ruins of a château at Vauguillain, outside town.

St Léger-Vauban *(2)*

The birthplace of orphan Sébastien le Prestre who became Marquess of Vauban and one of the most influential figures in France. The village was known as St Léger de-Foucheret but changed its name to honour its famous son. Vauban was a military engineer in the service of Louis XIV and rose to the rank of Commissioner General of Fortifications, and then Field Marshal. He was responsible for a chain of fortresses along France's borders and was regarded as the best siege director in

Europe. He is buried at a church in Bazoches in the Morvan, although his heart was placed in the Invalides in Paris at the orders of Napoleon I. There is an exhibition about his life in the community centre. The Renaissance Church of St Léger has some interesting and quite modern sculptures.

St Magnance *(1)*

This very fine twelfth-century church contains the carved tomb of St Magnance who was one of the escorts who brought the body of St German from Ravenna to Auxerre.

St Micaud *(2)*

The menhir of St Micaud was re-erected at the beginning of the twentieth century, and is the only one left of a group of three known as Pierre aux Fées (Fairy Stones). There is carving of a horned serpent on one side of the stone, which is thought to be protohistoric.

St Parize-le-Châtel *(1)*

The twelfth-century church is noted for its crypt with massive pillars capped by ornate and unusual carved capitals, including scenes depicting a woman acrobat, animal musicians, mermaid and a miser clutching his purse.

St Père *(2)*

The town stands on the banks of the River Cure, and is noted for its fine Gothic Church of Notre-Dame, built at the beginning of the thirteenth century but not completed until the mid-fifteenth century. It became the parish church and took its name from St Peter's Church which was burnt down during the Wars of Religion. It has a beautiful rose window, elegant belfry and unusual arch with three doorways.

There is the regional archaeological museum nearby located in the former seventeenth-century presbytery. It contains numerous exhibits found at the excavations at Fontaines-Salées, about 1 mile (2km) away.

St Pierre-le-Moûtier (1)

This quiet but important market town, with fifteenth-century ramparts and many delightful old streets and buildings was captured by Joan of Arc in November 1429, in what was her last victory.

The Fontaines Salées mineral springs, rich in salt, have been used by man since the earliest times. Oak trunks, hollowed out by fire, were used to carry the water and nineteen of these wooden 'pipes' have been found. The springs were also believed to have healing powers and excavations have unearthed the remains of a large circular sanctuary as well as an area where sacrificial offerings could be left. Near the temple is a bathing area, dating from the first century AD. The museum contains many exhibits found during the excavation, and at other sites in the region.

The church dates from the ninth century and was part of the Benedictine abbey. Of note are two fine capitals, and the carved tympanum.

St Révérien (1)

The earlier church was built in the twelfth century on the site of an oratory dedicated to the saint, martyred in the third century. The church was badly damaged by fire in 1723, but the chancel survived, and the capitals are especially beautiful and among the best examples of Romanesque art.

St Romain (2)

There is a well-marked footpath from the area known as Le Vieux Château (the Old Castle) to the rocky spur on which a medieval castle once stood. It was built in the twelfth century and added to over the next 400 years. Parts of it have been excavated and there are great views from the hilltop.

The museum has displays from the early Stone Age, artefacts used by first farms, and objects from the Bronze and Iron Ages, Gallic and Gallo-Roman settlements, medieval castles, Carolingian houses and agricultural tools used over the last 400 years. The museum is open during the summer.

St Saulge (1)

This small town has a fine Gothic church noted for its sixteenth-century stained glass windows.

St Seine-l'Abbaye (1)

The abbey, close to the source of the Seine, was built in the thirteenth century, on the site of a sixth-century sanctuary. The church was largely rebuilt in the fourteenth century after a fire, and the façade was added in the following century. Of interest is the beautiful nineteenth-century rose window and the many old tombstones in the transept.

St Thibault *(1)*

This is named after the saint whose bones were presented to nearby priory in the thirteenth century. The priory church has a lovely carved doorway, surmounted by statues, considered one of the finest examples of Burgundian architecture. The choir and apse date from the late thirteenth and early fourteenth centuries. The shrine of St Thibault is in the chapel of St Giles.

Saints *(1)*

The old water mill in 40 acres (16 hectares) of meadows and parkland, is now a farm museum, showing country life through the seasons.

Santenay *(2)*

Opposite the camp of Chassey, on the left bank of the Dheune are a number of ancient sites, a megalithic necropolis and burial tombs from the early Bronze Age, and the Temple of Mercury, excavated by Bulliot during the nineteenth century, which stands on top of the Mont de Sène. Access is by the RN6 from La Rochepot, or by Decize-lès-Maranges and the hamlet of Borgy.

Saône Valley *(2)*

The valley is a boater's paradise, criss-crossed as it is by rivers and canals. Apart from the Saône, there are the Burgundy, Rhine-Rhône and Marne-Saône canals. You can climb Mont Ardoux for fine views over the entry town of Pontailler-sur-Saône, downstream there is Auxonne with its attractive beach and well-preserved buildings, which have earned it a national award for heritage conservation. The river then flows on St-Jean-de-Losne, with France's largest inland marina. Every year on the third Sunday of June, boatmen from all over France come here to celebrate the Grand Pardon. Next is Seurre, like Auxonne a former military town, and now noted for its red brick buildings, which give a very Mediterranean air to this charming town. Visit the Eco Museum with its fascinating collection of vegetables, or stroll around the ramparts and visit the thirteenth-century church.

Saulieu *(2)*

The town is famous for its good food and Christmas trees, more than a million of which are marketed each year. One of the greatest chefs of all time Alexandre Dumaine reigned here for many years, and his traditions continue today.

The Basilica of St Andoche is noted for its remarkable series of sculptured capitals, and is open daily. St Andoche was martyred in Saulieu with two companions in AD177. By AD306 a church had been built over their graves, but this was destroyed by the Saracens. It was rebuilt by Charlemagne, who donated many of its treasures, including his own altar book, now kept in a special shrine.

The François Pompon Museum, considered one of the finest outside Paris, is open all year and has many galleries dedicated to the archaeology of the region, especially objects from palaeolithic and neolithic sites in the Auxois, and the Gallo-Roman town of Saulieu, formerly *Siduolocum*, and area. There are many fine carved funeral stones, and from the springs near the town, many sacrificial carvings, some carved from human bones. It also displays the works of Pompon (1855-1933), the noted animal sculptor, who was born in the town. He worked for a time with Rodin and he received a gold medal at the French Artists' Exhibition.

Seignelay *(1)*

An important town in the Middle Ages and now a pleasant country town surrounded by hills and woods. The château, once owned by Colbert, was destroyed during the Revolution, but the park, tower and gate lodge survived and can be visited. The town hall, formerly the courthouse, was designed by Colbert, and is in the place Colbert, which has many other fine seventeenth-century buildings.

The seventeenth-century covered market is opposite the town hall, and the fifteenth-century Church of St Martial has many Romanesque features from the one it superseded.

Semur-en-Auxois *(1)*

According to local legend, the city was founded by Hercules, although there is nothing to back this up, and the first mention of it dates from AD606 when the monks from the Abbey of Flavigny signed their charter in a village called Sene Muros (the 'Old Walls').

Today it is a small but charming market town with cobbled streets, archways and alleys to explore on a meandering bend of the River Armançon. The area is known for its pink granite, which is also the name of the local sweet. Much of the medieval city remains including towers — Margot, Prison, Géhenne and Orle d'Or — walls and the collegiate Church of Notre Dame. The Sauvigny Gate, built in 1417, has the town's motto inscribed under the archway, written in old French, which translates as 'The people of Semur welcome strangers'. The massive granite Tour de l'Orle d'Or, in rue Buffon used to be the prison of the château. Its walls are 16ft (5m) thick. The Couvent des Jacobines, the former seventeenth-century Dominican convent, houses the municipal museum and library, and is noted for its many rare volumes. The museum has many exhibits found in the Auxois, especially at Genay, and a collection of more than 12,000 fossils and minerals. There is also a fine collection of paintings and sculptures from the seventeenth to nineteenth centuries, and sacrificial objects found by the Sources des Seine. The museum is open most afternoons, and if closed, ask at the town hall to visit.

The Gothic Church of Notre-Dame has an ornate fourteenth-century façade, decorated with gargoyles, noted for its carved tympanum over the Porte des Bleds, which depicts the Doubting St Thomas. Note the carved snails crawling up the pillar, a typical feature of Burgundian art. The windows of the sixteenth-century Chapel of the Butchers, portray the slaughter and preparation of meat from that period.

Every 31 May, the oldest horse race in France, the Course de la Bague, takes place here, and in September the ancient theatre is used for opera. Close by are Lake Pont, the châteaux of Bourbilly and Époisses, and the remarkable Church of St Thibault, which set out to be a cathedral but never quite made it.

Semur-en-Brionnais (2)

The Romanesque church is one of the later and more fascinating works of Clunisian art. The choir and transept date from the early eleventh century and the name from the end of that century. The two tier tower is especially beautiful, and the carvings on the doors depict scenes from the life of St Hilary to whom it is dedicated.

Sène (2)

The Mont Sène is also known as the Montagne des Trois Croix, because of the three crosses on the summit. There are fine panoramic views from the top.

Sennecey-le-Grand (2)

The Church of St Julien dates from the eleventh and twelfth centuries topped by a two-storey square bell tower, and the town hall is all that remains of a fortified château which used to be protected by a moat

Sens (1)

For many centuries Sens was one of the most important centres of Christianity in France, and for a short time, the most important centre in the world. It was the capital of the Sénons, the Gallic tribe which captured Rome in 390BC, ensuring the town's early notoriety although it prospered for several centuries. In 1163 Pope Alexander III moved the Papacy to Sens, although this lasted only a year. Today it is a quiet town dominated by the cathedral, one of the most beautiful Gothic churches in France, and together with the Bishop's Palace, Cathedral Treasury and other religious buildings, they make up a remarkable group of museums. The Cathedral of St Etienne, started in 1140, is famous for its twelfth- to seventeenth-century stained glass windows, the oldest dating from around 1200 is in the north choir. The 240ft (73m) high south tower is a useful landmark. The façade used to have two towers, one was destroyed in the nineteenth century, and the other was partly demolished and replaced by a Renaissance bell tower in the 1530s. The Gothic south transept was built by master stonemason Martin Chambiges at the beginning of the sixteenth century. The nineteenth-century Statue Gallery has statues of former archbishops of Sens, while the statue of St Stephen, between the doors of the Central Portal, dates from the twelfth century. Streets around the cathedral have many fine half timbered medieval buildings, including the thirteenth-century church of St Pierre-le-Rond noted for its unusual wooden roof and sixteenth- century stained glass windows.

The Church of St Savinien is dedicated to the martyrs who died bringing Christianity to the area. Parts of the church date from the eleventh century and it has an elegant Romanesque tower.

Parts of the ramparts from the late Roman period and early Middle Ages have been preserved and are best seen near the medieval postern of Garnier-des-Prés, and Cours Chambonas. A number of Roman remains and mosaics are exhibited in the entrance hall of the Banque de France (Cours Tarbé). They were found when the building was being built.

The museum in the former thirteenth century Archbishop's Palace is open all year, and contains an impressive collection of flints found locally, swords from the Bronze and Iron Ages from the Yonne, and many items of dress found in Gallic tombs. The most impressive exhibits are the Gallo-Roman statues depicting first century life. These stones were used to build the ramparts of the old town, and were only discovered when the walls were demolished in the nineteenth century. The Cathedral Treasure House, one of the richest in France, is next to the museum, and has robes worn by Thomas à Becket, who fled from Canterbury to Sens. It was on his return to England that he was murdered in 1170. The art gallery also contains the hat worn by Napoleon at Waterloo.

Solutré *(2)*

There have been settlements at the foot of the rocks for at least 30,000 years. For more than 20,000 years camps were established here to hunt the huge herds of migrating horses. A layer of animal bones more than 10ft (3m) high in places, has been found. The small archaeological museum was opened in 1986 and was built into the hillside. Open all year, it contains objects found during the excavations, and has a slide and video show.

Sully *(2)*

The turreted Renaissance château, surrounded by a moat, is set in magnificent grounds, overlooked by a broad terrace. Inside there is a spectacular staircase. Marshal MacMahon, President of France from 1873 to 1879, was born here in 1808.

Taingy *(1)*

The quarries at Aubigny have been mined for many centuries, and the stone has been used to build many well-known buildings, such as the Paris Opera House and Town Hall, and the cathedrals of Auxerre and Sens. The underground quarries have resulted in huge, spectacular caves which can be visited between May 1 and early-September.

Above: Tornus is a sunny market town on the Saône with quaint streets and delightful cafés.
Below: The Hotel Dieu in Tonnerre was founded in 1293.

Taizé (2)

The little church, built in the twelfth century, is still a centre for prayer and meditation, thanks to the ecumenical community founded in 1940 by Pastor Schutz. Their aim is reconciliation and they work particularly with young people of all denominations. They built their own Church of the Reconciliation, noted for its flat roof, which was ordained in 1962.

Talmay (2)

This magnificent château is noted for its imposing thirteenth-century keep which is more than 150ft (46m) high and topped by a lantern tower. The tower is all that remains of the original château which was destroyed in the mid-eighteenth century, and replaced by the present Classical-style building. The rooms are very elegantly furnished.

Tamnay-en-Bazois (2)

The trade and craft museum has exhibitions of tools and items of every day life in the region at the turn of the century. It is open from Easter to the end of October.

Tanlay (1)

The Renaissance château dates from the sixteenth and seventeenth centuries and is surrounded by moats. The apartments and their furnishings are magnificent, as are the ornate wrought iron railings, elegant staircase and frescoed great gallery. There is a secret room in the tower, once used as a hiding and meeting place by Huguenot Protests during the religious wars of 1562-98. Guided tours are available. The Centre for Contemporary Art is open during the summer.

Ternant (2)

The dolmens of Ternant, in the Montfarbeau woods, are the first evidence of architecture found in Burgundy, and are believed to be family tombs dating from the late neolithic or early Bronze Age. The smallest dolmen, known as the Priest's Chamber, was used to shelter a priest during the French Revolution. The dolmens are well signposted and are on the right side of the road from Ternant to the hamlet of Rolle. They are also on the GR7 long-distance footpath.

Til-Châtel (2)

The fine Church of St Florent dates from the mid-twelfth century, and is noted for its carved doorway and tympanum, and carved capitals.

Tonnerre (1)

A charming hillside town overlooking the River Armançon, with a delightful old town and surrounded by vineyards. The town was almost completely destroyed by fire in the sixteenth century, but the hospital thankfully, was one of the few buildings that survived. The Hotel-Dieu was founded in 1293 and has celebrated its 700th anniversary. The impressive thirteenth-century ward — the 250ft (76m) long panelled Grande Salle — can be visited, and the museum has a number of permanent exhibitions on the role of the church between the thirteenth and nineteenth centuries, hospital life, the foundation of the Hotel-Dieu, a patient's room of 1850, and a surgery unit at the turn of the century. There is also a film presentation about the history of the hospital. The Church of St Pierre, like most of the town, was rebuilt after the huge fire in 1556, and it provides a good vantage point for looking out at the many surviving sixteenth-century houses. Other sights include the Fosse Dionne, a well fed by an underground stream and used as a wash house, and the Renaissance Hotel d'Uzès, now a bank, but the birthplace of the Knight of Eon, an eighteenth-century spy who frequently wore womens clothes as a disguise, which led to many rumours about his sexuality. After his death in London in 1810, however, a post-mortem confirmed that he was a man.

Toucy *(1)*

A small town on the River Ouanne and the birthplace of Larousse, the scholar and lexicographer. The town's church with its two towers has a fortified appearance because while being built it incorporated parts of the adjacent château.

Tournus *(2)*

A small, sunny market town on the Saône with quaint streets to explore and delightful cafés to lounge in and let the world pass you by. It is a great place for a rest and relaxation stop, although there are a few sights worth seeing. The sombre, almost fortified abbey Church of St Philibert was built by the monks of Noirmoutier who fled south from Norman invaders. The church was built near the tomb of St Valenan who was martyred in AD177 on a nearby hillside while trying to convert the locals. A sanctuary and then an abbey was built over the tomb. By the time the monks from Noirmoutier arrived, the old abbey had fallen into disrepair, and the new, larger structure was built. The abbey church houses the relics of their founder St Philibert, and is a fine example of early Romanesque architecture. The date of the church is unknown, but the oldest part is the crypt, believed to date from the first quarter of the eleventh century. The nave is noted for its unusual arrangement of bays, arches and pillars, and lack of decoration. The stark external aspect contrasts with the warm, light interior, a result of the many openings allowing light in to play on the rose-coloured stonework.

The Museum Bourguignon, next door, closed in the winter, portrays life in the area from palaeolithic times to the early Middle Ages. Many objects from the neolithic, Bronze and Gallo-Roman periods were dredged from the Saône. Others come from Iron Age and Gallo-Roman settlements in the northern Mâcon region, and from 'barbarian' tombs found in the western suburbs of Tournus. Other sights include the Geuze Museum devoted to the eighteenth-century painter, the twelfth-century Church of La Madeleine, and the Perrin-de-Puycousin folk history museum in a fine seventeenth-century house. Guided tours of the St Philibert Abbey and old town are available from the tourist office.

Uchon (2)

The town is set in desolate high country and its church was the centre for pilgrimages in the sixteenth century because of its statue of the Virgin in the oratory. About 1 mile (2km) south of the village is the Uchon Signal Station at 2,133ft (650m).

Vallery (1)

A small village noted for its rather sombre Renaissance château, with an isolated thirteenth-century tower, all that remains of a previous castle. The church with its chapel dedicated to Henry, Prince of Condé features statues of the four virtues; and the huge oak tree in Vallery Wood which is at least 350 years old.

Vareilles (2)

The eleventh-century church has received a number of restorations leaving the choir intact and the fine Brionnais bell tower.

Varenne l'Arconce (2)

The Romanesque church is noted for its Clunisian influence. Built in sandstone at the end of the eleventh century, it dominates the Charolais countryside. It is noted for the decorated tympanum over the south doorway.

Varzy (1)

The Chapel of St Lazare was built at the end of the twelfth century and is all that remains of the ancient leper hospital of Vaumorin. The small museum, open during the summer, contains objects excavated from the three prehistoric tumuli in the region, as well as Gallo-Roman objects from Entrains and Compierre.

Vault-de-Lugnu (2)

The tiny village has a fifteenth-century church noted for its massive sixteenth-century mural, more than 230ft (70m) long. A moated château with fifteenth-century keeps stands outside the village.

Vausse Priory (1)

Founded in the twelfth century, the Cistercian priory was dedicated to St Mary and Denis. It was sold after the Revolution and became a pottery factory, but was restored in 1869. The cloisters and fourteenth-century chapel are well restored.

Verdun-sur-le-Doubs (2)

An unusual wheat and bread museum is open daily from May to September between 3 and 7pm. It is closed on Tuesdays.

Vermenton (1)

This twelfth-century church has suffered considerable damage but is noted for its west doorway and four pillar statues, and lavishly-decorated capitals. The twelfth-century north tower has a handsome

Above: The pretty village of Chambolle-Musigny is a charming small town south of Dijon, just one kilometre from Vougeot.

stone spire, inspired by the one of St Germain at Auxerre.

Verneuil *(1)*

The charming church, dating from twelfth century, is adorned with the remains of some fine murals.

Vertault *(1)*

The site of the ancient town of *Vertillum* which is steadily being revealed by excavations. Many objects from the site are on display in the museum in Châtillons-sur-Seine.

Vézelay *(2)*

This is a hill town with cobbled streets, ramparts and many fine red-roofed buildings. The St Madelaine Basilica, is an outstanding Romanesque abbey church dating from the twelfth and thirteenth centuries, although the abbey was founded by Girart de Roussillon, a ninth-century duke of Burgundy. The original abbey at St Père was destroyed during a Viking raid, and a new more secure site on top of the hill at Vézelay was chosen. St Bernard preached the Second Crusade at Vézelay in 1146, and the church was a famous pilgrimage destination because it housed the relics of St Mary Magdalene, although the authenticity of the remains became increasingly in doubt in the thirteenth and four-teenth centuries.

The abbey was sold after the Revolution and only the basilica escaped destruction. It was beautifully restored by Viollet-le-Duc in 1840. It has a noted tympanum and outstanding sculpt-ured capitals. One of its charms is its construction in pink and ochre stone. The huge nave was built between 1120 and 1140 to accom-modate the many pilgrims who came to pray near the bones of the saint, and is remarkably light thanks to the ten two storey bays and tall windows above. It is noted for its fine carvings, capitals and friezes, and the carvings on the tympanum over the central door, depicting the Pentecost. The choir in early Gothic style and transept were built be-tween 1185 and 1215 in white stone, which adds further contrast to the colours of the nave.

The church contains the relics which are still sanctified by Rome. Guided visits are available. Sculpt-ures from the abbey can also be seen displayed in the former Franciscan monk's dormitory next door which has been carefully rebuilt. It was the first monastery of the Brotherhood of St Francis of Assisi founded in France.

Villeneuve l'Archevêque (1)

It was in the twelfth-century Church of Notre-Dame that the French King Saint Louis received the crown of thorns of the Crucifixion from the Venetians. The church has a very beautiful doorway.

Villeneuve-sur-Yonne (1)

This was a military town founded in the eleventh century and is famous for its thirteenth-century towers and fortified gates, and the eighteenth-century House with Seven Heads. There is a comprehensive exhibition detailing the area's history from the Acheulean stone industry to the iron mines in the forest of Othe.

There are also burial furnishings from the Bronze Age necropolis of Colombine, Gallic ceramics and Roman villa furnishings and pottery. If the exhibition is not open ask at the Town Hall for a visit. The church, with its massive Gothic nave, dates from the thirteenth century.

Vougeot (2)

The Château du Clos-de-Vougeot is the headquarters for the Brother-head of the Knights of Tastevin. See Clos de Vougeot.

BURGUNDY ADDITIONAL INFORMATION

Regional Tourist Offices

Comité Régional du Tourisme de Bourgogne
Conseil Régional
BP 1602
21035 Dijon Cedex
☎ 80 50 10 20

Comité Départemental de Tourisme de Côte-d'Or
Hôtel du Département
BP 1601
21305 Dijon Cedex
☎ 80 63 66 00

Comité Départemental de Tourisme de la Nièvre
3 rue du Sort
58000 Nevers
☎ 86 36 39 80

Comité Départemental de Tourisme de Saône-et-Loire
389 ave Maréchal-de-Lattre-de-Tassigny
71000 Mâcon
☎ 85 38 27 92

Comité Départemental de Tourisme d L'Yonne
1-2 quai de la République,
89000 Auxerre
☎ 86 52 26 27

Tourist Offices

AIGNY-LE-DUC 21510
Place de la Gare
☎ 80 93 85 03

ARNAY-LE-DUC 21230
15 rue Saint-Jacques
☎ 89 90 07 55

AUXONNE 21130
23 place d'Armes
☎ 80 37 34 46

BAIGNEUX-LES-JUIFS 21450
Chalet du Camping
☎ 80 96 51 27

BEAUNE 21200
rue de l'Hôtel Dieu
☎ 80 22 24 51

BIERRE-LES-SAMUR 21390
Point 1, Exit from A6

BLIGNY-SUR-OUCHE 21360
place de l'Hôtel de Ville
☎ 80 20 16 51

BROGNON 21490
Maison de la Côte d'Or
☎ 80 23 30 00

CHAMPAGNEY 21440
Musée-ecole
☎ 80 35 01 64

CHÂTILLON-SUR-SEINE 21400
place Marmont BP 78
☎ 80 91 13 19

DIJON CEDEX 21022
Office de Tourisme Dijon-Darcy
place Darcy, BP1298
☎ 80 43 42 12

Office de Tourisme Dijon-Forges
34 rue des Forges, BP1298
☎ 80 30 35 39

DIJON CEDEX 21033
Hotel de Ville, BP 1510
☎ 80 67 12 12

ÉPOISSES 21460
Town Hall
☎ 80 96 44 09

FLAVIGNY-SUR-OZERAIN 21150
Maison au Donataire
☎ 80 96 24 65

FONTAINE-FRANÇAISE 21610
Town Hall
☎ 80 75 81 21

GEVREY-CHAMBERTIN 21220
Place de la Mairie
☎ 80 34 30 35

GRANCEY-LE-CHÂTEAU 21580
Point 1
☎ 80 75 63 45

IS-SUR-TILLE 21120
1 rue Charbonnel
☎ 80 95 24 03

MARSANNAY-LA-CÔTE 21160
rue de Mazy
☎ 80 52 27 73

MEURSAULT 21190
Place de l'Hôtel de Ville
☎ 80 21 25 90

A6- Aire de Beaune Merceuil
☎ 80 21 46 43

MIREBEAU-SUR-BÈZE 21310
rue de Moulin ☎ 80 36 76 17

MONTBARD 21500
rue Carnot
☎ 80 92 03 75

NOLAY 21340
Maison des Halles, place des Halles
☎ 80 21 70 86

NUITS-ST-GEORGES 21700
Rue Sanoys
☎ 80 61 22 47

PONTAILLER-SUR-SAÔNE 21270
☎ 80 47 80 14

POUILLY-EN-AUXOIS 21320
Le Colombier
☎ 80 90 74 24

PRÉCY-SOUS-THIL 21390
Salle Sainte Auxille

RECEY-SUR-OURCE 21290
Place Silenrieux
☎ 80 81 05 41

ROUVRAY 21530
Syndicat d'Initiative
☎ 80 64 74 61

ST-JEAN-DE-LOSNE 21170
5 ave de la Gare d'Eau
☎ 80 29 05 48

ST-SEINE-L'ABBAYE 21440
☎ 80 35 01 64

SANTENAY 21590
Ave des Sources
☎ 80 20 63 15

SAULIEU 21210
24 rue d'Argentine
☎ 80 64 00 21

SAVIGNY-LES-BEAUNE 21420
rue Vauchey-Very
☎ 80 21 56 15

SELONGEY 21260
5 place des Halles
☎ 80 75 70 41

SEMUR-EN-AUXOIS 21140
2 place Gaveau
☎ 80 97 05 96

SEURRE 21250
5 rue Bossuet
☎ 80 21 09 11

SOMBERNON 21540
Town Hall
☎ 80 33 44 23

VENAREY-LES-AUMES 21150
place de Bingerbrück
☎ 80 96 89 13

VITTEAUX 21350
rue Hubert Languet
☎ 80 33 90 14

To most people Beaujolais is the place somewhere in France where the new red wine comes from each year accompanied by incredible hype. Most people do not know where it is, and few tourists take the time to visit, which is a shame, because if you are interested in wine, good food and spectacular scenery, Beaujolais has a lot to offer.

It is also a relatively small region and one can tour many areas on foot or by bike, and even if driving, no day's tour need cover more than 40 or 50 miles (60 or 80km) in order to take everything in.

The region lies to the east of the Massif Central, between the Mâconnais in the north and almost as far as Lyon in the south — a distance of less than 40 miles (64km). It is part of the Lyonnais and the Pays de Beaujolais is in the *département* of the Rhône. To the south its border is marked by the River Turdine and the lower Azergues, to the east by the River Saône, and to the west by the Monts de Beaujolais which run into the Loire Valley.

The hills rise to over 3,000ft (915m) in the north with deep gorges cut in the granite. The slopes are covered with gorse, pine forests and chestnut groves. The land towards the Saône tends to be limestone, and supports the vineyards, as well as orchards and lush grass meadows that feed the livestock.

This is an area of hills and gorges, of large fertile valleys and scattered villages. The villages, many of them high in the hills, used to have their own cottage industries, especially weaving from local wool, and then cotton, and in the western valleys there are still a small number of textile towns.

The area was travelled by the Romans but there were no large settlements in the area. Having settled in *Lugdunum* (Lyon), the Romans built the *Via Agrippa*, now the N6, and moved on to settle at *Augustodunum* (Autun), via Villié-Morgan. The Barbarians then invaded the area, followed by the Arabs and then the powerful noblility who created the principality. The first records of Beaujolais date back to AD957 when Beraud, the first Lord of Beaujolais, who created the state, had a castle — Pierre-Aigue — built overlooking Beaujeu. The state was tolerated by neighbouring nobles because it acted as a buffer between the constantly-feuding states of Mâcon and Lyon. In 1131 the Church of St Nicolas, built at the command of Lord Guichard III, was consecrated by Pope Innocent II. This was the great age of building Romanesque churches. Humbert III founded Villefranche-sur-Saône in the mid-twelfth century, and Belleville, whose church became the necropolis of the Lords of Beaujeu. Edouard II was the last Lord of Beaujeu and heavily in debt, he bequeathed his province to Louis, Duke of Bourbon in 1400. Although

Previous page: La Maison de Pays in Beaujeu, a town which is rich in history and surrounded by spectacular scenery.

the region lost its independence, it has never lost its individuality.

For 100 years, Beaujeu remained the capital of the area, but then Villefranche-sur-Saône took over in 1592 as the commercial and political centre. Villefranche-sur-Saône gained its charter in 1260 as an important trading and staging centre. It handled agricultural produce from the surrounding fertile plains and was on the main route from the south coast to the north.

At the end of the fifteenth century, Anne de France, Louis XI's daughter, and Pierre II of Bourbon, her husband were Regents of France, and they had the Gothic façade of the Church of Notre-Dame des Marais in Villefranche-sur-Saône built. François I and later in 1658, Louis XIV came to Villefranche-sur-Saône.

Then, the Grande Demoiselle Duchesse de Monpensier, the King's cousin, was appointed ruler of the region, and also of the Dombes to the south. The last Baron of Beaujolais was Louis Philippe Joseph d'Orléans, also known as Philippe Egalité. During the Revolution, the province was annexed to the Rhône *département* which, as a reprisal for the rebellious behaviour of the Lyonnais during the 'Terror', lost the Chapelle de Guinchay district. Napoleon 1 refused to rectify this injustice, and this explains why today, part of the wine producing territory of Beaujolais is in the Saône-et-Loire *département*. In the nineteenth century, Benoit Raclet, a grower in Romaneche, saved the vineyards from total destruction by finding the solution to *pyralis*, a parasitic worm, and forty years later, Victor Puillat saved them again by grafting local vines on to American rootstock to overcome the dreaded *Phylloxera*, which decimated most of the other vineyard areas of France.

Beaujolais is fun to visit because of its accessibility and small size. It is easily reached by car from Paris with its international airports, and the north-west by the A6. It is 285 miles (459km) from Paris, and it is only 34 miles (55km) from Lyon in the south to Villefranche-sur-Saône via the A43 and A6. From Marseille to Lyon using the A7 it is 195 miles (314km). There are also good high speed rail (TGV) links between Paris, Marseille and Lyons and a good local service from Lyons to Villefranche-sur-Saône and Belleville.

Today, **Villefranche-sur-Saône** on the N6 Paris-Lyon road and just west of the A6, is dominated by the wine trade, and makes a good touring base because of its hotels and restaurants, and there are old buildings and narrow, twisting streets to explore. When it was founded, Villefranche-sur-Saône was designed around three long streets running roughly north to south, which explains its present elongated shape. On either side of the main street with the principal buildings and shops was a 'back' street of smaller houses. Narrow alleys ran between the streets and a tax was changed for each 'toise' 6ft (2m) of frontage, which also explains why many of the buildings are very deep with narrow frontages. Many

The Church of Notre Dame des Marais (Our Lady of the Marshes) takes its name from the land on which it was built. Although originally Romanesque, many Gothic features were added with side chapels and ornate façade. It also has a fine carved front door, and beautiful stained glass windows.

Other places of interest include the Ancient Hospital with its chapel, Rentières and convalescents rooms. The carved and painted octagonal ceiling is 39ft (12m) in diameter, and was painted around 1682 although is now in need of restoration.

To the north-east on the D19 is **Salles-Arbuissonais-en-Beaujolais**, an ancient village with many fine old buildings, and an old priory with buildings dating from the eleventh and fifteenth centuries. **Tarare** in the Turdine Valley is famous for its muslin, and there are more textile towns along the Route de Sapins (The Road of Firs) in the western hills. The delightful town of **Anse** to the south has more than 2,000 years of history on offer, with Gallo-Roman remains, ramparts, medieval city and the thirteenth-century Château des Tours with its 70ft (21m) high keep. Beaujeu, the old capital, is in the north, in a narrow valley surrounded by vineyards and forests. The other major town is **Belleville**, also to the north, which makes a good alternative touring base.

Most people who visit Beaujolais do so because of the vineyards and wine, but the largely unspoilt countryside offers some very pleasant walks, especially at higher ground through the forested hills. There are also opportunities for horseriding and fishing.

Summers tend to be sunny and warm but there is always the threat of a heavy downpour or hail. Winters are chilly with average temperatures hovering just above freezing in the coldest months. Springs are warmer but often wet, while the autumn is the best time to visit, not only for the wonderful colours as the leaves turn, but also because it is the time of the harvest when the region is at its most vibrant.

When visiting Beaujolais, it is easiest to divide the region into three areas, the northern part which takes in the Haut Beaujolais and many of the best wine producing villages; the Valley of the Azergues; and the Monts du Beaujolais, the high lands to the west of the Azergues.

The Haut Beaujolais

To reach the Haut Beaujolais from Villefraiche, take the N6 north to Belleville and turn left on the D37 for Beaujeu. For the tours in this section, you are recommended to purchase a large scale route map locally. It will aid navigation on some of the country roads. They are really worth the effort of touring as some of the scenery is spectacular. This northern hilly region has a rich history and **Beaujeu** was the first capital of Beaujolais. The town developed because of its 'strategic position in the narrow Ardières Valley along an important trading route. Beaujeu has a twelfth-century Romanesque church and opposite, the fifteenth-century half-timbered Maison de Pays, built during the Renaissance, is well preserved. The town has many old buildings although some are not easily seen because of the narrowness of some of the streets. There is a fine collection of old buildings, however, around the Place de la Liberté. The tourist office is in the tree-lined Place de l'Hôtel-de-Ville with its ornate drinking fountain. Upstairs there is a museum with exhibits ranging from the geology and wine history of the area, to a doll collection. In the cellars, there is the Temple of Bacchus, where you can taste and buy the region's wines. Beaujeu is the centre for the Beaujolais Villages appellation. The town has several good restaurants, including Anne-de-Beaujeu on rue de la République. The restaurant in a charming old building, is named after the daughter of Louis XI.

There is a pleasant 5 mile (8km) round walk from Beaujeu which starts from the main street and crosses the Ardières by a small bridge and then makes its way steeply up to the small village of Château St Jean. It then follows a farm path past the farm of Ruettes and the ruins of a château, through the woods to Les Laforêts farm, before descending along a paved road to the village of Longefay and then back along the GR76 to Beaujeu. The farms sell wine and cheese so you can picnic along the way without having to carry supplies!

From Beaujeu take D136 past the ancient Hospice de Beaujeu. The road climbs up through vineyards, to an area of open heather and scrub littered with huge stones. This is the **Col du Fût d'Avenas** 2,499ft (1,762m), and there are fine panoramic views over Bresse and surrounding countryside, and on clear days the Alps and Mount Blanc can be seen. You can visit the nearby tasting centre of the Vignerons de Chiroubles, and then drive to the village of **Avenas**, via the D18. It has a delightful old stone church built in 1180 and recently restored, and a twelfth-century altar made from local limestone, which is a declared historic monument. The front of the altar has an elaborate carving of Christ surrounded by the Apostles. The modern stained glass windows are not incongruous. From Avenas there is a choice of routes you can take to St Mamert. The D18 is the direct route via Ouroux and the Grosne Oriental Valley, or via the D18e to the Col de Crie and then the D32 through the woodlands that make up the Forêt de l'Hospice de Beaujeu. **St Mamert** is surrounded by rich farmlands and pastures, with herds of grazing goats and flocks of turkeys. The village is dominated by the Romanesque church with its red tiles and central tower. The next village is **St Jacques-des-Arrêts** which also has a very attractive church with classical windows. The village is set in rich woodland noted for its many different species of trees. The D23 continues through the

Above: St. Joseph-en-Beaujolais, on the D26 north-east of Beaujeu.
Below: Elegant château near to Les Dépôts, west of Beaujeu on the D43.

Above: The Château de Varennes near Marchampt, south of Beaujeu.
Below: The church in the small village of St. Igny de Vers.

hills to the village of **Cenves** surrounded by the large farmhouses which are typical of the district. The average hill farm in the area is around 37 acres (15 hectares) and keeps cattle, sheep and goats. The D23 then drops steeply before joining the D68 which climbs up to the Col de Gerbe 2,000ft (610m). This is goat herding countryside and you have to take care when driving for stray animals on the road. Follow the road to the Col de Siberie — an indication that it can turn very cold in the winter — before the winding descent to the village of **Jullié**, the centre for the Juliénas vineyards. ✳ There is a tasting centre and an attractive avenue of plane trees leading up to the church. There is a notice board in the village square which details a number of walks in the area. The village is also noted for La Vigne Gournmand restaurant. From the village take the narrow D68e through the vineyards to Emeringes then on to the D26 for **St Joseph**, via the Col de Dirbize 1,804ft (550m), and Col du Truges 1,460ft (445m), both of which offer good views over the surrounding vineyard country. The St Joseph Church is noted for its twin towers and the Stations of the Cross can be followed through the vineyards. The road then descends into the valley back to Beaujeu.

The western part of the Haut Beaujolais can be explored by taking the D37 out of Beaujeu, past **Les Dépôts** to **Les Ardillats**, a pretty wine village tucked among the hills, then along the D43 through the Ardières Valley where there are a number of fish farm ponds. This is delightful countryside with rolling hills, vineyards, and ancient stone farmhouses, and forests of firs and pines. The road joins the D23 at the Col de Crie where you can get out to walk to the summit of **Mont St Rigaud** 3,319ft (1,012m), the highest peak in the Beaujolais. The path to the top is along a paved forest track and not strenuous if you take your time. A hermit once lived on the summit of the hill and the surrounding woods offer many attractive well waymarked walks.

Take the D43 from the col to the village of **Monsols**, a large sprawling settlement with lots of new buildings, then the D22 through the Grosne Occidental valley to **St Christophe**. There is a simple tenth-century church overlooking the valley and offering good views. The D52 runs to Vaujon and then you can turn right on the narrow country lane via Mussery, through charming countryside, to **St Bonnet-des-Bruyères**. The large church was built using local granite and sandstone, and is interesting for its pillars and corner stones. The D5 then goes past the headwaters of the Sornin to connect with the D987 and the commune of Aigueperse. Continue west along the D987 for a short way and then turn left on the D66 through the deciduous forests of mainly oak and beech.

The route connects with the D43 and the village of **St Igny-de-Vers**, where *ski de fond* can be practised in season, then on to the Col du Champ,

2,430ft (741m), then right on the D52 into more rugged countryside. To the east are the foothills around Mont St Rigaud. The road runs through the tiny village of **Ajoux** and then past the château of **La Farge** with its red and white tiles, which is nearly hidden in the trees, to **Propières** on the D10, and access to **Azolette** and **St Clément-de-Vers**, on the western boundary of the Haut Beaujolais. The D10 continues south to **Les Echarmeaux** where there are fine views, after which you can take the D37 straight back to Beaujeu, Belleville and Villefranche-sur-Saône.

Belleville, like Beaujeu and Villefranche-sur-Saône, was designed around a long central street although the Notre-Dame church is some way away. This is explained because it was originally the abbey church standing in the abbey grounds. The abbey was destroyed after the Revolution. The church was chosen by the Lords of Beaujeu for their necropolis. The church is a mixture of Romanesque and Gothic styles with a square bell tower almost 100ft (30m) tall and many beautiful carvings, including the ornate front door.

The Valley of the Azergues

The valley of the Azergues marks the boundary between northern and southern Beaujolais, and is an area of narrow lanes, forests and hills. If you want to explore the Haute Azergues, head for **Chénelette** in the hills at 2,168ft (661m), and almost at the head of a tributary valley surrounded by forests and chestnut groves, and overlooked by Mont Tourvéon at 3,126ft (953m). It is on the D23 and follow the road down to Claveisolles and the nearby forest of **Corcelles**, famous because it has the oldest and tallest stand of Douglas firs in Europe which were planted in 1872. Some of the trees are 185ft (56m) high. Take the D129 up to the **Col de la Casse** Froide 2,430ft (741m) where there are excellent views of Mount Soubrant 2,880ft (878m). Continue on the D129 on the , tree-lined road to **St Didier-sur-Beaujeu**, where there is a church with an unusual broached spire, and a large wine bottling plant. From the village follow the D129e and D139 past the southern slopes of Mont Tourvéon to Chénelette.

Another option is to start at Les Echarmeaux on the D37 and taking the D110 at La Scierie which follows the river, and the railway after Poule to Le Prunier on the D485. It then descends through a steep-sided valley, past the entrances to the spiral tunnels, to **Lamure-sur-Azergues**, a small town with the fifteenth-century Château de Pramenoux. Take the D44 along the very scenic road to the Col de Croix Montmain 2,417ft (737m), then the D88e along a narrow, wooded and twisting road to the Col de la Croix-Rosier, where there is, surprisingly, a nightclub miles from anywhere. Continue on the D72 to **Marchampt** which is surrounded by vineyards, orchards and woodlands. It is worth making the detour along the D9 to

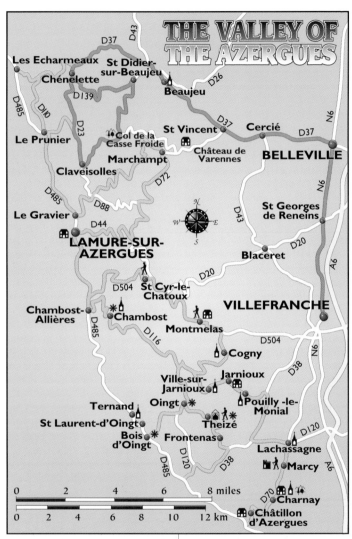

THE VALLEY OF THE AZERGUES

D37

D43

Les Echarmeaux

St Didier-
sur-Beaujeu

Chénelette

D139

D26

Beaujeu

D485

D110

D23

Le Prunier

Col de la
Casse Froide

Marchampt

Claveisolles

St Vincent

D37

Cercié

D37

N6

Château de
Varennes

BELLEVILLE

D72

N6

D485

D88

Le Gravier

D44

LAMURE-SUR-
AZERGUES

D43

St Georges
de Reneins

D20

Blaceret

A6

D504

St Cyr-le-
Chatoux

D20

Chambost-
Allières

Chambost

Montmelas

VILLEFRANCHE

D485

D116

D504

Cogny

N6

Ville-sur-
Jarnioux

Jarnioux

D38

Ternand

Oingt

St Laurent-d'Oingt

Bois
d'Oingt

Theizé

Frontenas

Pouilly -le-
Monial

D120

Lachassagne

D120

D485

D120

D38

A6

Marcy

| 0 | 2 | 4 | 6 | | 8 miles |
| 0 | 2 | 4 | 6 | 8 | 10 | 12 km |

D70

Charnay

Châtillon
d'Azergues

visit the Château de Varennes with its spectacular turrets and towers. You can return on the D9 via the Col de la Croix de Marchampt 2,247ft (685m), and then on to the Pont Gaillard, and then on to **Le Gravier** on the D485, where there are some interesting walks advertised in the Café Gravier. Continue to Lamure and then take the D485 down to

Above: Verdant fields and vineyards near to Cublize, west of the Azergues Valley.
Below: St Bonnet-le-Tracy, near to St Nizier d'Azergues.

Chambost-Allieres, a small industrial town with metal and plastic works. Take the D504 which climbs steeply to **St Cyr-le-Chatoux**, where there is a relaxing forest walk along a Sentier Botanique to the Source Font-Froide in the Cantinière Forest. Then continue on the D504. At **Le Parasoir** there are good views of Vaux and the Vauxonne valley, and then take the D44 to the village of **Montmelas**, which is where you set up to climb Mont-St-Bonnet at 2,230ft (680m). On the D44 outside the village is the spectacular fortress château of Montmelas, which was painstakingly restored by Villet le Duc in the nineteenth century. The route then joins the D19 to **Cogny** with its golden stone church, for Le Saule d'Oingt on the D116 where the Corniche begins. This road follows the crest of the hills past Col du Chêne 2,362ft (720m) and Col du Joncin 2,411ft (735m) to **Chambost**, set amid wonderful panoramic woodland scenery. The village is set off the road and has a small stone church, next to which is a huge lime tree reputed to have been planted in the reign of Henri IV, four centuries ago. The road then drops steeply to Chambost-Allières on the D485.

The Lower Azergues Valley

South of Villefranche-sur-Saône is the lovely Lower Azergues Valley which includes the Pays de Pierres Dorées, the new name given to the forty-one communes which have their own Syndicat d'Initiative at Châtillon d'Azergues. The name comes from the setting sun which shines on the ochre-coloured limestone used to build the houses, churches and châteaux of the district. The typical farmhouse has the living accommodation built above the ground floor storage area. It is reached by an outside staircase with a wrought iron or stone balustrade, and many properties also have porches with stone or wooden columns. To reach this area go south from Villefranche-sur-Saône on the N6 to its junction with the D485 near Limonest. Turn right up the D485 to Châtillon and continue to the D38. Turn right and eventually left off the D38 to Theizé. The best way to see this lovely area is on foot. There is a charming 5 mile (8km) walk in and around **Theizé**. It starts in the centre of the village by the old column with a cross erected in 1567, known as La Croix de Enfants de Theizé. It follows a track called Le Boîtier to the Close de la Platière, the home of Madame Roland, a writer guillotined during the French Revolution, and now a small museum. The path continues through the vines to the chapel of St Hippolyte, built in 1662, and then on to the D19 to **Frontenas** where there is a French Revolution inscription scored on the door of the fifteenth-century church. The path turns right to Moiré and then up the hill through attractive Beaujolais countryside, before descending back to Theizé through woods and vineyards. Below Theizé, with its narrow streets, is the huge fortified château of **Rapetour**. In the village the fifteenth-century church, no longer consecrated, has a gallery connecting it with the seventeenth-century Château Rochebonne, with its two towers and splendid staircase. Both buildings can be visited and are being restored by volunteers.

From Theizé, the D96 runs to nearby **Oingt** perched on top of the hill and dates back to medieval times. It has many fine old buildings, and the tower of Nizy, the only remaining fortified gate, offers fine panoramic views. There is also a thirteenth-century church, formerly the castle's chapel, with many old sculptures, and a village hall which dates from the sixteenth century. The village is involved with the wine industry and there is a tile works on the outskirts. There is also a road leading to the fourteenth-century Château de Prosny, which according to legend, was haunted by La Dame Blanche, the unfaithful wife of its seventeen-century owner who put her in a convent for two years. The village's name is believed to come from the Greco-Roman *Iconium*. The D96 quickly runs into **St Laurent-d'Oingt** where there is a Cave Coopérative offering tastings, before descending steeply into the valley of the Azergues. Take the D485 to Les Grandes Planches and then after crossing the river, visit **Ternand** along the twisting D31e. There has been a settlement on top of the hill for thousands of years, and the first ecclesiastical buildings date back to the fifth century when a crypt was built. The crypt was adorned with frescoes in the ninth century, and in the tenth century a church was built on the site. The settlement was fortified by the Archbishops of Lyon, and in the eleventh century, an exiled Archbishop of Canterbury was granted sanctuary here. The narrow lanes hide many very old buildings, some dating back to the fourteenth and fifteenth centuries. To the west is the Forest of Brou which offers many pleasant walking opportunities. Follow the right bank of the Azergues and then, after a few kilometres, join the D39 to cross the river for **Chessy-les-Mines** on the D485. There is a twelfth-century church and the wealthy Jacques Coeur owned the nearby copper mines in the fifteenth century. These mines were established by the Romans and only ceased working towards the end of the nineteenth century. The red slag heaps can still be seen towards the river.

The next village is **Châtillon d'Azergues**, with its splendid fortified twelfth-century château and keep. The building was carefully restored from a virtual ruin in the nineteenth century, and is today a private residence, although the chapel with its beautiful ornate paintings, can be visited. The village is the headquarters for the Syndicat d'Initiative of the Pierres Dorées, which has frequent exhibitions and holds tastings. From Châtillon take the D70e from the D485 for **Charnay** on the D70. The village also boasts an old château, an eleventh-century church and excellent views.

The D70 continues to **Marcy** with a ruined château atop the summit of Montézain, and a tower which looks out over the Saône Valley.

❉ The tower was restored by the French Post Office and is the only one left from the Chappe telegraph system installed in 1799, which revolutionised communications throughout France. The system used mechanical flag-like arms to relay messages, which were passed on from tower to tower. The system was used nationwide until the adoption of the electronic Morse code. There is also a fascinating well-tended walk near the quarry and cement works along rock layers which indicate the geological history of the region. The walk follows a heavily-eroded fault in between clay and limestone strata, and you can see the various rock layers that have been laid down over millions of years.

The route then heads for **Lachassagne** where the church is famous for a crib which took eleven years to make. From Lachassagne, take the D39 which climbs up to the west to meet the D38. Turn right and then after 2 miles (3km) turn left into Pouilly-le-Monial where there is a fifteenth-century church and La Forge, a restaurant noted for its traditional fare. Continue on a country lane leading to the nearby hamlet of **Jarnioux** with its fabulous Château de Jarnioux. Originally built in the thirteenth century, it was largely rebuilt and extended during the Renaissance with six pepper pot towers, and a magnificent entrance. It is considered one of the finest grand houses in the south-east of France, and the courtyard can be visited. There are also a number of very old houses nearby. Also worth visiting close by is **Ville-sur-Jarnioux**, noted for its church with Austrian frescoes, a reminder of the area's occupation in 1814.

From Ville-sur-Jarnioux take D116 to St Clair and then return on the D120 to Oingt and then on to **Bois d'Oingt**, with its tasting cellar run by the *Cave Coopérative*, and fine old honey-coloured stone houses.

The Monts du Beaujolais

This is the high land to the west of Azergues Valley, between the Rhône and the Loire. It is an area of rugged, wooded uplands and steep valleys and a great place to get out and walk.

The Route de Sapins (Road of Firs) is the best way to explore the area. It starts in **Lamure-sur-Azergues** which is on the D485, north-west of Villefranche-sur-Saône. The route starts on the D485 and head northwards to the D9 above Le Gravier and St Nizier, a small village perched on the hillside. The road continues to climb through forests with occasional views through the trees of La Croix Nicelle 2,578ft (786m), and Mont-St-Rigaud in the distant to the north, to St Bonnet-le-Troncy before descending to **St Vincent-de-Reins**. Although the village has quite a lot of light industry, there is a pleasant 10-and-a-half mile (17km) round walk from the church which offers great views as it climbs via the Col Burdel 2,230ft (680m) to above La Chapelle de Mardore 2,453ft (748m), before descending via the forest to the village.

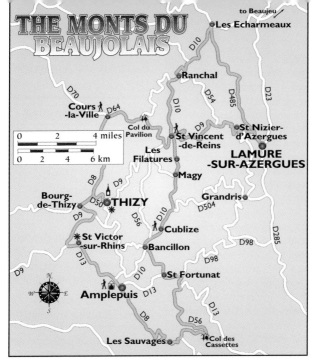

THE MONTS DU BEAUJOLAIS

to Beaujeu

Les Echarmeaux

Ranchal

Cours-la-Ville

Col du Pavilon

St Vincent-de-Reins

Les Filatures

St Nizier-d'Azergues

LAMURE-SUR-AZERGUES

Magy

Bourg-de-Thizy

THIZY

Grandris

St Victor-sur-Rhins

Cublize

Bancillon

St Fortunat

Amplepuis

Les Sauvages

Col des Cassettes

| 0 | 2 | 4 miles |
| 0 | 2 | 4 | 6 km |

The car route continues on the D108 through very mixed woodland to the Col du Pavilon 2,280ft (695m), and then on the D64 for the climb up to **Cours-la-Ville**, a small textile town, set in very scenic countryside and offering a number of local round walks, ranging in distance from 10 to 21 miles (16 to 34km). Details of the walks are available locally and they are well waymarked in yellow and white. Take the D8 through the Trambouze Valley to the Thizy. The wooded area along the way also offers lots of opportunities for walks.

Thizy and neighbouring **Bourg-de-Thizy** have a number of very old houses, and the former has the eleventh-century Chapelle St Georges. The town can be bypassed, however, by taking D9e to D9a for **St**

Victor-sur-Rhins, which is a quiet village best known for its large railway viaduct, and eleventh-century church, formerly part of the priory of Cluny. You have now entered the *département* of the Loire which is why Rhins is used rather than Reins. The D9 (which also runs part of the way as the D13) continues to the textile town of **Amplepuis**, with its Monnier Museum, named after the inventor of the sewing machine. There is a 11 mile (18km) round walk from the Place Belfort, through the woods and taking in the Château de Rochefort. Follow the yellow waymarks.

The D8 from Amplepuis climbs to **Les Sauvages** 2,371ft (723m), where there is a monument commemorating a meeting between François I and James IV of Scotland. There is a small mountain road on the left up to the Col des Cassettes 2,040ft (622m), then you join the D56 for a delightful drive through beech and fir forests and meadows with stunning views, to Ronno, then through woods to Bancillon in the Reins Valley on the D504 and the scenic Lac de Sapins, which has a path all the way round.

Continue to **Cublize**, which also offers a number of walks. The shorter walks have yellow way-marks, and the long, round walk of 19 miles (31km) is waymarked in blue and white and forms part of the GR7. The D504 joins the D10 which travels through pretty countryside, the textile village of **Les Filatures** and the wooded upper Reins and Ranchal. The D10 climbs the shrine at Notre Dame la Rochette to the Col des Escorbans 2,798ft (853m), and then drops down through the forests before rising again to the Col des Aillets at 2,348ft (716m). From the col it is clear how extensive the forests of Haut Beaujolais are. A British aircraft crashed into the forest in the 1950s and it was not found until a party stumbled across it by accident in November 1960. From the col drive on to Les Echarmeaux and back to Beaujeu on the D37 or via Lamure-sur-Azergues on the D485.

An alternative route into the Monts du Beaujolais is to take the D485 from Cambost-Allières to the D98 and St Just d'Avray, famous for its Château La Valsonière, and pleasant well-marked walks, and then on to either Ronno or Amplepuis.

Beaujolais Additional Information

Markets in Beaujolais

Beaujeu
A market is held each Wednesday morning
Belleville
A market is held each Tuesday morning
Villefranche
A market every Monday morning, all day Friday, Sunday morning and the **Quartier des Marais** a craft market is held on the second Sunday of each month.

Horse Riding in Beaujolais

Association Beaujolaise des Amis du Cheval
Denicé
☎ 74 67 33 27

Société Hippique des Pierres Dorées
Le Bois d'Oingt
☎ 74 71 81 57

Centre Equestre des Silmarils
Cublize
☎ 74 89 51 36

Le Carruge
Ouroux
☎ 74 04 60 05

Events in Beaujolais

January
Villefranche — Fête des Conscrits is held on the last Sunday of the month.

April
Chiroubles — Festival of the Crus of Beaujolais

June
Cenves — cheese festival
Villefranche — Midsummer night festival

July
Letra — Tasting Room open house, four Saturday of the month.
Villefranche — Festival

September
Gleizé — Harvest festival
Oingt — Street organ festival, first weekend of the month
St Lager — Festival of the Friends of Brouilly

October
Lacenas — New wine presentation, first Friday of the month
Odenas — Festival of the First Pressing
Romanèche-Thorins — Benoît Festival, last Sunday of the month

November
Beaujeu — Festival of Beaujolais Nouveau, third Tuesday in the month
Bois-d'Oingt — Wine Competition
Fleurie — Wine Market
Juliénas — Victor-Peyret Prize Competition

December
Beaujeu — Hospices wine sale, second Sunday in the month
Villefranche - Les Deux Bouteilles Wine Competition, first weekend of the month

Tourist Offices

AMPLEPUIS
place de l'Hôtel de Ville
☎ 74 89 01 71

ANSE
place du 8 Mai
☎ 74 60 26 16

BEAUJEU
square de Grandhau
☎ 74 69 22 88
Open: mid-March to December.

BELLEVILLE
105 rue de la République
☎ 74 66 17 10

BOIS-D'OINGT
Town Hall
☎ 74 71 60 51

CHÂTILLON D'AZERGUES
Golden Stones Pavilion
☎ 78 47 98 15

COURS-LA-VILLE
54 rue de Thizy
☎ 74 64 72 11

LAMURE-SUR-AZERGUES
rue du Vieux Pont
☎ 74 03 13 26

MONSOLS
route de St-Igny-de-Vers
☎ 74 04 70 85

TARARE
place de la Madeleine
☎ 74 63 06 65

THEIZÉ
Tourist office in the old church
☎ 74 71 64 27

THIZY
Animation Gallery
☎ 74 64 35 23

VILLEFRANCHE-SUR-SAÔNE
290 rue de Thizy
☎ 74 68 05 18

Above: Hot-air ballooon drifts serenely over the skyline of Lyon.
Below: The town of Lyon was originally founded in 43BC, and throughout the centuries has developed into the huge industrial centre it is today.

Lyon and Surrounding Area 3

Most visitors to Lyon know it as the city plagued with traffic jams that they have to negotiate on their way to and from the Mediterranean. It is a wonderful city and well worth exploring, not only for its history and many beautiful old buildings, but also for its restaurants, which offer some of the best food on earth.

The Lyonnais are rightly famed for their gastronomy and this is partly because of the wealth of excellent produce all around them, and partly because of the culinary traditions that date back many centuries. The area has more top starred restaurants than anywhere else in France.

Lyon was founded in 43BC by one of Julius Caesar's lieutenants, in an ideal defensive position on a hill overlooking the confluence of the Rivers Rhône and Sâone. The first settlers were refugees who had escaped from an attack on Vienne 19 miles (31km) to the south but it quickly became an important Roman military colony known as *Lugdunum* and within thirty years was the capital of the Roman Province of Gaul. It reached its peak of classical development in the second century AD during which Christianity was introduced. In AD177 the Christian community was persecuted by Emperor Marcus Aurelius and in AD197 the settlement was virtually wiped out by Lucius Septimus Severus.

In 1032 Lyon was absorbed into the Holy Roman Empire and it became one of the most important ecclesiastical centres in Europe with the line of Lyon archbishops holding enormous power and influence. Famous ecumenical councils were held in Lyon in 1245 and 1274, although in 1312 the city was annexed by the Kingdom of France.

Lyon thrived during the Renaissance and became an important trading centre. International commercial fairs were established in 1464, printing was introduced in 1473, Italian merchants set up businesses and important banking houses moved in. By the seventeenth century it had become the silk manufacturing capital of Europe.

While initially welcoming the Revolution, the city rebelled after the execution of Louis XVI and retaliated by guillotining Maire-Joseph Chalier, the chief officer of the Revolutionary Council in Lyon. Revolutionary leaders in Paris ordered that Lyon be destroyed, and in 1793 the city was besieged by Republican forces of the Montagnards. After two months Lyon surrendered, many parts of the city were destroyed and thousands of people were killed. Many businesses collapsed during this period and the Revolution virtually halted international trade, hitting Lyon's silk industry very hard. After the Revolution the importance of

Lyon was again recognised, and Napoleon himself laid the first stone in the reconstruction of the city, and founding the Museum of School of Fine Arts. New bridges were built across the rivers and prosperity slowly returned in the nineteenth century helped by massive industrial expansion, and there has been a huge urban expansion in the last fifty years so that zones of factories and suburbs now surround the city. The Old City, however, on the right bank of the Sâone remains one of the largest and finest surviving collection of Renaissance architecture and art. To the south, along the Rhône, Feyzin and St Fons make up one of the largest oil refinery complexes in Europe.

The city now relies on the chemical, metal and textile, especially rayon and silk, industries, together with food processing, printing, plastics, oil products and construction. It is the most important centre of learning outside France with a fine university, and a rich cultural life. It also lays claim to be the second city of France, after Paris, although Marseilles challenges this.

Lyon has many beautiful sights, interesting places to visit and many things to see and do. There is a wealth of accommodation, a galaxy of great restaurants, and one of the best things of all, most of the sights can be seen on foot.

Lyon's traffic problems are legendary and caused because most of the city is trapped between the two rivers. Once in the city, find a car park and then explore on foot. The area between the rivers is known as the Presqu'ile and there is a massive **underground car park** in the tree-lined **place Bellecour**, close to the tourist information office. You can purchase a one day pass to all the museums which is great value. The pass can also be purchased at any of the museums. The square is one of the largest in France with many elegant buildings with their classical façades. The large bronze statue of Louis XIV on horseback is the work of local sculpture Jean Lemot and was erected in 1828, to replace the original destroyed during the Revolution. From the square, head down to the river and cross the Sâone by the pont du Bonaparte to the old town with its many interesting sights.

St Jean Cathedral was begun in 1180 and took 300 years to complete, which accounts for its mixture of architectural styles from Gothic to Romanesque. The choir and the apse are the oldest parts with thirteenth-century stained glass in the lower windows. Near the choir is a rare elaborate fourteenth-century astronomical clock which bursts into life on the hour between 12noon and 4pm each day. During medieval and Renaissance times, the cobbled Rue St-Jean in front of the cathedral, was the city's main thoroughfare, and there are many wonderful buildings along its length. Opposite the cathedral is the Manecanterie, the old choir school founded in 1180.

You can either continue your tour of the old town, or detour to take the funicular railway (*ficelle*) from the

Gare-Saint-Jean, next to the cathedral, to the summit of **Fourvière Hill** to view the Roman ruins.

The original Roman settlement was established on Fourvière Hill, and the original and now well-restored **Roman amphitheatre** is the largest in France. It was built in the four decades before the birth of Christ and enlarged in the second century AD by Emperor Hadrian to hold 10,000 spectators. It, and the smaller **Odeon Roman theatre** nearby, are still used for plays and concerts, particularly during September.

Close by is the **Gallo-Roman Museum** (Musée Gallo-Romain), partly built into the hillside, and with splendid views over the Roman theatres. Its treasures include the unique bronze tablet, found in La Croix Rousse in 1538, engraved with the speech given by Emperor Claudius to the Senate in AD48, asking that citizens of Lyon, where he was born, be given Roman citizenship as well. There are also many fine exhibits and statues depicting Roman life in *Lugdunum*.

Also overlooking the old town is the garish **Basilica of Notre-Dame-de-Fourvière**, built after the Franco-Prussian war in 1870. One critic said of the basilica that the only good thing about it was the view it offered over Lyon. You can climb the 287 steps to the basilica's observatory. Behind the basilica is the Tour Métallique, built in 1893 and now a television transmission tower, and close by are the stone steps, the Montée Nicolas-de-Lange, which

lead back down to the old town, emerging near the funicular station.

Once back in old town, look out for one of the intriguing features of this old quarter, the little tunnels that connect many of the streets. These vaulted passages, known as *traboules* (short cuts), are public rights of way and often lead from one street to the inner courtyard of a Renaissance dwelling, and then continue to emerge in the next street. They are very common in the St-Jean quarter and in the old silk weaver's district on the hills of La Croix Rousse, where they were used to carry the silk between buildings, protected from bad weather. If you take the *traboule* at 19 rue St-Jean it brings you out into Rue des Trois-Marie where numbers six and seven have ancient religious statues on their façades. Crossing the place de la Baleine takes you back into rue Saint-Jean: number eleven has a magnificent courtyard with a huge, splendid Gothic staircase, the façade of number seven is equally impressive. Cross the place du Change, with the **Loge du Change** on one corner. This church was built by Soufflot, the architect of the Panthéon in Paris, in 1747. Enter the rue de Lainerie for the St Paul quarter where there are many examples of fine Renaissance architecture, as there are in the rue Juiverie. The Gadagne mansion in the street of the same name is the largest Renaissance building in Lyon built by the Gadagne brothers in 1445 after having made a fortune from banking. Today it houses the

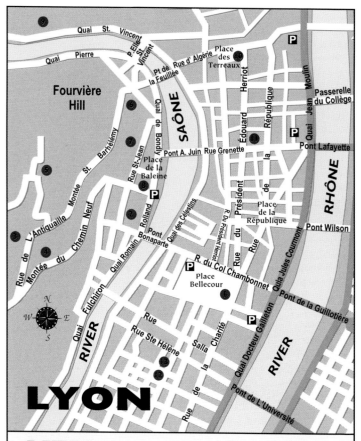

LYON

KEY

P Car Parking

1. Tourist Office
2. St Jean Cathedral
3. Roman Theatres
4. Gallo-Roman Museum
5. Basilica of Notre-Dame-de-Fourvière
6. Loge du Change
7. Historical Museum
8. Archaeological Gardens
9. Jardin des Plantes
10. Museum of Fine Arts
11. Museum of Printing and Banking
12. Historical Textile Museum
13. Museum of Decorative Arts

Historical Museum and the **International Museum of the Marionette**.

The rue Boeuf runs off rue Gadagne, and on the corner is a small statue of a bull, a throw back to medieval times when few people could read and so statues and symbols were used to indicate street names. The statue was the work of Giambologna, a famous French sculptor who lives from 1529 to 1608. Many other street names are represented by figures and symbols depicted on wrought-iron signs. Number 17 is Maison du Crible famous for its round tower and rose coloured frontage, from which the excellent restaurant on the corner, the Tour Rose is named. During the summer this is a delightful area with lots to see, and plenty of cafés and restaurants, many with charming shaded terraces for when you want a refreshment.

A short distance away is the rue de la Bombarde which leads to the **Archaeological Gardens** where the remains of four churches, all built on the same site, have been excavated.

Also worth visiting are the botanical gardens of **Jardin des Plantes**, off rue de l'Annonciad, which also contain the remains of the Amphithéâtre des Trois Gauls, a massive circular amphitheatre built in AD19. The gardens are close to the Croix Rousse quarter, which is where the city's famous silk industry first thrived. By the nineteenth century, over 30,000 silk weavers were working in the city, many of them packed into the small houses of this quarter. This is still a warren of narrow streets and *traboules*, but great fun to explore. The Maison des Canuts, in rue d'Ivry has exhibits on weaving and a miniature loom which children are shown how to use.

Lyon has a number of excellent museums. These include:

The **Museum of Fine Arts** (Musée des Beaux Arts) in the massive Palais St Pierre. It is the largest art collection in France outside the Louvre, and contains many Dutch Masters, but concentrates on French art from the seventeenth century with a priceless collection, including a very large exhibition of Impressionists. It also has works of art, ceramics and sculptures from around the world. On the other side of the Place des Terreaux, with its lively cafés, is the Hôtel de Ville, largely rebuilt after a fire in 1674, although parts of the early seventeenth-century building survived. The monumental fountain in the centre of the square was designed by Bartholdi, who also was responsible for the *Statue of Liberty*, a gift from France to the United States. The fountain's four horses represent the four great rivers of France, the Loire, Rhône, Garonne and Seine, galloping to the sea.

The **Museum of Printing and Banking** (Musée l'Imprimerie et de la Banque), with many fascinating exhibits. Lyon, for instance, was the first city in Europe to set up a Stock Exchange and issue cheques.

The **Museum of Decorative Arts** (Musée Lyonnais des Arts

Decoratifs), rue de la Charite, is housed in a beautiful eighteenth-century mansion and dedicated to the elegance and splendour of eighteenth-century life. On display are some fine examples of the period's furniture, tapestries, porcelain and gold and silverware.

The **Historical Textile Museum** (Musée Historique des Tissus), next door, was founded more than 100 years ago, and is devoted to the history and development of cloths, fabrics and tapestries over the last 2,000 years. Exhibits include the wall hangings made in Lyon in 1771 for Russia's Catherine the Great.

Other museums include: the Museum of Telecommunications, rue Burdeau which traces the history of communications. Le Musée des 150 Aitomates, in rue Saint-Georges, with its animated exhibits and *son et lumière*. The Historic Museum of Lyon, place du Petit Collège; Maison des Canuts, rue d'Ivry; Palais de la Miniature, rue Juiverie; the Natural History Museum, boulevard des Belges; Musée Africain, Cours Gambetta; Dental Museum, rue G. Paradin; the Museum of Military History, ave Yves Farges; and the Museum of the History of Medicine and Pharmacy, ave Rockefeller.

The **Parc de la Tete d'Or**, named after a legend that a golden head of Christ was found here, is one of the finest botanical gardens in France. In late summer more than a million roses can be in bloom, and there are huge glasshouses full of tropical plants to visit, as well as an alpine garden, zoo, and an exotic aviary.

You cannot stay in Lyon without indulging in the magnificent cuisine. Fine restaurants abound in and around the city. Some are so popular that you have to reserve weeks and sometimes months in advance, and cooking of this standard does not come cheap, but if you enjoy great food prepared by some of the world's finest chefs, a visit to one of these prestigious restaurants can be a gastronomic treat of a lifetime. There are many other restaurants and cafés, however, where you can still enjoy good local food and wine without having to worry too much about the cost.

Things To See Around Lyon

Vienne is 19 miles (31km) to the south, and after Marseille, the oldest city in France. It was a prosperous Roman town with many well pre-served monuments and remains, as well as early Christian churches and the magnificent Cathedral of St Maurice, which was started in the twelfth century but took 300 years to complete. The wonderful west front is 98ft (30m) high, 125ft (38m) wide with three highly elaborate portals and the central arch is noted for the magnificence of its carvings. On the left hand side of the nave there is a thirteenth-century carving of Herod and the Three Wise Men, as well as earlier statues of St Peter, John and Paul. The Roman theatre could seat 13,000 spectators, making it larger than those in Lyon and Orange. The theatre was completely buried in

1926 when excavations started, and it took six years to uncover the forty-six layers of seating and the stage. It has now been fully restored and is used for summer performances.

The Temple of Augustus and Livia is Vienne's finest ruin, and one of the two best preserved Roman temples in France, the other being in Nîmes. The temple has survived so well because it was adopted by the early Christians and used as a church. The spaces between the columns were walled in preserving the interior, which was restored to its original state in the late nineteenth century.

The archaeological museum, well worth a visit in its own right, is housed in the former Church of St Pierre, one of the oldest churches in France and dating back to the fifth century. The north, west and south walls date from the sixth century, and the bell tower was built in the twelfth century. The Church of St Andre-le-Bas, at the other end of town, dates from around the same period but was mostly rebuilt in the mid-twelfth century when an adjoining cloister was added.

St Romain-en-Gal, opposite the river from Vienne, was the upmarket suburb of Roman Vienna, with fine paved streets, luxury villas, an artisans quarter and a spa, although none of this was discovered until 1967, when excavation started to build a new school. There is now a small museum exhibiting some of the mosaics and artefacts found.

About 7 miles (27km) north of Lyon, on the D433 is the **Rochetaillée Motor Museum** on the banks of the Saône. Over 200 veteran and old cars, trams and buses are on show, including Hitler's armoured Mercedes.

To the west of Lyon is the **Monts du Lyonnais** where there are many scenic drives and good walking. Both the GR7 and 76 traverse the hills. There is a game park at **Courzieu** on the D30 which specialises in European animals, including those which used to roam the region wild. There is also a nature trail through the 50 acres (20 hectares) of woods and parkland.

Close to **St André-la-Côte** on the D113, there is a footpath to the summit of Signal St André 3,063ft (934m). The round trip only takes about forty-five minutes and there are fabulous views of the Alps and the Rhône Valley from the top.

In the north of the Monts du Lyonnais, near **L'Arbresle**, is the Convent d'Eveux, built in the late 1950, and designed by Le Corbusier, considered one of France's best modern architects.

To the east of Lyon is the medieval fortified town of **Pérouges**, which is so well-preserved that it has often been used for period film. During the Middle Ages it was famous for its linen, but its remoteness meant it could not compete with factory produced cloth after the industrial revolution. Over the past few years, the village has been faithfully restored, and the centuries-old houses are now used by artisans and craftsmen, much as they were 500 years ago.

Other things to see and do

Bourg-en-Bresse, formerly the administrative centre for Savoy, is a quiet town noted for its superb appellation poultry and the church of Brou, on the outskirts of the town. It was built between 1506 and 1532 as a memorial to the husband of Archduchess Marguerite of Savoy who died in 1504 aged only twenty-four. It is a beautiful showy, Gothic building with a fine interior and rare triple-arched rood screen. There are many fine marble statues, three ornate Royal tombs and seventy-four individual monks' stalls carved in oak in front of the choir, and the original stained glass windows made by Lyon craftsmen. It is the setting for a *son-et-lumière* held on Thursday and weekends from May to September. The nearby cloisters house an art museum with many works by Dutch, Flemish, French and Italian Masters from the sixteenth to nineteenth centuries. The area south of Bresse, once covered by a huge glacier, is now known as La Dombes, and is covered by lakes which attract both anglers and birdwatchers. The Parc des Oiseaux at **Villars-les-Dombes**, about 18 miles (29km) south of Bourg-en-Bresse, is regarded as one the best bird sanctuaries in Europe, with more than 400 species of local and exotic species.

Châtillon-sur-Chalaronne, between Villars-les-Dombes and Bourg-en-Bresse, is famous for triptych on wood in the Town Hall's council chamber which depicts the taking down of Christ from the Cross and the Resurrection. The fully restored work dates from 1527 but the artist is unknown, although obviously a Master. The red brick and red tiled Church of St André dates from the fifteenth century, as does the covered market, although most had to be rebuilt after a fire in 1670. The thirty-two pillars are from oak trees donated by La Grande Mademoiselle, the niece of Louis XIII, from her estate.

ADDITIONAL INFORMATION

Places to Visit

ANNONAY
Safari Park Haut Vivarais
Open: 9.30am-7pm 15 March to 1 November, 11am to 5pm rest of year.

COURZIEU
Game Park
Open: daily 10am to sunset.

L'ARBRESLE
Convent d'Eveux
Open: daily July and August. Afternoons only rest of the year

LYON
Musée de la Civilisation Gallo-Romaine
Open: Wednesday to Sunday daily.

Musée des Beaux Arts
Open: daily 10.45am to 6pm, except Tuesday and public holidays.

Musée de l'Imprimerie et de la Banque
Open: Wednesday to Sunday daily.

Musée Lyonnais des Arts Decoratifs
Open: Tuesday to Sunday daily.

Musée Historique des Tissus
Open: Tuesday to Sunday daily

Rochetaillée
Musée de l'Automobile Henri Malartre
Open: Daily to 6pm (7pm in summer).
Villars-es-Dombes

Parc Ornithologique
Open: Daily 8.30am-7pm (earlier in winter)

Tourist Information Offices

Lyon
Comité Régional du Tourisme de la Vallée du Rhône
2 place des Cordeliers
69002 Lyon
☎ 78 92 90 34 for the Rhône Valley and Lyon areas

also at:

place Bellecour
69002 Lyon
☎ 78 42 25 75

Bourg-en-Bresse
Office de Tourisme
6 ave Alsace-Lorraine
01000 Bourg-en-Bresse
☎ 74 22 49 40

Travel

Getting to Lyon

By air
Satolas International Airport is 16 miles (26km) from Lyon. There are frequent bus and train connections between the airport and city

By train
The TGV from Paris to Lyon takes two hours and there are frequent daily services

By car
A6 Nord from Paris 287 miles (462km). Lyon is notorious for huge traffic jams at peak times

Boat trips on the Saône and Rhône

Aqua Viva
Les Berges du Rhône
60 ave Leclerc
69007 Lyon
☎ 78 58 36 34

Navig-Inter
3 rue de l'Arbre Sce
69007 Lyon
☎ 78 27 78 02

Hotels

Amberiéux-en-Dombes **01330**
Les Bichonnieres ££
route de Savigneux
☎ 78 42 75 75

Bourg-en-Bresse **01000**
Hotel Ariane ££
boulevard Kennedy
☎ 74 22 50 88

Hotel de France ££
19 place Bernard
☎ 74 23 30 24

La Petite Auberge
St Just
☎ 74 22 30 04

Châtillon-sur-Chalaronne **01400**
Auberge de la Tour ££
place Republique
☎ 74 55 05 12

Lyon
Cour des Loges £££
6 rue du Boeuf
69005 Lyon
☎ 78 42 75 75

Sofitel ££
20 quai Gailleton
69000 Lyon
☎ 72 41 20 20

Royal ££
20 place Bellecour
69002 Lyon
☎ 78 37 57 31

Hotel des Artistes ££
8 rue Andre
69002 Lyon
☎ 78 42 04 88

Hotel Bayard ££
23 place Bellecour
69002 Lyon
☎ 78 37 39 64

Hotel des Savoies ££
80 rue Charite
69002 Lyon
☎ 78 37 66 94

Pérouges ££
Ostellerie du Vieux
☎ 74 61 00 88

Vienne
La Pyramide £££
14 boulevard Fernand Point
☎ 74 53 01 96

Hotel de la Poste ££
47 Cours Romestang
☎ 74 85 02 04

Restaurants

Bourg-en-Bresse
Le Poulet Gournmand £-££
7 rue Teynière
☎ 74 22 49 50

L'Auberge Bressane
166 boulevard de Brou
☎ 74 22 22 68

Collonges-au-Mont d'Or
Paul Bocuse £££
pont de Collonges
☎ 72 27 85 87

Lyon
Le Vivarais ££-£££
1 place du Docteur-Gailleton
☎ 78 37 85 15

La Tour Rose ££-£££
22 rue de Boeuf
69005 Lyon
☎ 78 37 25 90

Le Mere Brazier ££-£££
12 rue Royale
69001
Lyon
☎ 78 28 15 49

Café des Federations ££
8 rue du Major-Martin
☎ 78 28 26 00

Brasserie Georges £-££
30 Cours Verdun
69002 Lyon
☎ 78 37 15 78

Léon de Lyon £££
1 rue Pléney
☎ 78 28 11 33

Vienne
Le Bec Fin £-££
7 place Saint-Maurice
☎ 74 85 76 72

THE GASTRONOMY OF BURGUNDY

The Burgundians eat well, and it is generally true that the best meals are to be had as a guest of a family rather than as a diner in a restaurant. Because of the thousands of tourists who visit the region every day, the restaurants and hotels have tended to become more international than Burgundian in their style, although there are still those which stick faithfully to the local cuisine.

As a rule, it is wise to avoid any menus advertised as *touristique* or *gastronomique*, unless you know the establishment well. They are likely to cost the earth and the high price is unlikely to be matched by a similar culinary excellence.

The Burgundians do not go in for extremely elaborate cooking, although some chefs do, but they work hard and eat well. Quality counts, but quantity is often more important. They have always had a preference for large scale entertaining and the banquets of some of the Dukes of Burgundy are legendary. Up to 500 people would sit down to a gargantuan feast of a dozen or more courses, and the eating and drinking lasted well into the night.

The region benefits from its strong mix of wine and agriculture. In the south, the woodlands and forests of the Mâconnais provide excellent game, there is first class

beef from the Charolais, truffles and mushrooms, good vegetables and hams. The finest food is generally found in the Côte d'Or, but there are many good restaurants throughout Burgundy, and many small establishments specialising in traditional local cuisine, offered with the finest of the local wines.

There are also distinct styles of regional cooking as you travel from Chablis, through the Côte de Nuits, Côte de Beaune, and into the Chalonnaise and Mâconnais.

Before a meal, you can enjoy an aperitif, and Burgundy's most famous pre-dinner drink — and a great drink at any other time — is Kir, a mixture of Burgundy white wine and *crème de cassis*, a blackcurrant liqueur made from locally-grown fruit. Ideally it should be made from Crème de Cassis de Dijon and Bourgogne Aligoté wine. Kir is believed to have been created by accident at the end of the nineteenth century although it owes its world-wide fame to Canon Kir (1876-1968), who was Dijon's deputy mayor for twenty-two years. He made it so popular that it was later named after him. There are a number of other variations of Kir, such as Kir Royal when the Aligoté still wine is replaced by sparkling Crémant de Bourgogne.

There are many other fruit liqueurs, sold as *crème de fruits*, including raspberry, mulberry and vine peach. These aperitifs are often served with local specialities such as *gougères* (choux pastry), *apérichèvres* (goat's cheese appetizers), or *feuilletés d'escargots* (snails in puff pastry).

Dijon is internationally famous for its mustard, and *crème de cassis*, but try the gingerbread with honey, known as *pain d'épices*, which can also be made with spices. Regional specialities include *andouille* and *andouillette*. The first is a very rich sausage made from pig tripe, usually already cooked and served cold as a starter. The second is another pork sausage but usually grilled and served hot with mustard. Chablis, Mâcon and Clamecy are all noted for their *andouillette*.

Perhaps the region's most famous dish is *boeuf à la Bourguignonne*, a rich stew of beef cooked in red wine with onions, mushrooms and cubes of bacon. A Savigny-lès-Beaune is an ideal accompaniment.

Other first courses can be *jambon persillé*, ham flavoured with parsley in jelly, or *jambon de Morvan*, delicious raw ham from the area to the west of the Côte d'Or. *Jambon en saupiquet* is ham braised in wine and served with a piquant sauce (it is also known as *à la creme*, or *à la Morvandelle*). *Jambon cru* is raw ham, and from Morvan it is especially good, and *jambon rosette* from Mâcon, is a sort of Burgundian salami. There is a very light cheese-flavoured choux pastry ring called *la gougère*, which is normally served cold, and *fouée*, which is a cream and bacon flan with walnut oil, which come from the walnuts which grow

in abundance in the Mâconnais. Burgundy even produces some magnificent *foie gras*.

You will see *morilles* on the menu either by themselves or as an accompaniment to other dishes. They are field mushrooms picked locally in the spring and highly regarded.

Beef is served in many forms, as simply Charolais steaks, or *boeuf à la mode*, which is beef stewed in red wine with vegetables and herbs and served either hot, or cold in its own jelly.

Coq au vin is also a speciality, and Chambertin should be used, but the recipe varies throughout the region. The chicken is cooked in the red wine together with vegetables, mushrooms and onions. Chicken also figures in many other regional dishes and local specialities. *Poulet demi-deuil* is breast of chicken cooked with slices of black truffle; and there is *poulet en matelote*, chicken cooked in red wine with sliced eel, bacon and onions.

Snails are a speciality of the region and can be found everywhere. The edible snail *helix pomatia*, has even been found as fossils, and it can be seen painted and sculptured on many of the Romanesque buildings. It is thought that snails were first eaten in Burgundy around the third century AD and in the Middle Ages, all the monasteries and convents had snail enclosures for home consumption or sale. Today the most sought after snail is the vine snail, but it is now quite rare. *Escargots de Bourgogne* (if the snails are local or *à la Bourguignonne* if they

Above: Hotel Les Arts in Meursault. Although the Meursault borders on Volnay, it is the largest white wine producer in the Côte D'Or.
Below (*left*): Place des Fontaines, Dornecy (*right*): Le Vieux Moulin, Chablis.

come from elsewhere) are snails served in a hot garlic and parsley butter sauce. *Garbure* is a really thick soup made with pork, cabbage, beans and sausages.

A lot of game appears on the menus. *Rable de lièvre* is saddle of hare cooked in red wine. A variation of this is *lièvre à la Piron*, which is saddle of hare marinated in *marc*, the spirit distilled from the grape juice, and then cooked with shallots and grapes and served with a pepper and cream sauce. It is a speciality of Dijon.

Boudin is Burgundian black pudding, made with blood, and *quenelles de volaille* are finely-minced balls of chicken meat, moulded into a sausage shape and served with a sauce. Sausage also figures in *saucisse en brioche*, a large sausage in some form of pastry or dough. *Marcassin farci au saucisson* is young wild boar, from the Mâconnais, stuffed with sausage, and *meurette* describes a sort of red wine sauce which can be served with fish, eggs or meat.

Pouchouse (or *pochouse* from the Burgundian dialect word for a fisherman) is a stew of freshwater fish from the Saône, a Burgundian freshwater *bouillabaisse*. Usually pike, perch, eel and tench are used, although carp is sometimes added. They are all cooked in white wine to which cream and garlic is added, and served with croutons rubbed in garlic. The secret is to use a very good wine. Many towns along the Saône and the Doubs rivers lay claim to creating the recipe which is certainly very old. Its first mention in print was in 1598 when it appeared in the St Louis Hospital register at Chalon-sur-Saône. *Matelote* is a freshwater dish, usually eel, pike or trout cooked in red wine. The rivers and likes provide an abundance of fish, including crayfish. Dishes are offered *en meurette* (in a wine sauce), *à la Bourguignonne*, *à la Morvandelle* and *à la Mâconnais*. Each region has its own specialities and special ways of preparing even classic recipes. If eating a dish like *pouchouse*, drink a lively wine such as Aligoté, Pouilly-Fumé or a white Mâcon. For fish dishes cooked in wine, try a young wine served slightly chilled to reduce its acidity, and forget the white wine with fish rule and try a red Burgundy from Auxerrois, a Côte Chalonnaise or a Côte de Beaune Village.

Salade à la Bourguignonne is made from a curly lettuce, liberal quantities of garlic, and diced bacon. *Haricots au vin rouge* speaks for itself, and *jambon à la lie-de-vin* is a meal in itself and quite delicious. It is ham which has been braised in the red wine left in the barrels after bottling the lees. Liberal quantities of bread are essential to mop up every drop of the sauce. *Queue de boeuf des vignerons* is oxtail stewed with white grapes.

Burgundy is noted for its poultry and the very best chickens come from Bresse which was entirely in Burgundy until 1789, when it was split up after the Revolution. The best poultry, however, still comes from the area of Bresse now in the

Saône et Loire département. The first reference to Bresse poultry is in the Bouy archives in November 1591, and the poultry is so highly regarded gastronomically, that it received its own appellation in 1919, the only animal product allowed to use an AC label. As for fish, a light red wine is often better for roast poultry than a white, so try a Mercurey, Morey-St-Denis, St Aubin, Volnay or Beaune. For chicken with a cream sauce try a supple white such as Pouilly-Loché, St-Véran, Chablis Grand or Premier Cru, Chassagne or Montagny. For *coq-au-vin*, try a Premier Cru de Côte d'Or, or Côte Chalonnaise.

The hills of Morvan and Nivernais to the west of the Côte D'Or also have some speciality dishes including *sansiot*, calf's head, served with onions and mushrooms; *rapée Morvandelle*, grated potato baked with cream, eggs and cheese; and *potée Bourguignonne*, a vegetable stew to which one or several meats can be added, mostly pork, but chicken, beef or garlic sausage can be used. An *omelette au sang* has a sauce filling thickened with blood, and blood is also used to thicken a rich sauce in which a chicken is cooked for *du poulet au sang*. Pig's offal, cooked in red wine, is also popular, and served on the menu as *fressure*: it can sometimes be calf's offal, but it is cooked with onions, and eaten cold.

The Burgundians tend to prefer cheese to desserts, but if you like puddings, you will not be disappointed. There is a wealth of *pâtisserie*, and many towns have their own special desserts, such as *bûchettes in Sens*, the biscuits of Chablis, the *anis* of Flavigny-sur-Ozerain, the *Jacquelines*, *Colombier* and *pain d'épice* of Dijon, *pavés* from Autun and Chalon-sur-Saône, and *nougatines* from Nevers. Auxerre is famous for its Marmottes cherries which appear in a number of their desserts. You may also be offered *rigodon* or *tartouillat*. The first is a brioche flan with nuts and fruit, and the second is apple tart. Check the *rigodon* carefully because it is sometimes served with bacon as a savoury. Two other dessert delicacies are *Le Cacou*, pastry and fruit cake using black, unstoned cherries and a speciality of Paray-le-Monial; and *La Poire Belle Dijonnaise*, whole pears peeled and poached with their stalks in a vanilla syrup and served covered with raspberry purée. It should also be accompanied by blackcurrant ice cream and roasted almonds.

There are more than two dozen regional cheeses, both from cow's and goat's milk, or a mixture, and they are worth seeking out because it is unlikely that you will find many of them outside Burgundy. They are always served after the main course to allow you to finish off the last of the red wine. Although many white wines also go superbly with these cheeses, this may be considered heresy in Burgundy! The goat cheeses include *Charolais*, made around the town of Charolles, to the west of the Mâconnais. It is rolled into the shape of a log, has a blue rind and a firm, nutty tang. *Claquebitou*, made with added herbs and garlic, is only available from June to October. *Chévreton de Mâcon* again has a nutty taste when a little mature, but can be creamy when young. *Montrachet* is also log-shaped and wrapped in a vine leaf. It is creamy and mild. The cow's milk cheeses include *Aisy-Cendré*, which can be served in a variety of shapes but is always covered in wood ashes. It is a firm, fruity cheese with a strong smell and sometimes cured in *marc*. *Cîteaux* is a tangy cheese made by the monks in the monastery of Cîteaux, to the east of Nuits-St-Georges, and *Epoisses* is a soft, tangy cheese in a distinctive orange-red rind. *Les Laumes* is made on farms. It has a strong flavour and a dark brown rind, a result of being dyed with coffee. The monastery near St-Léger-Vauban, gives its name to *Boulette-de-la-Pierre-Qui-Vire*, a strong cheese always sold on a mat of straw, but it can be eaten fresh when it is much milder. It is usually rolled into a ball and can be flavoured with herbs. *St-Florentin* is a flat round cheese, with a spicy smell and shiny rind; *Soumaint-rain* is similar, but can be eaten young when creamy. Other cheeses to look out for include: *Chaource*, a creamy cow's milk cheese made to the west of Les Riceys and best eaten during the summer and autumn; *Ducs*, a soft cow's milk cheese from Tonnere and best drunk with St. Bris whites; and *Pourly*, a soft, slightly nutty goat's milk cheese.

Finally, when you have finished your food, enjoy a Burgundian liqueur or spirit, appropriately known as *les digestifs*, because they do aid digestion, especially after a little over indulgence. Many of the liqueurs and spirits are based on the distillation of infusion of grapes or fruit. *Marc de Bourgogne* and *Fine de Bourgogne* are considered as traditional digestifs to go with refined cuisine. Newer liqueurs are based on raspberry, blackberry, peach and sloe.

Marc de Bourgogne is by far the oldest spirit of Burgundy. It is made from the distillation of the '*genne*', the skins, pips and stems of the grapes left after pressing. The alcohol which comes from the still is white and it gets its colour after being kept in oak barrels by absorbing tannin in the wood. The wood storage also develops aroma. It is traditionally drunk at the end of the meal, but may be offered during the *trous bourguignons* the waiting period between courses. At the end of the meal, it is best served in the still warm coffee cup which brings out its full aroma.

Food Markets

Bouhans
The Balme Fair, last Saturday and Sunday in August

Chablis
The Burgundian wine and food market every Sunday morning

Louhans
The Bresse poultry market, every Monday

Marcigny
The turkey and goose fair, second Tuesday in December

Moulins-Engilbert
The sheep and farm produce every

Above: Restaurant and bar in Place de L'Europe, Pommard.
Below (*left*): The restaurant La Côte D'Or, Nuits St Georges. (*right*): Even the house white wine is extremely full-flavoured at L'Arc en Ciel in Rully.

Monday, cattle and farm produce every Tuesday

St-Bris-Le-Vineux
New Year's Eve Market at the Bally Cellars

St Christophe-en-Brionnais
A cattle and food market, every Thursday

Saulieu
The national Charolais cattle fair, the Saturday and Sunday after 15 August

---

THE GASTRONOMY OF BEAUJOLAIS

Beaujolais is part of the Lyonnais and there are many who argue that this is the culinary capital of France. Certainly Lyon boasts more than its share of starred restaurants, and just north of the city, slightly over the edge of Beaujolais country, is the Auberge Paul Bocuse, named after its patron chef, rightly acclaimed as one of the finest in Europe.

Lyonnais is a large area able to draw on the resources of many types of agricultural and horticultural enterprises. It is bordered to the north by the Mâconnais which offers a similar, but less accessible cuisine. To the east are the Jura and the Alps, the lower slopes of which are grazed by dairy cattle, the source of many fine cheeses. To the west is the Massif Central, and its foothills which are the home of the Charolais cattle. To the south there is the Rhône Valley with its fruit and vegetables, fish and access to the coast and the Mediterranean catches.

There is no distinct style of Lyonnais cuisine; rather, it is a collection of menus and dishes which vary according to the chef. Some dishes can be plain, while a neighbouring establishment will offer the same dish adorned with cream and truffles. The region also includes in the north-east the area of Bresse, noted for its special chickens, the only poultry in the world to have their own *appellation contrôlée*. The chickens are free range, fed on maize and buckwheat, and then plucked by hand so that only a ruff of feathers remains, the sign of a Bresse bird. The chicken is then soaked in milk which boosts the whiteness of the meat. Bresse also harvests a host of other produce from its fertile land. Apart from vegetables, there are many dairy cattle, and these provide the milk for the world famous *Bresse Blue*, or *Bleu de Bresse*, which is a strong flavoured creamy cheese.

Beaujolais itself makes fine tarts and the delicate white goat's cheese, *Chèvre*, although this is found in other regions as well; the Saône and the Rhône provide the freshwater fish, including pike, used in many of the region's speciality dishes.

As with the rest of Burgundy, Beaujolais is not the place for the weak-hearted or those on a diet; the helpings are generous and many menus, even the more modestly priced ones, expect you to eat your way through several courses.

In addition to many of the dishes mentioned in the Burgundy section, such as *coq au vin* and *boeuf Bourguignonne*, you will find that lamb and pork also figure heavily on the menus of the Lyonnais. The lamb comes from the lush grass meadows of Beaujolais, and the pork from around Lyon, which is famous for its charcuterie. There is also game from the Forez, the high, tree-covered hills between the Loire and the Massif Central.

The area is known for its frogs, and there are many different *grenouille* dishes. They can be served in butter, with a cream and herb sauce — *grenouilles à la Bressane*, or simply cooked in butter — *grenouilles sautées*. Quenelle is also a speciality; it is a very light, delicate poached mousse. *Quenelles de brochet* is pike, *quenelle de volaille* is chicken.

There are marvellous local soups, both fish and meat, and for many people they can be a meal in themselves. Especially, there is potage à la *jambe de bois*, a Lyonnais speciality. It is soup made from leg of beef on the bone as well as other meats and assorted vegetables.

A much lighter dish is *écrevisses à la crème*, crayfish from the Saône served in a cream sauce.

Lyonnais cuisine is also famed for its sweet pastry fritters, *bugne*, which at certain times may be served decorated with acacia flowers.

Cardon is another name you might not have come across before. The English 'cardoon' looks like celery, is related to the thistle family and has a taste a little like that of a Jerusalem artichoke. In the Lyonnais it is baked with bone marrow to create *cardons à la moelle*, and it can be served with a cheese sauce.

Pork figures in many of the dishes, but especially sausages and the excellent prepared hams. There is blood pudding cooked with apples, *boudin aux pommes de reinette*; a large pork sausage, similar to salami, called *rosette*; and *sabodet*, a sausage made from the pig's head and served hot in thick slices. There is also *cervelas*, a soft smooth pork sausage, similar to a Saveloy. It was originally made with brains, and is now lightly smoked, poached and can be eaten hot or cold. The Lyonnais style is *cervelas en brioche*, baked in a brioche dough.

Chapon de Bresse gros sel is a Bresse capon with sliced truffles under the skin, covered in rock salt and baked. Other Bresse poultry dishes include *poulet* (or *poularde* or *volaille) Celéstine*, with tomatoes, mushrooms, wine and cream (and named after Napoléon III's chef); *poulet aux écrevisses*, with crayfish in a white wine and cream sauce; *poulet en vessie*, poached inside a pig's bladder; *poulet à la Mère Fillioux*, stuffed with sausage with sliced truffles, and served with a cream sauce, and *poulet au vinaigre*, a speciality, chicken served with shallots, tomatoes, white wine, vinegar and cream.

The presence of cattle is also felt with many ox, beef and calf dishes. *Gras-double à la Lyonnaise* is sliced ox tripe, fried with onions, vinegar and parsley; *saladier Lyonnaise* is a gargantuan salad of calf's head, pig's and sheep's trotters, sausage and ox muzzle (the nose and lips) all tossed in a vinaigrette dressing and diced shallots. *Tablier de sapeur*, which literally means 'fireman's apron', originated in this region; it is a thick slice of ox tongue, coated in egg and breadcrumbs, grilled or fried, and served with a sauce, usually either tartare, mayonnaise or Béarnaise.

Jambon au foin, used to mean ham cooked in fresh hay, in the same way that some cheeses are cured in it. Although the practice is still continued, it is more likely now to mean ham cooked in herbs.

Hare is a feature of Bresse cuisine, and *lièvre* (or *civet*) *de Diane de Châteaumorand* is stewed hare with red wine, mushrooms and onions. It is named after a seventeenth-century beauty who divorced her husband for his brother, and then ignored him and turned to her greyhounds for company. They, presumably, caught the hares.

Other speciality dishes are *pommes Lyonnaisse*, sauté sliced potatoes cooked with onions; *omelette à la Lyonnaise*, an omelette filled with onions and parsley; *civet à la Lyonnaise*, hare stewed with chestnuts; *galette Lyonnaise*, a cake of puréed potatoes and onions; and *saucisson à la Lyonnaise*, sausage served with a hot potato salad. Lyonnais cuisine is also famed for its desserts and pâtisserie. There are *marrons à la Lyonnaise* (chestnut cake); *cocons* (marzipan sweets, often filled with liqueur in the shape of a cacoon); *pogne* (a brioche cake filled with fruit and jam) which is really a speciality of further south, but is now widely available here, and tendresses (flavoured nougat in a meringue case).

The most famous cheese is the *Bleu de Bresse*, a mild creamy blue cow's milk cheese similar to a Gorgonzola; it is now almost all factory made. *Cervelle de Canut* (also called *Claqueret*), is a home-made mixture of curds, vinegar, white wine, oil and garlic. It means 'silk-weaver's brain' and was traditionally made by their families. *Fromage fort du Beaujolais* is a strong, firm cheese, often soaked in marc, and *Fourme de Montbrison* comes from the Forez foothills and it is a firm cheese that is uncooked, unpressed and ripened for two months. It has a fruity taste, is lightly blue-veined and has its own appellation. *Rigotte de Condrieu* is a small, mild cheese made by the small dairies around Condrieu. It has a mild, milky taste and a reddish rind. And, *Mont d'Or* from just north of Lyon is a very delicate, soft cheese.

There are two main goat's cheeses available locally; one comes from Bresse and the other from Forez. Bressan, also known as *Petit Bressan*, is a soft, small, mild goat's cheese still made on farms, with a slightly fruity taste. The other *Brique du Forez* is also known as *Chévreton d'Ambert* and *Cabrion du Forez*. It is named after its brick shape. It is a mild cheese with a nutty flavour, made on farms in the Ambert and Monts du Forez region. Also, you should not leave the region without trying *fromage blanc*, a fresh cream cheese eaten with fresh cream and sprinkled with sugar.

Burgundy stretches from Chablis, which is 114 miles (184km) south-east of Paris, southwards almost to Lyon. It is an area of forest and arable land, but above all, of vineyards. The vineyards are on the slopes of the Morvan Hills, on the right hand bank of the River Saône. The area is not one long stretch of vineyard, but rather a number of clearly-defined separate areas, which include many of the great names in wine. From the north you travel from Chablis and the Auxerrois, to the Côte de Nuits, the Côte de Beaune, the Côte de Chalonnaise, the Mâconnais, and then finally Beaujolais.

Although for hundreds of years a dukedom in its own right, Burgundy was separated after the French Revolution and now forms part of the *départements* of the Yonne, Côte d'Or and the Saône-et-Loire.

The vineyards of Chablis, less than two hours' drive from Paris, lie in the Yonne *département*. Chablis produces only dry white wines from the vineyards on the slopes of the hills. The soil is mostly limestone, and the chief grape is Chardonnay, which produces all the finest Burgundian white wines. Nearby is the Auxerrois, which also grows Sauvignon and Aligoté and produces the sparkling wine of Burgundy, the Crémand de Bourgogne.

The Côte d'Or, or Golden Slope, is divided into two areas, the Côte de Nuits in the north, and the Côte de Beaune in the south. The area is believed to have got its name from the golden colour of the vine leaves in the autumn just before they fall. Both areas stretch for just under 40 miles (64km) from Dijon to Santenay. Almost all the vineyards are east facing, but the soils and sub soils vary considerably as you travel through the region, which is why the wines differ so much from area to area. Throughout the Côte d'Or, the vineyard strip is narrow, nowhere more than 1 mile (2km) wide. In the Côte de Nuits, the vines are planted on the hillsides, almost up to the tree-lined summits. The vineyards face east or south-east, and get many hours of sunshine without the grapes being scorched. The Côte de Beaune is flatter and the soil is richer and thicker, but the vineyard belt is again restricted to quite a narrow strip, never more than 2 miles (3km) wide. The best wines come from grapes grown on the slopes.

The Côte de Chalonnaise is another centre for sparkling wines, and efforts are being made to revitalise the still wine industry with some encouraging results. Some excellent white wines are made, and because they are overshadowed by their neighbour to the north they tend to be cheaper.

The Mâconnais is a large producer of white wines, notably Pouilly-Fuissé, Bourgogne red and white, Bourgogne Aligoté, and Mâcon, both red and white.

The area is very hilly, and the vineyards fill the slopes leaving the

Previous page: The elegant Château de Rully.

fertile valleys free for other agricultural enterprises.

Burgundy has unpredictable weather. The summers can be very hot and the winters very cold. Severe frosts in 1956 destroyed thousands of vines in Chablis. Hail is another problem, and a severe hailstorm can cause very serious damage to harvest prospects in minutes. On average it rains in Burgundy 155 days a year. Even in summer there can be heavy rainfall and travellers are advised to have waterproof garments or an umbrella with them. June and October are the wettest months. Summer rains tend to be light and constant, rather than torrential downpours, but cloudbursts are common. There is a record of more than two inches of rain falling in just one hour on 16 July 1947. Heavy rainfall in June can be a problem because it is the time when the vines are in flower. The rains can damage the flowers which can affect fertilisation and lead to poor yields. Rain can also cause the onset of various diseases, especially rot. Most of the rain comes up from the south, and therefore it is heaviest in the southern parts of Burgundy. It decreases as you travel northwards through the Côte d'Or. The hillsides afford the vines some protection and do assist drainage. July is normally the hottest month of the year with temperatures of about 70 to 75°F (21 to 24°C), December, January and February are the coldest months. They are the times of the frost, which around Dijon occur on about sixty days of the year. The vines bud late,

and this generally protects them from frost damage unless the temperature falls below 0°F (-18°C). But a late spring frost, during the time when the vines are shaking themselves back into growth and the sap starts to rise, can be disastrous.

Despite its inland location, and its situation in the hills, Burgundy gets a surprising amount of annual sunshine — an average 2,000 hours — and temperatures can occasionally rocket. There are records of temperatures in excess of 85°F (29°C) in May, but these most often occur in mid-summer. The high sunshine readings are part of a typical continental climate of long hot summers as high pressure areas are trapped over land masses. The sunshine is nature's compensation for the high rainfall, much of which falls at the wrong time of the year for most vineyard owners. The sunshine helps to dry out the vines, ripen the grapes and a combination of warmth and wind can prove an effective natural deterrent to the development of rot after rain.

Burgundy is one of the best places to study the geology of a wine growing area, because the contrast of soils is clear to see as you travel from district to district through the region. The rocks in the hills of Burgundy were formed during the same geological age as the Alps. They were subjected to enormous pressures, which accounts for the many rifts and valleys.

For millions of years, the whole of the area now known as Burgundy was part of a massive inland sea, and this explains why so many shells and fossils are to be found in the rocks and subsoil, and why the ground is so rich in minerals. When the inland sea drained away, the mountain-building which was to create the Alps, the Pyrenees, and the Atlas Mountains in North Africa began.

Most of the vineyards are now on limestone, laid down over millions of years as vegetation and marine life died and fell to the bottom of the sea. As the layer grew bigger and heavier, it was compressed into rock. There are also isolated areas of grave and marl, a limey clay. The limestone ridge extends as far south as the Mâconnais, where it merges into granite, the main geological feature of the Beaujolais area. The colour of the soil also changes as you travel south through Burgundy, because while the covering is predominantly limestone, it consists of a large number of different varieties.

The best grapes come from vines on the first part of the slopes, which have soils containing a high proportion of silts and clay. The stony, chalky tops of the slopes are best suited for white wines, while the flat land at the foot of the hills is often turned over to other agriculture.

Many of the vineyards have stony soils which act as storage heaters, trapping the sun's heat during the day and releasing it slowly during the night. Stones and pebbles in the soil also aid drainage, which can be a particular problem in Burgundy.

Grape varieties in Burgundy are Pinot Noir and Gamay for reds, and Chardonnay, Pinot Blanc, Pinot Gris

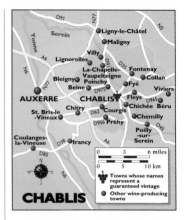

CHABLIS

and Aligoté for whites. The Pinot Noir produces all the classic red wines of Burgundy, while the Gamay, which is believed to have originated in the Côte d'Or, is now the grape of Beaujolais. It is still planted, however, in parts of northern Burgundy where it is blended with Pinot Noir to make Bourgogne Mousseaux and Bourgogne Passe-Tout-Grain.

Chardonnay, likewise, produces the great white wines of Burgundy and it is interesting that the two — Chardonnay and Pinot Noir — when blended, produce the 'Queen of wines', Champagne. Aligoté is an important variety in Burgundy, producing highly acidic, refreshing white wines which are best drunk young. Its advantage is that it is a sturdy vine, which produces good yields and can be planted on ground not suitable for Chardonnay. The Pinot Blanc and Pinot Gris are both planted, but their acreage is declining, and they are being used less for blending.

THE WINE DISTRICTS OF BURGUNDY

Chablis

The twenty communes of Chablis sit among the limestone hills in the most northerly part of Burgundy, and produce a white wine which is famous the world over. Certainly Chablis is the most-ordered white wine in restaurants, perhaps because the name is easy to say, but also because it drinks so well. The wines are light-coloured, pale and dry but balance masks the high acidity. They are superb with seafood, oysters in particular.

The district of Chablis is just under two hours' drive from Paris, down the A6, the main autoroute south. You leave the autoroute at Auxerre and head for the town of Chablis, which is well worth a visit in its own right. Formerly owned by the Crown, the town of Chablis and surrounding land was one of those areas presented to the Church. It was a gift from Charles the Bald in AD867 to the monks of St Martin-de-Tours in the Loire. It stayed in the hands of the Church until the French Revolution in 1789, when the lands were again distributed among the peasants.

The town lies in the valley of the River Serein and in Roman times there was a ferry here which made it an important crossing point. The cluster of stone houses now looks out over the limestone slopes to the east, where the grapes for the seven Great Growth (Grand Cru) Chablis are grown. Chablis has had a long and troubled history, being so close to the border. Although part of Burgundy, it was captured several times by the French during the Hundred Years' War, and then retaken by the English and their allies. Its greatest disaster, however, occurred during World War II when in June 1940 Mussolini's airforce bombed the town. Why Chablis was chosen, no-one knows, but the centre of the town was destroyed and fires raged for three days.

Much of the prestige of the area comes from the religious orders, especially the Cistercians, who gained permission to plant vines around Chablis from the monks of the Order of St Martin. They selected the best sites for the vines, improved the quality of the wine, and established a tradition that has continued for centuries.

The seven Grand Cru growths are Vaudésir, Preuses, Les Clos, Grenouilles, Bougros, Valmur, and Blanchots, and their popularity was greatly enhanced because of their proximity to Paris where it was very fashionable to drink the wines favoured by the Court.

Chardonnay has always been the dominant grape here, and is known locally as the Beaunois, because it was introduced to Chablis by the Cistercians from Beaune in the Côte D'Or. It is not a heavy producer, but the soft, northern sunshine, the soil and the slopes combine to produce a magnificent wine. The best Chablis vines are all grown on chalky clay, littered with pebbles and stone overlying the limestone rock. Obviously quality does vary, and a lot of the production is actually bottled further south in Beaune and Nuits-St-Georges.

The other major problem of producing wine in this area is frost, which seems to linger for days. In the worst years, and there have been several since the end of World War II, entire vintages have been wiped out. In the 1950s, half the vintages of the decade were totally lost.

There are four categories of Chablis: Grand Cru, Premier Cru, Chablis and Petit Chablis. The best growths are obviously the Grand Crus, seven in all, on the hills above the River Serein, a tributary of the Yonne, which gives its name to the *département*. Only in the very best years are wines labelled under their Grand Cru title which gives them enormous cache and a price tag to match. If they do not meet all the strict criteria needed for a Grand Cru, they will be downgraded to Premier Cru, or simply Chablis. The Grand Crus must contain eleven per cent natural alcohol, and be made only from the Chardonnay grape. The vines are carefully manicured by hand, and only the best grapes are selected for harvesting. If a Grand Cru is made, the output is only about 1,800 bottles an acre. In the best vintages the seven Grand Cru will produce between them only about 5,000 cases, which is reflected in their subsequent high price. The wines are bottled about a year after the vintage, and then spend up to four years in cellars before being sold. The classic Chablis has a pale colour with a green tinge on the rim. It is bone dry but with a mouth-filling flavour of fruit, which lingers on long after the first sip. Although dry, the fruit gives an impression of sweetness.

Chablis Premier Cru is the next quality category. These wines must have an alcohol content of at least ten per cent natural alcohol, and production is limited to about 2,080 bottles an acre. There used to be about two dozen vineyards allowed to use the title Premier Cru, but in 1967 the list was reduced to eleven for the sake of simplicity, and these vineyards are: Beauroy, Côte de Lechet, Vaillons, Melinots, Montmains, Vosgros (all on the south side of the Serein); and Fourchaume, Montée de Tonnerre, Mont de Milieu, Vaucoupin, and Les Fourneaux (all on the north side of the river).

One of the problems of Chablis is the small size of the vineyards. After the Revolution, the great estates were split up, and since then, on the death of the vineyard owner, the land has been subdivided between all the members of the family under French inheritance laws. As a result, this continual division has led to thousands of small vineyards, which would be totally uneconomic if they were left to produce wine themselves. Most survive by pooling their grapes and producing wine under one or other of the vineyard names allowed under the Premier Cru appellation.

The Chablis appellation yields up to 1,250,000 bottles in a reasonable year, and the vineyards extend away from the town of Chablis towards Auxerre in the west. The wine must have a minimum of ten per cent natural alcohol, and must comply with all the other rules laid down for the cultivation and vinification of Chablis. Again the smallness of the individual producers means that the wine is always blended, and because it can come from a wider area than allowed for Grand or Premier Cru, problems in one village can be overcome by blending with grapes from another. The best appellation Chablis is produced in and around the villages of Maligny, Beine, Lignorelles, Chemilly and Bertu. They are dry and best drunk young.

Petit Chablis is not widely known outside France, and some growers have campaigned to have the appellation changed to Chablis Villages to make it more meaningful. The appellation covers a score of villages circling the town of Chablis. The wine must reach a minimum nine-and-a-half per cent natural alcohol, and volume is restricted to that of the Chablis appellation. A lot of vineyard replanting over the past few years has taken place in the Petit Chablis area, as growers try to cash in on the world-wide popularity of the wine.

Although the Chardonnay is the only grape allowed in Chablis, wine producers do grow some Aligoté, which is used to produce Bourgogne Aligoté, a very crisp, dry wine for everyday drinking which is ideal when served chilled on hot summer days. Also made is the sparkling Crémant de Bourgogne which comes from the area around Auxerrois. It is made in the *méthode Champenoise*, using the Sacy grape, which is high yielding, high in acidity and reasonably low in alcohol — all ideal for the production of sparkling wines.

Côte de Nuits

The Côte de Nuits is the northern half of the Côte d'Or, and is to Burgundy what the Médoc is to Bordeaux. Just travelling through the villages of the district is like flipping through an atlas of the world's best wines. There are names such as Chambertin, Clos St Jacques, Clos de la Roche, Clos St Denis and Gevrey-Chambertin. In the south of the area there is Musigny, Clos de Vougeot, Clos de Tart, Nuits-St-Georges and many others.

The Côte de Nuits, which gets its name from Nuits-St-Georges, starts at Dijon in the north and runs south for just over 12 miles (19km) to Corgoloin in the south. The vineyards are rarely more than half a mile deep, and in places less than a quarter of a mile wide, as they hug the south-east facing slopes of the continuous range of small hills making up the Côte d'Or. There are three main areas of excellence in the Côte de Nuits, around Chambertin, Musigny and Romanée-Conti, and the vineyards here constitute some of the most expensive agricultural land in the world. Not all the land is

Above: Château de Marsannay, south of Dijon. The area produces a marvellous rosé from the Pinot Noir grapes.
Below: Some of the major vineyards of the Côte de Nuits are signposted.

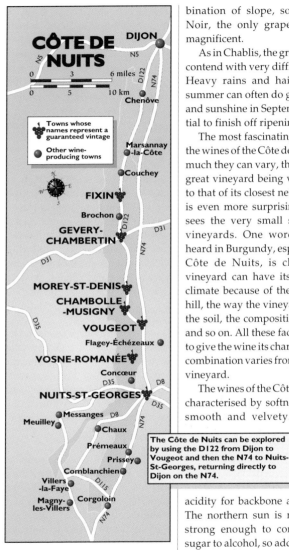

bination of slope, soil and Pinot Noir, the only grape allowed, is magnificent.

As in Chablis, the growers have to contend with very difficult weather. Heavy rains and hail in the late summer can often do great damage, and sunshine in September is essential to finish off ripening.

The most fascinating thing about the wines of the Côte de Nuits is how much they can vary, the wine of one great vineyard being very different to that of its closest neighbour. This is even more surprising when one sees the very small size of these vineyards. One word frequently heard in Burgundy, especially in the Côte de Nuits, is climate. Each vineyard can have its own micro-climate because of the slope of the hill, the way the vineyard faces into the soil, the composition of the soil and so on. All these factors combine to give the wine its character, and the combination varies from vineyard to vineyard.

The wines of the Côte de Nuits are characterised by softness. They are smooth and velvety. They have

The Côte de Nuits can be explored by using the D122 from Dijon to Vougeot and then the N74 to Nuits-St-Georges, returning directly to Dijon on the N74.

devoted to vines, and the best wines come from the vineyards in the middle of the predominantly clay and chalk soil. Here, the com-

acidity for backbone and long life. The northern sun is not generally strong enough to convert all the sugar to alcohol, so additional sugar frequently has to be added. This is a legal process, called *chaptalisation*. The wines also have very complex noses and scents of truffles, violets and raspberries can often be detected. They age magnificently, and many of the great Côte de Nuits need ten to twenty years to reach their peak.

Larrey

Larrey is the most northerly village in the Côte de Nuits and can also be included in the Côte de Dijon. Over the last hundred years many of the vineyards have been swallowed up by the spread of Dijon and the best known is now Les Marcs d'Or, which is unusual in that it has a north-east aspect.

Chenôve

This village has also seen better days, and once boasted of some fine vineyards with an international reputation. There is a story that the village got its name from *chanvre*, or cannabis, which was reputedly grown here. Today it is worth a visit to see the massive presses dating back to the fifteenth century. The wines from the villages are sold under the Bourgogne Rouge label.

Marsannay-la-Côte

Marsannay-la-Côte is 5 miles (8km) south of Dijon, and the first major producer encountered after leaving the city. Its claim to fame lies in the marvellous rosé produced from the Pinot Noir grapes. The majority of the production comes from the *Cave Coopérative* and *Clair-Dau*. Vines have been grown here for at least 1,200 years (and probably much longer), and with neighbouring Couchey, many of the vineyards were turned over to Gamay to satisfy the demands of Dijon which doubled in size in the eighteenth century. Since the last war, plantings of Pinot Noir have increased and growers are now striving to win the right to call their wines Appellation Contrôlée Côte de Nuits.

Fixin

Fixin is 2 miles (3km) south of Marsannay-la-Côte, off the N74, and the first village south of Dijon to have AC status. For many years the wines of Fixin were used for blending with those of Chambertin, but it gained AC status in 1936 and many new vineyards are now producing wines with great depth of colour and robustness. A tiny amount of white Fixin is also produced.

Brochon

This is the next village south and its wines are used for blending. The northern vineyards are used to produce wine for blending with Côte de Nuits Villages, while those in the south are often used for blending with Gevrey-Chambertin.

Gevrey-Chambertin

This village has given its name to some of the finest wines in the world. It is the home of Chambertin, the favourite red wine of Napoleon, and includes other classic vineyards such as Latricières-Chambertin, Chambertin-Clos-de-Bèze, Mazis-Chambertin, Ruchottes-Chambertin, Charmes-Chambertin, Mazoyères-Chambertin, Griottes-Chambertin and Chapelle-Chambertin. The

Gevrey-Chambertin AC is the largest village AC in the Côte de Nuits and has again been producing wine since Roman times, but the Church had the biggest influence on wine production.

In AD630 the Duke of Amalgaire donated a plot of land to the Abbey of Bèze and the vines planted started the long and illustrious history of Clos de Bèze. The name Chambertin is supposed to have come from the name of a peasant farmer who owned land next to the abbey's vineyard. He was called Bertin, and his vineyard was known as *Campus Bertini*, then *Champ de Bertin* (the Field of Bertin), and eventually, simply Chambertin. The Abbey of Cluny acquired its first land in the area in AD895, a gift from the Duke of Burgundy, and it continued to expand, buying land whenever possible. In 1257 work started on the château on the orders of the Abbot Yves de Poissey. The fortified château was used for centuries to protect the villages when attacked, and parts of it still remain and can be visited. Gevrey-Chambertin has more Grand Crus to its name than any other village of Burgundy and more than a score of Premiers Crus. The Gevrey-Chambertin vineyards cover almost 1,250 acres (500 hectares), and average annual production is about 1,900,000 bottles.

Morey-St-Denis

Morey-St-Denis is the home of the famous Clos de Tart vineyard, in the hands of the Mommessin family of Mâcon. In 1120 part of the village,

then known as *Mirriacum Villa*, was given to the Abbey of Cîteaux, and in 1171 another parcel of the village was donated to the Abbey of Bussières by Guillaume de Marigny, the High Constable of Burgundy. The effort devoted to the vineyards by the monks, and especially the Cistercians, helped create the magnificent wines of today. There are four Grand Crus of Morey-St-Denis: Bonnes Mares (although much of this vineyard is in neighbouring Chambolle-Musigny), Clos St Denis, Clos de Tart and Clos de la Roche.

The Clos St Denis property can trace its history back to the College of St Denis de Vergy, which was established in 1203. The title of Morey was extended in 1927 when St Denis was added to the name. Clos de Tart was owned by the nuns of Notre Dame de Tart. They bought it in 1141 and the sale was ratified by a Papal Bull signed by Lucius III in 1184.

Chambolle-Musigny

The village was known by the Romans as *Campus Ebulliens*, the boiling field, not because of heat, but because of the turbulence of the stream which runs down the hillside during the floods following the spring rains. The wines of the commune have been noted for many years for their delicacy, and while this may now no longer be the case, they command very high prices. There are two Grand Crus here, Musigny and Bonnes Mares. Musigny is near the Clos de Vougeot and is first mentioned in 1110. Pierre Cros, the Canon of St Denis de

Top: The fifteenth century wine press belonging to the Dukes of Burgundy at Chenôve, south of Dijon.
Above: The Clos de Vougeot was built in the sixteenth century.

Vergy, is recorded as having given a parcel of land known as Musigné to the Abbey of Cîteaux. The origin of Bonnes Mares is not known. There are two schools of thought: the first is that the name comes from the pools of water from which the animals used to drink, and the second, is that it comes from an old French verb *marer*, which means to tend or care for the land. A small quantity of Musigny white wine is also made.

The Premier Cru vineyards include Les Amoureuses (the first vineyard as you approach from the north), Les Charmes, Les Cras, Les Borniques, Les Baudes, Les Plantes, Les Hauts Doix, Les Châtelots, Les Gruenchers, Les Groseilles, Les Fuées, Les Lavrottes, Derrière la Grange, Les Noirots, Les Sentiers, Les Fousselottes, Aux Beaux-Bruns, Les Combottes and Aux Combottes. The two best-known are Les Amoureuses and Les Charmes. The wines of the commune are fine and elegant, and unlike many of the big, powerful red Burgundies which are clearly masculine, the wines of Musigny can best be described as feminine.

Vougeot

Vougeot plays host to the Confrérie des Chevaliers du Tastevin which holds its dinners, with suitable pomp and ceremony, elaborate robes, trumpet blasts and drum rolls, in the medieval château, the Clos de Vougeot. This is one of the most important buildings in Burgundy and a sight which should not be missed.

The château was built by the Cistercians in the sixteenth century, although there had been a building on the site for almost 500 years before that. The building has very low walls so that the high sloping roof could trap as much water as possible when it rained. The water was then stored in huge wells.

The Confrérie was founded in 1934 in order to promote the wines of Burgundy. They bought the Clos in 1944 and have since painstakingly restored it, as a result of donations from all over the world. Every year

the Confrérie meets about twenty times and up to 500 people sit down in the banqueting hall for a superb dinner. The Confrérie has a more serious role, however, which is to maintain and improve quality. In 1950 all growers and wine merchants were invited to submit their wines to the Chevaliers for tasting. Those that met with their approval were allowed to carry the *Tastevinage* label and all the bottles were numbered. This continued a tradition started by the Cistercian monks, centuries before. The monks had three categories of wine, and the best were not for sale, but were reserved as gifts for the hierarchy of the Church, the nobility and royalty. There is no doubt that this grading stimulated interest and the monks had little trouble selling both the other categories. After the French Revolution, the vineyards of the Clos were confiscated and auctioned. For a time they were in the hands of a single owner, M. Focard, but in 1889 they were divided and are now owned by about eighty different growers. A share in the Clos de Vougeot vineyard is still much sought after.

There are some other vineyards in the commune which are worth attention: Close de la Perrière, Le Clos Blanc, Les Petits-Vougeots, Les Cras, and Clos du Prieuré.

Flagey-Échézeaux

This is a village lying on the flat plain opposite the Côte de Nuits, on the other side of the N74 highway. In 1188 it belonged to the Abbey of St

Vivant, and it now has two of Burgundy's most famous vineyards, both of which are Grands Crus. These are Grands Échézeaux and Échézeaux. Les Grands Échézeaux extends to 22 acres (9 hectares) and Les Échézeaux covers just over 74 acres (30 hectares) and comprises eleven vineyards. Between them they produce about 12,500 bottles in an average harvest.

Vosnée-Romanée

This village, about 1 mile (2km) north of Nuits-St-Georges, is reached by one of three turnings off the N74. There are so many famous vineyards bunched together around the old stone houses of the village, that it is easy to pass a great name without knowing it. The best way to explore the village and its vineyards is on foot, and there are various wine maps available locally to help; the best is the Larmat map of the Côte de Nuits.

Over two centuries ago, the Abbé Courtépée declared that only fine wines were made in the village, and while this is not strictly true today, the majority of the wine can be considered as such. There are five Grands Crus, in the hillsides above the village they are: Richebourg, Romanée, Romanée-St-Vivant, La Tâche, and lastly, perhaps the finest red wine of Burgundy, Romanée-Conti.

The village gets its name from the Romans and their vineyards, which were already famous in the fourth century. The church again had a major influence on the development of the vineyards, and for a time, the vineyard of Romanée-Conti, was owned by the Priory of St Vivant, who simply called it Le Cloux, which meant 'the best'. The vineyards of Romanée-Conti have an interesting history; a feud between Louis François, the Bourbon Prince of Conti, and Madame de Pompadour led to them both bidding for it in 1760.

Louis François was successful and became the new owner, adding his name to the vineyard, but he lost his prestige at court and had to relinquish his position as chief minister. He died in 1776; during the French Revolution the land was taken over, and it changed hands a number of times between then and 1869, when it was purchased by Monsieur Duvault-Blochet. It has been in the family ever since. M. de Villaine, the great grandson of M. Duvault-Blochet and co-owner Henri Le Roy, created the Société Civile du Domaine de la Romanée-Conti, which now controls all or parts of six of the greatest vineyards in the area — perhaps the finest collection of Burgundian red wine.

The Romanée-Conti wines are magnificent, round and velvety, full of lush fruit and bouquet. They are the classic Burgundies, and unless bought young and laid down, their prices can be staggeringly high. Premiers Crus are Aux Malconsorts, Les Beaumonts, Les Suchots, La Grand Rue, Les Gaudichots, Aux Brûlées, Les Chaumes, Les Reignots, Les Clos des Réas and Les Petits Monts.

Nuits-St-Georges

The town of Nuits-St-Georges gives its name to the wines of the area and is surrounded by vineyards, but there is not a single Grand Cru in the immediate area. There are, however, twenty-eight Premiers Crus from the Nuits-St-Georges commune, and a further ten from the commune of neighbouring Prémeaux. Needless to say, the town is the centre of the region's wine industry and not only houses the shippers, *négociants* and brokers, but all the other associated businesses necessary to keep the industry going; the label-makers for instance. Much of the fruit is grown locally and in the town there are also fruit juice factories and wineries producing sparkling wine.

It is interesting to note that as you travel to Nuits-St-Georges southwards, all the vineyards on the right are the ones producing the best wines and those entitled to the village appellation status. The vineyards on the left, between the road and the river, are generally providing grapes for AC wines.

Nuits-St-Georges is surrounded by vineyards, trees and a number of quarries which have provided stone for houses in the area for centuries. The best vineyards lie to the south of the town along the road to Beaune. The small village of Prémeaux, just to the south, is allowed to carry the Nuits-St-Georges appellation. There are just over 900 acres (360 hectares) of vineyards in the appellation, and only one Premier Cru is on the 'wrong' side of the road, Clos des Grandes Vignes, which skirts the northern boundary of Prémeaux.

Prémeaux

The vineyards here are at least 700 years old, and they hug the narrow strip of land between the main road and the hilltop. They only produce Premier Cru, and Clos de la Maréchale, its southernmost vineyard, is the last wine allowed to call itself Nuits-St-Georges.

A small quantity of white wine in produced in the commune, mostly from La Perrière and Clos Arlots in Prémeaux. The vineyard of La Perrière is worth a visit for curiosity's sake, as well as for the quality of the wines. By a freak of nature, a part of the vineyard planted with Pinot Noir produces white grapes. Part of the vineyard has been re-planted using grafts from these vines, and a small quantity of remarkable white wine is now produced every year. Even in a good year, only about 2,500 bottles are made and so the wine is both rare and expensive. It is much more like a Rhône white than a Burgundy. It is straw-coloured, full, fruity and marvellously balanced and a treat to drink.

Prissey, Comblanchien and Corgoloin

These are the last villages of the Côte de Nuits on the southern boundary, before the transition to the Côte de Beaune. The three villages in the commune sell their wines under the Côte de Nuits Villages appellation, as do the two most northerly villages, Brochon and Fixin. The limestone that is so treasured in the vineyards to the north has here been quarried to provide the grand homes of the nobility in Paris. The pink limestone, known as Rose de Prémeaux, was excavated for many years, as was the marble which runs in strata above it. This granite was used in the construction of the Paris Opera House, and it is to be seen as flooring in many of the more elegant residences of the Côte d'Or.

The red wines of the Côte de Nuits villages are more robust than their cousins to the north and south, but full of colour and fruit. They have fragrant noses with a hint of burnt oak, and they age well, often better than the other wines of the Côte de Nuits.

Côte de Beaune

The Côte de Beaune is the southern end of the Côte d'Or; the division is marked by a dramatic change in scenery. After Corgoloin the vineyards suddenly end, and you enter an area of old quarries and huge piles of discarded stone. Between the stone-workings, there are a number of small farms, but hardly a vineyard to be seen. The vineyards start again at Ladoix-Sérrigny and then for the next 15 miles (24km) or so they follow the N74 south. The northern vineyards of the Côte de Beaune are all on the west of the main road, hugging the many small hills that make up the Côte d'Or's southern tail. Only at its southernmost tip, around Volnay, do the vineyards switch to the left-hand side of the road.

The Côte de Beaune takes us from Ladoix, through Aloxe-Corton to Beaune (after a small detour west to Savigny), and then on to Pommard and finally Volnay. In this area, covering about 7,500 acres (3,000 hectares) of vineyards (twice the growing area of the Côte de Nuits), are to be found some of Burgundy's greatest wines, and some of the world's finest dry white wines. These are the Grands Crus which all bear the Corton appellation and these include the magnificent white Burgundy, Corton Charlemagne. There are almost thirty Premiers Crus under the appellations of Corton, Pernand, Beaune, Pommard and Volney.

The town of Beaune is the most important one in Burgundy, and it is the capital of the wine trade. It is, therefore, an excellent place to stay, and to make a base for your visits to the vineyards and cellars. It is quite possible to park your car and explore many of the vineyards on foot — and sensible if you plan to taste. The commune of Aloxe-Corton to the north is just over 2 miles (3km) away, Savigny to the north-west is about 2 miles (4km), and all the vineyards of Mersault are within 3 miles (5km) of Beaune. If the weather is fine, and your legs are strong there is no better way of visiting the vineyards, stopping for a picnic and a glass of wine or two along the way.

Apart from the annual vintage, the most important event in the wine calendar is the annual auction of

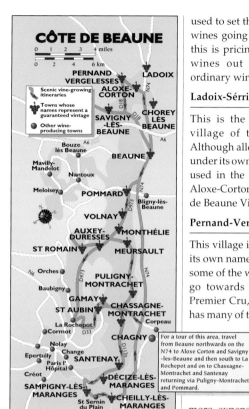

CÔTE DE BEAUNE

0   1   2   3   4 miles
0   2   4   6 km

PERNAND
VERGELESSES
LADOIX

Scenic vine-growing itineraries

Towns whose names represent a guaranteed vintage

Other wine-producing towns

ALOXE-CORTON
CHOREY LÈS BEAUNE
SAVIGNY -LÈS- BEAUNE

Bouze lès Beaune   A6
BEAUNE
A6

Mavilly-Mandelot
Nantoux

Meloisey
POMMARD
Bligny-lès-Beaune

VOLNAY

AUXEY-DURESSES
MONTHÉLIE

ST ROMAIN
MEURSAULT

Orches
PULIGNY-MONTRACHET
Baubigny

GAMAY
ST AUBIN
CHASSAGNE-MONTRACHET
Corpeau

La Rochepot
Cormot   D33

CHAGNY

Nolay
Change
Epertully
Paris l'
Hôpital
SANTENAY
Créot
DÉCIZE-LÈS-MARANGES
SAMPIGNY-LÈS-MARANGES
St Sernin du Plain
CHEILLY-LÈS-MARANGES

For a tour of this area, travel from Beaune northwards on the N74 to Aloxe Corton and Savigny -les-Beaune and then south to La Rochepot and on to Chassagne-Montrachet and Santenay returning via Puligny-Montrachet and Pommard.

used to set those of other Burgundy wines going on to the market, and this is pricing most of the greatest wines out of the reach of the ordinary wine drinker.

Ladoix-Sérrigny

This is the first wine-producing village of the Côte de Beaune. Although allowed to produce wines under its own name, they are usually used in the production of Corton, Aloxe-Corton Premier Cru and Côte de Beaune Villages.

Pernand-Vergelesses

This village is also allowed to carry its own name on the label, although some of the wine from its vineyards go towards Corton. It has a fine Premier Cru, Ile des Vergelesses. It has many of the qualities of its much more expensive neighbour to the south, and is usually a sound investment. Grapes for the Corton-Charlemagne are also produced here.

Aloxe-Corton

Aloxe-Corton has been making wine certainly since Roman times and it is associated with many of the great names in French history. Several Kings of France have owned vineyards here, the most famous being Charlemagne, whose name is now used for the best white wine of

wines at the Hospices de Beaune, the magnificent Hôtel Dieu, founded in the fifteenth century to look after the poor and care for the sick. The auction is always held on the third Sunday of November, during a weekend of true Burgundian wining and dining. The prices paid are always high but in the last few years they have frequently reached astronomic heights. In a way this is commendable, because the proceeds go to charity, but the prices are often the region. In AD858 the Bishop of Autun presented his vineyards to the cathedral. Other famous owners included the Knights Templar and the French Kings Henri II and Louis XIV. Charlemagne made a donation of some of his vineyards to the Abbey of Saulieu in 775 which is why the village still carries an eagle on its coat of arms — Charlemagne's own symbol. The vineyards of Corton-Charlemagne are now jointly owned by shippers Louis Jadot and Louis Latour and a few local growers. Many of the vineyards producing grapes for this white wine are westerly-facing, so that they get less sunshine which keeps the sugar content down, and the alcohol levels up — both necessary for making great white wines. In the village itself there are two tasting cellars worth visiting, although they are well advertised and can get very crowded. One is owned by the Château Corton-André, and the other by a consortium of local growers, and the wines offered by the growers are superb.

Altogether there are only about 580 acres (232 hectares) of vineyards in Aloxe-Corton. Chardonnay is planted on the limestone near the top of the hills which rise to about 1,275ft (389m). The red wine all comes from Pinot Noir, planted lower down where the soil is reddened by the iron present below.

Savigny-lès-Beaune

This village lies between Pernand-Vergelesses and Beaune. It is an important wine producer with about 950 acres (380 hectares) of vineyards and well worth a visit, not only because of the spectacular views over the surrounding countryside, but also because the village itself is interesting. There is a lovely old church; the tower dates back to the twelfth century and there is a fine fifteenth-century fresco. One of the novelties of the village is the number of houses which have delightful inscriptions carved into the stone lintels over the doors. There are also two châteaux, one large and one small.

Savigny is also important in the history of viticulture. Vineyards were first planted in straight rows here, and Guyot developed a new system for pruning, now widely used around the world and still bearing his name. The first 'mechanised' vineyard cultivator was also made here. Horse drawn, the cart with huge wooden wheels was pulled along straddling the vines.

There are no Grands Crus in the commune, but almost two dozen Premiers Crus from all or parts of the vineyards on either side of a stream which splits the area. The stream, which has the rather grand name of the River Rhoin, divides the commune into two very distinct areas of production. The vineyards to the north produce fuller wines from the clay soils, while those south of the stream, on gravelly soil, give rise to much lighter wines. The grape in the southern vineyards also ripen at least a week before those to the north.

Chorey-lès-Beaune

This is a small commune to the east of Savigny with about 300 acres (120 hectares) of vineyards, mostly producing red wine sold under the Côte de Beaune Villages appellation. It does have the right to use its own village appellation. Almost all the vineyards are sited on the plains, and because of this, it produces a firm wine that is perfect for blending although not outstanding.

Beaune

The most famous town of Burgundy, its capital and the commercial and trading centre for the whole Côte d'Or is Beaune. The origin of its name is unknown, although there are many theories. It is known, however, that Julius Caesar camped with his legions here about 50 years before the birth of Christ.

Beaune is now similar to many French towns, a mixture of old and new buildings. From certain vantage points one can see the ramparts which circle the old town, and then see the suburban sprawl encroaching on the vineyards beyond. Beaune is also a huge wine making commune, and vineyards cover 1,400 acres (560 hectares). Again, there are no Grands Crus but thirty or so Premiers Crus. A very small amount of elegant, light white Côte de Beaune is produced.

The most famous building in Beaune is the Charitable Hospices de Beaune, and over the years the vineyards, donated by wealthy benefactors, have funded the work of the Hospices, and the sale of wine still contributes a significant proportion of its income. Wines from the 140 acres (56 hectares) or so of vineyards now owned by the Hospices are blended into special *cuvées*, and these are offered for sale at the world famous auction held annually on the third Sunday in November.

The wines do not only come from Beaune itself; the Hospices now have plots of land in Meursault, Aloxe-Corton, Savigny-lès-Beaune, Pommard, Volnay, Gevrey-Chambertin, Monthélie, Auxey-Duresses and Pernand-Vergelesses. With names such as these, and pockets of the bidders loosened by lavish hospitality, one can see why the wines command such high prices. All the wine is sold as Premiers Crus of the Côte de Beaune.

The vineyards are each under the control of one man, and in addition to a regular wage, he also receives a share of the proceeds from the annual auction, an incentive which helps to guarantee the high quality of the wine, year after year. The wines have been sold at public auction since 1859 and only in the very worst years has this been cancelled. All the wines are vinified in the winery behind the Hôtel Dieu, and today there are twenty-three red *cuvées* and nine white, together with some distilled wine.

The Sunday sale, which attracts buyers from around the world, is preceded by a dinner in the Château Clos de Vougeot. Thousands of people cram into Beaune for the auction; which is by invitation only

Above: Château Corton-André, Aloxe Corton with Premier Cru vines (Les Fournière) in the foreground.
Below: The Caves of Henri de Villamont at Savigny-les-Beaune.

Above: Beaune is a popular tourist centre and has numerous wine shops.
Below: Volnay, the last major vineyard supplying grapes for the Côte de
Beaune reds.

and the preceding two days of tasting, and the sale itself, which takes place in the market, is followed by another magnificent dinner in the Hospices. It is an honour to be invited to either. The celebrations continue on the Monday with a lunch for the growers, and the three days of celebrations known as Les Trois Glorieuses.

Pommard

This is another ancient town, and there was once a Gallic temple here. Now, you can look instead at the square bell tower on the church and explore the narrow little lanes which mix incongruously with the wider modern thoroughfares. Pommard used to be an important fording point across the River Vandaine, which still floods, and inns sprung up to cater for the passengers from the stagecoaches. The wines were a favourite of Victor Hugo, and to many people the wines of Pommard are the epitome of fine red Burgundy. There are now around 850 acres (340 hectares) of vineyards in the commune and twenty-six Premiers Crus. Alas, the reputation of the wine has pushed up prices and demand, and while Pommard can produce extraordinary wines in good years, the ease with which growers can sell it, has led to a relaxation of standards by some. The best producers, however, still make great wines, and these are universally acclaimed as Les Epenots (also called Epeneaux) and Les Rugiens. Other fine producers are Clis de la Commaraine (with its château dating back to the twelfth century), Les Jarollières, Château de Pommard, Les Pézerolles, Clos Micot and Les Arvelets.

Pommards age well and should never be drunk until they are at least three years old, and for the Premiers Crus at least double this. If you stick to the Premiers Crus you will avoid disappointment.

Volnay

The village of Volnay is up on the hill just beyond Pommard but nearer still to Meursault. It is the last major vineyard area supplying grapes for the Côte de Beaune reds. From here we move into white wine country. Because it is on the boundary, both white and red wines are produced. Volnay is a small village with a big reputation, and there are magnificent views from the square across to the Jura. Because neighbouring Meursault is famed for its whites, the two villages have reached an understanding. White wine from Volnay is sold as Meursault, while Meursault's reds are sold as Volnay. There used to be a château at Volnay built by the Dukes of Burgundy, but this was totally destroyed about 250 years ago. The village was also famous for a company of cross-bowmen who served first the Burgundian Dukes and then the Kings of France. The champion bowman, decided at an annual competition, was given a whole year off from working in the vineyards.

Because the vineyards of Volnay are higher than its neighbours, frost is a danger and you might see pots scattered among the vines. These are known as smudge pots and are filled with charcoal which is lit when the temperatures fall too low.

The red wines of Volnay are light and elegant, fruity and velvety and quality shines through. There are about 525 acres (210 hectares) of vineyards and two dozen Premiers Crus. The rest of the red is sold as AC Volnay.

Monthélie

This village is also on a hill, but the vineyards are sheltered and the grapes are said to get more sun than any other vineyards in the Côte d'Or. Only grapes could survive on the very poor soil, and they have been grown here since the fourteenth century.

There are now ten Premiers Crus, 325 acres (130 hectares) of vineyards, and all but 6,000 bottles of the production is red. The wines are very fine, well balanced and fragrant, and can be drunk quite young. They are always good value, but because of their limited production, they can be difficult to find outside France.

Auxeu-Duresses

This is another commune on the border between red and white production. About seventy per cent of the production is red, and the remainder white. The red wines are good, similar to those of Volnay; the whites can be great, rivalling those of Meursault, although generally they are no so long-lived. There are nine Premiers Crus, including Les Duresses, 2 acres (1 hectare) of which is owned by the Hospices de Beaune.

St. Romain

This village is surrounded by steep gorges, and while it is in the Côte de Beaune, it is really part of the Hautes-Côtes. It has the highest vineyards in the Côte d'Or, and the Chardonnay grapes planted on the higher ground tend to do better than the Pinot Noir lower down. The views from the hillsides are superb. There are no first growths here, and about a third of the production is white wine.

Meursault

The largest wine producer in the Côte d'Or is Meursault. The twisting streets and the church with its fifteenth-century tower, which is one of the tallest in the region at 187ft (57m), are a delight; and there is much to see and do; but everywhere one is reminded that this is above all else, a wine centre. There is a campsite just outside the town which is truly international during the summer with visitors from almost every country in Europe, and many from further afield. After Beaune, Meursault attracts more visitors than anywhere else on the Côte d'Or, mostly to drink the white wines as this is the capital of the Côte des Blancs.

The main festival in Meursault takes places the day after the auction at the Hospices de Beaune, when 400 people sit down to an enormous banquet with the very best wines.

There are three types of

rainfall throughout the year, and often snow during the winter. The commune includes the village of Gamay which gives its name to the grape variety which used to be so common throughout the Côte d'Or. It is a typical Côte d'Or village with old stone houses, narrow twisting streets and a church which has been largely restored, and is worth a visit because skeletons of plague victims were discovered here.

Almost everyone in Gamay is concerned with growing or making wine. About two thirds of the production is red and the remainder white. Despite its height, there are a few sheltered vineyards and these include the eight Premiers Crus: La Chatenière, En Remilly, Les Murgers-des-Dents-de-Chien, Les Frionnes, Sur-le-Sentier-du-Clou, Sur Gamay, Les Combes and Champlot. The reds are rarely outstanding, but they have a sort of rarity value as they are not widely known outside France. Much of the other red wine production goes towards Côte de Beaune Villages. There have been significant strides forward in the quality of the white wines, thanks to the introduction of new vinification techniques, and this is an area to watch.

Santenay

This is the last wine-producing commune of any importance at the southern end of the Côte de Beaune. Unlike the other towns in the Côte d'Or, however, Santenay has strings to its bows other than wine. There is a spa famed for its therapeutic properties, but like almost all other spas in Europe, it is only a shadow of its former elegant self. There is also a casino which is very popular during the summer months, and efforts have been under way for some time to improve both.

Santenay makes almost exclusively red wine which is strong and deep coloured, and there are seven Premiers Crus: Les Gravières, Le Clos-de-Tavannes, La Comme, Beauregard, Le Passe-Temps, Beaurepaire and La Maladière.

The white wines are easily overshadowed by their neighbours.

Décize-lès-Maranges
Cheilly lès-Maranges
Sampigney-lès-Maranges

These three red wine villages sell their production as Côte de Beaune Villages. They are at the southernmost tip of the Côte de Beaune and make strong, fine wines, which age well. The wines are best drunk after five years and will go on for some years after this.

Côte de Beaune Villages and Côte de Beaune

The Côte de Beaune appellation carries more weight than Côte de Beaune Villages, and denotes a wine from within the boundaries of Beaune itself or from a score of neighbouring properties that have been judged worthy of the name. You will also see Côte de Beaune used before the name of a particular commune such as Décize, Cheilly, Sampigny, Chassagne, Puligny,

Meursault, Auxey and Chorey, and this upgrades the wine over that of just the village appellation.

The appellation Côte de Beaune Villages can be used by sixteen villages and any two or more of these can blend their wines to produce reds, or they can sell under their own village name. Quality can vary enormously, but the commune of Chorey-lès-Beaune, which sells its wine under the Côte de Beaune Villages appellation is an exception because the standard is consistently high. All the forty or so produces strive constantly to improve their wines and they are now much sought after.

Chalonnaise

After travelling south through the Côte d'Or, the next area of Burgundy reached is the Chalonnaise. The area has been overshadowed by the Côte de Beaune, and for many years the wines of the five villages that make up the Chalonnaise were sold as Côte de Beaune. Recently the vineyards have come into their own and fine wines are now produced red, white and sparkling.

There are a number of good hotels, pensions and bed and breakfast establishments in the area, especially in Chagny and Chalon-sur-Saône, which make a good base for touring the Chalonnaise. The museum at Chalon, the Musée Denon, is well worth a visit, and there are a number of good restaurants offering local specialities and excellent local wines. Pinot Noir still provides the grapes for the red wine, and Chardonnay and Pinot Blanc are used for the white. The Aligoté also does well and is used for the acclaimed Bourgogne Aligoté de Bouzeron.

The vineyards of the Chalonnaise are fragmented, scattered along a 20 mile (32km) long stretch from Chagny in the north to Montagny in the south.

Rully

Rully is the first village one comes across entering the Chalonnaise from the north. For more than 150 years it has been making a sparkling Burgundy from a blend of Aligoté and Chardonnay. The still whites are dry and full-bodied, fruity and fresh, and should be drunk young, say after 3 years. They are excellent as an aperitif or with shellfish. Only white wine made from the Chardonnay can carry the Rully appellation. There are nineteen Premiers Crus.

Mercurey

This is perhaps the most famous village of the Chalonnaise, and its popularity has increased enormously in the last few years. Almost all the production is red wine from the Pinot Noir, which does well on the poor soil, similar as it is in composition to that of the Côte d'Or.

Only the finest red wines from three communes are permitted to carry the label Mercurey — St Martin-sous-Montaigu, Bourgneuf-Val-d'Or and Mercurey. There are five Premiers Crus and the growers have formed their own Confrérie to

The Mâconnais

The Mâconnais is the area between the Chalonnise and the Beaujolais, and produces wines that have become world famous — Pouilly-Fuissé in particular. The Mâconnais is trapped between two rivers; the Saône on which Mâcon stands, which flows along the eastern sides of the region, and the Grosne which meanders its way round the other three sides. Tournus is the first town of any size in the Mâconnais and the vineyards then run south for less than 30 miles (48km) to the west of the A6 and D103.

The Chardonnay grape produces pleasing whites, clearly Burgundies but a fraction of the price of their cousins from the Côte d'Or. In the past most of the wine produced was red made from the Gamay, the vineyards dotted on the slopes of the many small hills. The region has a mixed agriculture and Charollais cattle, named after the hills to the west, graze in the water meadows. There are woods and groves of sweet chestnuts and the area is rich in game, the hunting of which is a favourite local pastime after the vintage is over.

Mâcon is the capital of the region, built in a strategic position dominating the Saône. The area was covered in forest for thousands of years, but the Romans cleared the land and planted the vineyards, and there are early records of vines being grown around Tournus and Mâcon. There are also traces of the weapons made in Mâcon, arrow heads and spears, used for hunting game in the surrounding forests.

Today, the Mâconnais produces both red and white wines and while the reputation of the whites is already established, that of the reds is growing quickly. Much of the wine is now made by *coopératives*, and enormous investments have been made in new technology and equipment, which has clearly resulted in an improvement in quality.

The various appellations of Mâconnais are:

Mâcon Blanc is generally made from Chardonnay, must come from delimited areas and have a natural alcohol content of 10°. If the alcohol content increases to 11° the wine has the right to the appellation Mâcon Supérieur.

Mâcon Villages appellation can be used by the forty-three villages which are considered the best producers in the Mâconnais. They are generally to be found in the eastern part of the region.

St Vérnan comes from eight communes in the south, some of which overlap into Beaujolais. The wine can be sold under the village name, or as Beaujolais Blanc, Mâcon Villages, or Bourgogne Blanc.

Mâcon Rouge is made from the Gamay and must have 9° natural alcohol. It is also made as Mâcon rosé.

Mâcon Supérieur Rouge must have a minimum 10° natural alcohol and must come from a delimited area. It also has the right to carry its particular Villages after the title Mâcon.

Pouilly-Fuissé comes from the communes of Pouilly, Fuissé, Solutré, Vergisson and Chaintré. It must have 11° of natural alcohol, and 12° if it also carries the vineyard's name.

Pouilly-Vinzelles has to follow the same rules as Pouilly-Fuissé except that the grapes must come from the communes of Vinzelles and Loché. It is not quite up to Pouilly-Fuissé standards but costs a lot less.

A WINE TOUR OF THE BURGUNDY REGION

This tour concentrates primarily on the wines and wine sights of Burgundy. There is inevitably some overlap with the general tours described in this chapter, but it is more practical that some inform-ation is repeated, rather than having to search back for it.

The best way of touring Burgundy to see the wines is simply to drive from north to south, and stop off where you please.

Here, a six day tour is offered which allows time to explore and taste the different styles of wine, but the trip can be extended almost indefinitely. Indeed, it is possible to spend several months in Burgundy and still not have an opportunity to taste all the magnificent wines available or to visit the many fascinating châteax in the area.

Tour of Dijon

Dijon is the ideal place to begin the tour, and well worth visiting, thanks to its wealth of treasures and archi-tectural heritage. It is also close to the Côte de Nuits, the most northerly section of vineyards that make up the Côte d'Or.

The first day can take in the communes of Marsannay-la-Côte, Couchey, Fixin, Brochon, Gevrey-Chambertin, Morey-St-Denis, Chambolle-Musigny, Vougeot and Vosne-Romaneé. It is obviously impossible to visit all of these villages in a single day even though they are quite close together, and Fixin and the area south of Gevrey-Chambertin is likely to be most rewarding for the wine lover. Almost everywhere you will see the famous names of Burgundy, wines you have read about but which few are able to afford. There are wines like Les Hervelets, Les Perrières and Clos du Chapitre, all famous Premiers Crus from vineyards to the west of Fixin, and Grands Crus such as Chambertin, Chambertin-Clos-de-Bèze, Clos St-Jacques, Chapelle-Chambertin, Clos de la Roche and Clos St-Denis below Gevrey-Chambertin. This small area of vineyards, from Marsannay-la-Côte to Vosne-Romanée, is only about 10 miles (16km) long, but every signpost is full of famous names.

Marsannay to Nuits-St-Georges

From Dijon, head south through the small village of Marsannay-la-Côte to **Fixin**, which contains half a dozen

MÂCONNAIS

Prissé
Vergisson — D177
Charnay — MÂCON
Davayé
Solutré — La Patte d'Oie
POUILLY
Chasselas — FUISSÉ
LOCHÉ
Leynes
ST VÉRAND — VINZELLES
Varennes
St Amour — Chaintré
Chânes
Crêches

0 — 3 — 6 miles
0 — 5 — 10 km

Towns whose names represent a guaranteed vintage
Other wine-producing towns

excellent vineyards, and the famous statue, the *Awakening of Napoléon*, sculptured by Rudé and commissioned by Claude-Charles Noisot, a veteran of the Napoleonic wars. The statue is in the park founded by Noisot in 1846. His dying wish was to be buried in the park, upright, sword in hand, so that he could continue to serve and defend Napoléon. There is also a small museum devoted to the imperial campaigns. A fine lunch is offered at Chez Jeanette, and the restaurant also has a number of inexpensive rooms should the exertions of the day prove too much.

Just to the south is the village of **Gevrey-Chambertin**, which has been the centre of a vineyard area since Roman times, and today produces two of the world's most famous red wines — Chambertin and Clos-de-Bèze. Like many other famous wines of the region, the latter owes its dominance to the Benedictine monks who nurtured the vineyards, while the former achieved international fame because it was the favourite wine of

Napoléon, and is said to have first sustained him, and then comforted him during his calamitous invasion of Russia.

Gevrey-Chambertin boasts a number of hotels and restaurants, the latter including the excellent La Rôtisserie du Chambertin and Les Millésimes. The Rôtisserie has an incredible wine list and food to match. The sights to see are in the old part of the village. You can visit the château, parts of which date back to the tenth century, although it was mostly rebuilt in the thirteenth century. From here, travel to Morey-St-Denis, famous for its Clos de Tart vineyard; many of the vineyards in this area were formerly owned and run by the Cicerstian monasteries.

Other vineyards worth visiting are those of the Clos de la Roche and Clos St-Denis. Then down the road again to Chambolle-Musigny and Vougeot, and another clutch of Grands Crus; there are the vineyards of Clos de Vougeot, Vignes Blanches de Clos de Vougeot, Musigny and Echézeaux.

In **Chambolle**, visit the church which has some fine religious paintings, and there good views across the vineyards. There is also some marvellous countryside just a stone's throw away from the vineyards, with bubbling rivers rushing through wooded gorges, a marvellous place for a picnic lunch and a gentle walk.

Vougeot is of interest, apart from its wines, because of the Clos de Vougeot, built by the Cistercian monks and now the headquarters of the Brotherhood of the Knights of the Wine Taster, which is well worth a visit. The roof of the building was constructed in such a way to trap as much rainwater as possible, which was then stored in huge vats. The building dates from the twelfth-century, when it was enclosed by a wall. The Clos was rebuilt by the monks in the sixteenth century but the original wine cellars, thirteenth-century dormitories, winemaking equipment and giant press remain. The next port of call should be Vosne-Romanée, with its narrow streets and granite houses. The village is surrounded by world-renowned vineyards including Richebourg, Romanée-St-Vivant, La Romanée and La Tâche. The most famous of all, and the only Premier Grand Crus, is La Romanée Conti.

Most of the vineyards are older than the houses in this pretty village which has often seen troubled times. The wines of Romanée were first mentioned in a poem written in AD312 in honour of the Emperor Constantine. The vineyard of Romanée-Conti featured in a feud between Madame de Pompadour, mistress of Louis XV, and Louis François de Bourbon, Prince of Conti. She wanted the vineyard but he managed to buy it in 1760 and immediately lost favour in court and was ostracised. The vineyard, still bearing his name, survives and produces one of the supreme Burgundies.

Nuits-St-Georges is an ideal place for the first overnight stop. It is a small town, and another bustling commercial centre, housing the cellars of many famous shippers. Before visiting the surrounding vineyards and cellars, have a look at the twelfth-century church of St Symphorien, and the nearby Gallo-Roman and Merovingian excavations. Because of the narrow streets and busy traffic, it is best to park and explore the town on foot.

The Hospice de Nuits-St-Georges, founded in 1692, is well worth visiting. After the Revolution, the Augustinian monks were deprived of control of the Hospice, which was handed over the local Mayor. He appointed two nuns to look after the thirty-six patients. The Hospice originally had twelve beds and now has 166 and it has changed its role over the years. In the nineteenth century, it concentrated on caring for tuberculosis victims, now it specialises in treating the poor and the old.

Many of the local vineyard owners are benefactors and in 1938 the first auction of wines donated to the Hospice took place. The war halted the practice and it was not resumed until 1962 but is now firmly established once again.

Tour of the Beaune Area

From Nuits-St-Georges, continue south to the medieval fortified town of **Beaune**, famous for its hospice, museums, works of art and fine old buildings. To many it is the true capital of Burgundy, and some hours exploring the town is a rewarding experience. Beaune, too, can trace its origins back to at least Roman times, when it was called *Belna*. It has always been a successful trading and commercial town, receiving city status in 1203, and therefore subject to attack from its enemies which is why the huge ramparts were built in the reign of Louis XI (these now house the cellars of many of Beaune's growers and shippers). Today, the town has spread, and the sprawling suburbs now house many of the wineries and bottling plants formerly to be found in the heart of the old town.

For centuries the town and its surrounding land has changed hands at regular intervals. It was the seat of the Burgundian Parliament, and home of the Dukes of Burgundy until the fourteenth century. At different times it has been owned by the Church, the Monarchy, the Knights of Malta, and then after the Revolution, private ownership following the splitting up of the estates and a massive auction.

Many of the vineyards are now owned by the shippers who operate from the town, and the battlements which used to house the troops are now used for storing the wine. There are many buildings surviving from this period in the town's history. The Musée de Vin was formerly one of the town houses of the Duke of Burgundy. There is the church of Notre-Dame, dating back to the eleventh and twelfth centuries and containing fifteenth-century tapestries illustrating the *Life of the Virgin*, and the thirteenth-century church of St Nicolas in the old wine merchants quarter. A few miles outside town is the Archéodrome, off the A6, which contains life-size models depicting the history of the region from the earliest times.

Beaune's most famous building is, however, the Hospices de Beaune. It comprises the Hôtel Dieu, and the Hospice de la Charité, and was founded in 1441 by Nicholas Rolin, then Chancellor of Burgundy. He and his wife, Guigonne de Salins, decreed that all their worldly goods should be endowed to allow a hospice to be built to care for the poor and sick. It took eight years to build the Hôtel Dieu and the result is one of the finest examples of Flemish-Burgundian architecture; the Flemish craftsmen commissioned to aid the work built the patterned roof, one of the most notable features of the building.

A Flemish nursing order, the Dames Hospitalières, still runs the Hospices; naturally, conditions have improved over the centuries. When the Hôtel Dieu was opened, patients used to lie two or more to a bed. The beds were larger than those used today, and all were arranged in such a way that every patient could see into the chapel. The beds were still in use until 1948. The building has been beautifully looked after, and apart from the original beds which can be seen in the Salle des Pauvres (which is 170ft, 52m long), there is a magnificent art gallery, housing priceless exhibits such as Roger van der Weiden's masterpiece, *The Last Judgement*, and also a museum, full of interesting exhibits, and the kitchen and dispensary containing original artefacts. A guided tour of the Hospices is available and lasts about an hour.

The Hospices, like the one in Nuits-St-Georges, benefit from the patronage of local wine growers and merchants, and more than 100 acres (40 hectares) of hugely valuable vineyards have now been donated to the Hospices to help maintain them. Every year since 1859 special *cuvées* from these vineyards have been sold at 'public' auction, and even though the event is for charitable purposes, the prices now being paid are ridiculously high, because few people can afford their subsequent resale price. The auction is held during the third weekend of November and attracts buyers from all over the world. The number of *cuvées* offered at the auction has been steadily increasing, and there are now twenty-three reds, nine whites as well as some brandies and marcs. Although Beaune is famous for its red wine, it is usually the whites which command the highest prices at the auction, especially the Cuvée François de Salins which is produced from a half of an acre Corton-Charlemagne vineyard. While the three days of the auction, the Trois Glorieuses, are exhilarating, the town is so packed with buyers and others, that it is not a good time to visit unless you have a ticket for the sales, which is why it is not a true public auction.

From Beaune you can visit the vineyards of many Premier and Grand Cru wines. To the west of

Ladoix, just north of Beaune, and surrounding the village of Aloxe-Corton are the vineyards of Corton Renardes, Corton Clos du Roi and ten or more other Grands Crus reds. Just to the west of Aloxe-Corton is the vineyard producing the Corton-Charlemagne Grand Cru white, while south of the road to Savigny, are the vineyards of Premiers Crus reds such as Les Marconnets, Les Perrières, Aigrots, Vignes Franches and Clos des Mouches.

Pommard to Santenay

From Beaune, travel still further south to **Pommard**, famous as a Protestant centre and home, in the time of Louis XIV, to the Huguenots. They were forced to flee the town when the King revoked the Edict of Nantes, but the name they gave to their wine still lives on, and it is one of the most famous of all Burgundian reds. There have been problems in the past with the name Pommard — the wine was so popular that at one stage its consumption around the world apparently exceeded its production! Now the wine is either bottled locally or under licence in Burgundy, and most of the abuses, which usually occurred because the wine was shipped in bulk and bottled abroad, have now been stamped out. There is no doubt, however, that while Pommard produces some of the greatest Burgundian wines, it also produces a wide range of quality which can cause problems. The most famous vineyards, and quite magnificent, are Les Rugiens Bas, Les Rugiens

Above: Château Pommard. This village has a reputation for producing fine red Burgundies.

Hauts, Les Epenots, Clos de la Commaraine, Clos Blanc, Les Arvelets, Les Charmots, Les Argillières, Les Pézerolles, Les Boucherottes, Les Saucilles, Les Croix Noires, Les Chaponières, Les Fremiers, Les Bertins, Les Jarollières, Les Poutures, Clos Micot, La Refène, Clos de Verger, Derrière-St-Jean, La Platière, Les Chanlins Bas, Les Combes Dessus and La Chanière.

Just to the south of Pommard is **Volnay**. The village is a steady uphill climb and most of the vineyards are on the left below you. On a fine day, this is another ideal place for a picnic lunch and a chance to fully appreciate the Burgundian countryside, sipping a glass of Volnay, considered by many to be the finest wine from the Côte de Beaune. Wine has been produced here for centuries, and many of the names have re-

mained unchanged for 700 years or more. Then, many of the vineyards were owned by the Order of Malta. Since then they have changed hands many times, from the Crown, to the Dukes of Burgundy, through the Revolution and so on, but the tradition of the very finest winemaking has never been lost. The best vineyards today are En Cailleret, Cailleret, Dessus, Champans, En Chevret, Fremiet, Bousse d'Or, La Barre, Clos des Chênes, Les Angles, Les Mitans, En l'Ormeau, Taille-Pieds, En Verseuil, Carelle sous la Chapelle, Ronceret, Les Aussy, Les Brouillards, Clos des Ducs, Pitures Dessus, Chanlin, Les Santenots, Les Petures and Village-de-Volnay.

Monthélie, the next village on the route, also produces fine wines, which until recently used to be sold as Pommard. The tiny village hidden in the hills is a natural sun trap; since it received appellation status in 1937 it has produced consistently good, fragrant, delicate wine. Although most of the production is red, there is some very good white and this should be tried in the village café, or the *coopérative* cellars at Les Caves de Monthélie.

Continue to cut through the hills driving south past the village of **La Rochepot** with its ancient château, through Auxey-Duresses which has a fine restaurant, La Cremaillère, to **St Romain** and Volnay. This commune received its appellation in 1967 and has the highest vineyards in the Côte d'Or. It produces very good wines, both red and white, and has magnificent views from the vantage point up a steep path from the village. From Volnay, travel down the hill to **Meursault**, home of some of the world's most famous white wines. The small town is capital of the Côte de Blancs, which includes other such famous names as Blagny, Puligny-Montrachet and Chassagne-Montrachet. The houses are granite-built and typically Burgundian. Although the village has a long history, little remains of it today although there is still a fourteenth-century church with a steeple that guide you to the town.

Its most famous vineyards are those of Les Perrières and Les Charmes, but there are many others of importance — Genevrières, Blagny, Goutte d'Or, Bouchères, Les Santenots, Les Caillerets, Les Petures, Les Cras, La Jennelotte, La Pièce-sous-le-Bois and Le Poruzot. The tiny village of Blagny, up on the hill, is also noted for its white wines but it produces a fine, delicate red which should be tried.

Many vineyards are passed on the route south via Puligny-Montrachet and Chassagne-Montrachet. Almost all deserve a stop, but the amount of time devoted to this area must depend on the flexibility of your timetable. If you are a lover of Burgundy wines, the answer has to be to make as much time available as possible.

Santenay is also worth a visit both for its casino and its spa waters. The Source Carnot is a spring which is said to produce a water helpful in the treatment of gout and rheumatism. The springs were already well-

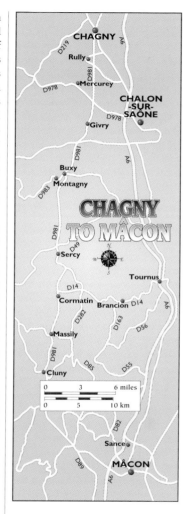

known in Roman times. Over the years, the original wells were polluted and new ones had to be drilled, and now there are a number drawing up water from several hundred feet below ground, each claiming to have different beneficial properties. A modern hotel has now been opened and this, with the Casino de Santenay (a popular attraction at weekends) has helped boost the town's popularity.

Santenay really consists of three villages, Santenay-le-Haut which houses the hotel, spa and casino; Santenay-le-Bas (or Bains) where the villagers live and the wine is made; and St Jean, which boasts a fine thirteenth-century Romanesque-Gothic church.

From Chagny and Chalon to Mâcon

Just outside Santenay, on top of the hill, is a statue of winged horses, placed there to commemorate three lovers of Burgundy wine who died in the Paris air crash of 1974. And then it is on to **Chalon-sur-Saône**. Chalon is the commercial heart of the Côte Chalonnaise, and another bustling industrial town. It has a twelfth-century cathedral, many other fine churches and buildings, and museums worth a visit. The drive from Beaune to Chalon takes less than half an hour, but as you can see, it is quite easy to spend several days wandering through the magnificent vineyards along the way.

Chagny is the first village of the Chalonnaise, although Rully, its neighbour to the south is the first to have its appellation. The Côte Chalonnaise runs along the hillsides for about 20 miles (32km) south from Chagny, which marks the dividing line between it and the Côte d'Or to the north.

Rully produces some fine white wines, and for over 150 years has been making sparkling Burgundy, but its products are overshadowed by the wines of Mercurey just to the south.

Mercurey which, it is claimed, is named after a Roman temple to Mercury, has wine charters going back to AD557. It is the most important commune of the Chalonnaise and there are five vineyards with Premiers Crus status — Clos du Roi, Clos Les Voyens, Clos-Marcilly, Clos des Fourneaux and Clos des Montaigus.

To the west of Chalon is **Givry**, which is now striving to retain its former glory. It once supplied wines to the best establishments in Paris, but between the wars, other wines became more popular. Givry received its appellation for good, full-bodied, almost sharp reds which are ready for drinking much earlier than those of its neighbours.

Chalon itself has much to attract the visitor, including fine hotels and restaurants. It has good shops and wide streets. Places of interest to visit include the twelfth-century cathedral, the seventeenth-century church of St Peter, and many sixteenth- and seventeenth-century houses. There is an archaeological museum, the Musée Denon which includes a photography museum housing the works of Joseph Nicéphore Niepce, who took the first photograph — a view of Chalon. He later teamed up with Daguerre, whose part in the development of photography is much better known.

The last port of call in the

Chalonnaise is Montagny, just over 5 miles (8km) south of Givry which produces clean, pleasant, refreshing white wines.

From Montagny, continue south just a couple of miles into the Mâconnais, a region trapped between two rivers: the Saône in the east, and the Grosne which wriggles its way in a wide sweep to the west from north to south. The Mâconnais combines agriculture and viticulture, and is an excellent place to end our tour of the region because both fine wines and tremendous food can be enjoyed. Although the town of Mâcon is the largest, it is Tournus that is reached first if you are travelling south from Chalon. If you are still in Montagny, travel to Tournus by going south on the D981 towards Cormatin. Before the centre, turn left on the D14. It goes to Tournus, but detour into medieval Brancion on the way, if time permits. **Tournus** has a wonderful abbey church and has long been a place of pilgrimage. In AD179 St Valerian was martyred here, and many buildings still remain from the Middle Ages. The abbey church was started in the ninth century, but there are architectural gems to be seen everywhere, two interesting local museums and lots of interesting streets close to the river, where you can park. The Mâconnais produces both red and white wine, but the whites have the edge, and Pouilly-Fuissé is known everywhere. The reds tend to be light and fruity, similar in style to the Beaujolais, but less fruity, although the best can be

very good indeed. The vineyards around Tournus produce mostly red wines, while the white production is concentrated to the west and south of Mâcon around Pouilly and St Véran.

If time permits, it is worth the detour to **Cluny**, about 10 miles (16km) from Mâcon. It is noted for its Benedictine Abbey, founded in AD910, which was once the largest in all Christendom. Cluny also boasts Romanesque houses and a Renaissance palace. The abbey church foundations can be seen. Get a ticket for the abbey at the museum. There is a good panorama from the top of the Cheese Tower above the Tourist Office. Next to the abbey is one of the national stud farms, with its lovely horses.

Mâcon is a pleasing town, home of the poet Lamartine, full of the red-tiled buildings which become even more numerous as you journey on towards the Mediterranean. The town is surrounded by hills which provide pleasant walking, and there are many Romanesque churches scattered about. There is good food to be had in the restaurants in and around Mâcon, and the remains of the twelfth-century church of St Vincent to explore.

The advantage of the Burgundian vineyards is that they run conveniently in a line that is easy to follow. A week could be spent exploring just one village, but this brief itinerary does allow enormous flexibility so that you can visit all the important areas but at a pace that suits you best.

The Wines of Beaujolais 6

Although Beaujolais is part of Burgundy, the wines from this region are so different from other Burgundies that they deserve a section of their own. Beaujolais is part of the Lyonnais and the inhabitants enjoy the good food that comes from this fertile region, which extends south into the northern Rhône. The Beaujolais vineyards start at the boundary with Mâcon, and run almost continuously to the Lyon suburbs, along the whole length of the motorways, the A6 and N6, yet by the time most motorists reach Lyon, they usually have their foot hard down on the accelerator and are racing for the Mediterranean. Few tourists stop to visit this delightful part of the countryside with its good food, reasonably-priced hotels and marvellous wines. The Beaujolais, for all that, is still one of France's leading wine producers. There are ninety-six villages (eighty-five in the Rhône and eleven in the Saône-et-Loire *départements*), about 4,500 growers, and 55,000 acres (22,000 hectares) of vineyards producing an average 170 million bottles a year. The average vineyard covers 15 acres (6 hectares).

Although the Beaujolais has the highest density of vines to the hectare, up to 13,000, it has one of the lowest yields among AC regions.

Although wine has certainly been grown in Beaujolais for hundreds of years, it was never very commercially significant because of the problems involved in moving it. The road network was not very good, although things improved in 1642 when the Canal de Briare was opened, with access to the Loire. Only in the last 200 years, however, have the wines gained in popularity, partly because of the French Revolution and partly because of the demand for the lighter, fruitier style that Beaujolais was able to produce.

Records show that before the Revolution, much of the land of Beaujolais was in the hands of a few very large agricultural estates. After the confiscation of land, it was divided into small parcels and this encouraged repopulation of the area.

The success of Beaujolais is that, in spite of its many vineyards and growers, it has just one product to sell, even though quality varies enormously. The staggering success of Beaujolais Nouveau allows the growers to dispose of their wine quickly. The better quality is kept for release the following year as Beaujolais Villages, and the best quality is reserved for the Crus Beaujolais.

Beaujolais is bounded on the east by the Saône, and in the west by the foothills of the Massif Central. The

Opposite: Domaine Croix near to Beaujeu.

vineyards are planted on these slopes, sheltered by the worst of the weather by the Rigaud Massif, which rises to 3,320ft (1,012m). These hills, the Monts de Beaujolais, protect the vineyards from the worst weather from the north and west, and help keep temperatures several degrees higher than in surrounding areas. This micro-climate rules out the very worst winter weather, except in freak years, and can push the summer temperatures up well over 100°F (37°C).

Vines grow everywhere, and even decorate the houses and gardens. It also becomes increasingly evident that you are approaching the Mediterranean because the houses are made of stone with red tile roofs — a familiar sight in southern France and northern Italy.

The different geology of the region is pronounced. The Mâconnais has a chalky soil which suits the Chardonnay grape so well, but the Beaujolais soil is mainly granite as far as Villefranche, and then limestone and clay further south.

The only grape variety allowed in Beaujolais is the Gamay, and all the nine crus are grown in the north of the region, on the granitic soil.

This area is sometimes called the Haut-Beaujolais, and apart from all nine crus, contains all the villages entitled to the Beaujolais Villages appellation.

Although the soil is a major factor in the quality of the wine, the weather also plays a critical role, despite the protection afforded by the mountains. Hail can devastate vineyards in minutes, and in 1975 about 5,000 acres (2,000 hectares) of grapes were destroyed. The growers have tried many devices to try to beat the hail, and even use aircraft to scatter silver iodide filings into the clouds, to try to release their water content before they reach the vineyards.

A special method of fermentation has been developed to produce the special fruitiness of Beaujolais, and the Gamay grape needs to be handled carefully if its full potential is to be realised. Fermentation is similar to the system of carbonic maceration but takes place much more quickly, over five or six days. The temperature of the fermentation is also high because this draws out the full flavour, fruitiness and bouquet of the Gamay. Some white Beaujolais is produced from Chardonnay grapes, and there is also a little rosé, but the vast majority of the production is of red wine, which can appear under a number of appellations.

The straight Beaujolais appellation applies to wine with an alcohol content of 9°. If it has an alcohol content of 10° or more it can call itself Beaujolais Supérieur. A wine needs a relatively high alcohol level to travel well, so almost all the Beaujolais exported is Supérieur. Beaujolais Nouveau and Primeur becomes available each November, only two months after the grapes have been picked. The popularity of Beaujolais Nouveau is waning and the mad rush to see which shipper could get it to the UK or US first is largely a thing of the past, but the idea of selling the new wine is perhaps the best example of marketing the world has ever seen. Although the Nouveau is perfectly drinkable, and fun to have, there is no doubt that it does improve with a little ageing. Yet up to a third of the entire harvest can be sold as Nouveau each year, relieving the growers of much expenditure on storage and further maturation.

The Nouveau is made by carbonic maceration. The grapes are not pressed, but placed in vats where the weight of grapes causes a little juice to be released, but fermentation actually starts inside the grape itself. This helps to trap the fruity flavour of the Gamay grape and produces the light style we associate with Beaujolais. A good Nouveau (and they can vary enormously), should have a fine red colour with just a tinge of purple, a warm, fruity nose and a taste that fills your mouth with fruit and flavour. Beaujolais is a very refreshing drink and even more so when served chilled.

The Nouveau is always released a few weeks after the harvest, while the Beaujolais Villages is not available until the following spring. Thirty-nine villages in the Haut-Beaujolais have the right to this appellation and they must meet certain rules. Yields must be under 45 hectolitres per hectare and there must be a natural alcohol content of 10°. Of the thirty-nine villages allowed this appellation, thirty-one are in the *département* of the Rhône

and the remainder in the Saône-et-Loire *département*. Although the growers are allowed to sweeten their wines, they must not let the alcohol content rise above 14°.

The flagships of the Beaujolais are the nine crus: St Amour, Juliénas, Chenas, Moulin-à-Vent, Fleurie, Chiroubles Morgon, Brouilly and the Côte de Brouilly, the order in which the vineyards are met when driving south. The crus must have at least 10° of natural alcohol, but if the name of the vineyard is also on the label, the alcohol content must be 11°.

The Districts and Villages of Beaujolais

St Amour

This village consists of the four hamlets Le Bourg, Le Plâtre-Durand, La Ville and Les Thévenins. It is unspoilt, and the church with its frescoes, is worth a visit. Legend has it that a Roman soldier fell in love, married a local girl and settled here, and thus the name. That may be dubious, but it is a fact that the wines from the village age well in the bottle for a year or two, but they should not be kept for more than four or five years. Production from the 700 acres (280 hectares) of vineyards is now about 1,800,000 bottles a year.

Juliénas

Juliénas, with 1,450 acres (580 hectares) of vineyards, claims to get its name from Julius Caesar. Château de Juliénas is one of the best vine-

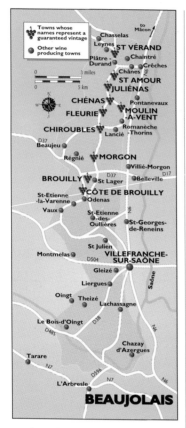

to Mâcon

Chasselas

Leynes

ST VÉRAND

Plâtre - Durand

Chaintré

Chânes

Crêches

ST AMOUR

JULIÉNAS

Pontanevaux

CHÉNAS

FLEURIE

MOULIN -A-VENT

CHIROUBLES

Romanèche -Thorins

Lancié

D37

Beaujeu

Régnié

MORGON

Villié-Morgon

D37

BROUILLY

St Lager

D17

Belleville

St-Etienne -la-Varenne

CÔTE DE BROUILLY

Odenas

Vaux

St-Etienne -des-Oullières

St-Georges- de-Reneins

St Julien

Montmelas

VILLEFRANCHE- SUR-SAÔNE

D504

Gleizé

Liergues

Oingt

Theizé

Lachassagne

Le Bois-d'Oingt

D38

D485

Chazay d'Azergues

Tarare

N7

L'Arbresle

N7

D596

N6

Saône

BEAUJOLAIS

0   3 miles

0   5 km

so, but the majority of the 300 growers do not have their own facilities and belong to the village *coopérative*. This is housed in the Château du Bois de la Salle, which dates back to the sixteenth century. It has a modern tasting room which is very popular throughout the summer. There is a second tasting centre in the old church in the village, a new church having been consecrated in 1868. The wines of Juliénas are longer lasting than those of St-Amour and require more bottle age.

Chénas

This is the smallest of the Beaujolais cru producers covering 650 acres (260 hectares) of vineyards, and the wines in the past have often been used for blending with the grapes of the Côte d'Or, or they have been sent south and sold as Moulin-à-Vent. Chénas produces a full-bodied but light wine, with lots of fruit, that can be kept for some years.

The wines of the village can be tasted at the Cellier de Chénas, which also boasts a sculpture by Renoir showing woodcutters felling an oak tree (*chêne*) to clear the ground for a vineyard. The oak forests, long since gone, gave the village its name.

Moulin-à-Vent

This area in the commune of Chénas produces deep coloured, full, fruity and quite heavy wines which age better than any of the other crus. The growers produce about 4,250,000 bottles a year from the 1,625 acres

yards in the village, and the foundations of the house date back to the beginning of the fourteenth century when the Seigneur de Beaujeu ordered work to start. There is also a sixteenth-century tithe barn, the Maison de la Dîme. The Cathedral of St Vincent took a tenth (*dîme*) of the crops in taxes, and this is presumably the origin of the US. dime coin, one tenth of a dollar. There are a number of quite large vineyards in Juliénas, of 25 acres (10 hectares) or

Above: The statue of Bacchus at Beaujeu.
Below (*left*): Gathering the harvest during the summer months. Below (*right*): Harvesting in Clochemerle.

(650 hectares) of vineyards, although the styles can be very different. There are many producers who prefer their wine to be drunk young so be sure you know what you have bought if you want to lay it down.

The commune used to be called Romanèche-Thorins, but the name was changed in 1936 to Moulin-à-Vent to salute the windmill which still stands, without its sails, in the middle of the vineyards. It is the only windmill in Beaujolais and now a national monument. There are two tasting cellars in the village.

Fleurie

Fleurie produces light, elegant, flowery wines best drunk within two years of the vintage. The *cave coopérative* and the *caveau* both offer tastings, and it is worth walking up to the nineteenth century chapel on top of the hill overlooking the village for splendid views over the 2,000 acres (800 hectares) of vineyards.

Chiroubles

This village has a wine history spanning back more than 1,000 years, and is the highest cru of Beaujolais in terms of altitude. The vines are planted very high on the hillsides, and had to be individually planted into holes dug into the granite. Today there are about 400 growers in the village, mostly working on rented ground for which they agree to give the landlord part of the harvest. The wines produced from the 850 acres (340 hectares) of vineyards, are light both in colour and style. They have an intensity of colour, are very fruity and must be drunk young.

Morgon

This village is the largest of the cru producers, with Brouilly, its neighbour to the south. The wine is full, almost fat, and long-lasting, but it does not lose its youthfulness and freshness. Because of the sand and gravel soil, the wine of Morgon from the 2,700 acres (1,080 hectares) of vineyards, has a very distinctive taste of wild cherries. The wines can be tasted in the cellars of the fifteenth-century château, which attracts thousands of visitors every year.

Brouilly

Brouilly is special among the crus because it contains a number of estates producing very fine wines. The 3,000 acres (1,200 hectares) of vineyards are around the five villages of St Lager, Charentay, Odénas, Quincié and Cercié, at the foot of the mountains. It is the largest producer among the crus.

There are two magnificent châteaux worth visiting, and the cellars of the Château de la Chaize are the largest in Beaujolais. Production amounts to almost nine million bottles a year and there are a number of styles, depending on the estate from which the wine comes. Generally the wine is light, with a very intense bouquet. It is best drunk between one and two years old, but can go on a little longer with a good vintage.

Côte de Brouilly

This is the name given to the vineyards on the slopes of the hills above those of Brouilly. The wines are stronger, and the alcohol content can reach 14° because of the amount of sunshine on the grapes. The wines from the 725 acres (290 hectares) of vineyards are big and powerful, fruity and with a hint of violets on the nose.

A Wine Tour of the Beaujolais Region

The Beaujolais region is part of the Lyonnais and lies just to the south of Mâcon. It can be visited as part of an tour of Burgundy, or one can use either Belleville or Villefranche as a base for a longer stay.

There are a number of wine routes signposted, which lead through the winding lanes of this historic area. The vineyards run just to the west of the busy Autoroute 6 and Route Nationale 6, but motorists on these see little as they speed past, usually either on their way to or returning from the Mediterranean resorts.

The Route de Beaujolais is clearly signposted, both by name and by the symbol of a bunch of grapes on a red background. The best vineyards are to be found in the north, where the Beaujolais Villages produce the best of the wines — names such as Juliénas, Moulin-à-Vent, Fleurie, Chiroubles and the velvety, fruity Brouilly.

Two or three days are needed to visit the various vineyards properly.

However by using either Bellevue or Villefranche as a base, it is possible to tour the northern vineyards on the first day, and the southern ones on the second which involves less than 40 miles (64km) driving each day.

The history of the Beaujolais stretches back more than 1,000 years, but it was in the tenth century that it became a territory in its own right, established as a buffer to separate the warring states of Mâcon and Lyon. In 1031 it was known as *Bellijocum*, and its leader was Beraud, the first Lord of Beaujeu.

The region has always been devoted to a mixture of agriculture and viticulture and much of it is still quaintly rural. Its agricultural produce and wine made Beaujolais famous throughout France.

The completion of the Canal de Briare in 1642 meant that wine producers could ship their wares to Paris. Even though the journey, first by horse and cart, then by canal and river boat on the Loire, took a month, it was much cheaper than the overland route and the wine was not disturbed as much.

Beaujolais still retains a special charm and a gentle pace of life. There are few tourist attractions other than the wineries and the villages have hardly changed in hundreds of years. Almost everyone is involved in the growing of grapes or making and selling of wine.

There are more than 5,000 vineyards covering 54,500 acres (21,800 hectares) in this small area, and at least 200 shippers. There are three main types of Beaujolais: the good wine drunk soon after the harvest; the wine from designated villages which is at its best the following spring; and that from the north entitled to its own appellation which can go on improving for some years.

Beaujolais also has a deserved reputation for its gastronomy, which is not surprising considering the area by which it is surrounded and the supplies from which it can draw. There is magnificent beef from Charollais to the north-west; Bresse to the east is famed for its dairy produce and cheeses; there are freshwater fish from the Saône, and sheep and game from the mountains that form the backbone of Beaujolais. With such a larder to draw on, and such excellent wines it is not surprising that Beaujolais has its fair share of first class restaurants.

Belleville has already been mentioned earlier, and Villefranche is the other suggested base for your wine tour. When the houses were built in the Rue Nationale, a frontage tax was imposed which explains why so many of the buildings are very narrow. Instead of building wide homes and having to pay the tax, the houses were built long and narrow and often lead into charming courtyards, with galleries and spiral staircases. Many of the houses date from the fifteenth to eighteenth centuries. Number 834 with its wonderful vaulting, still bears the arms of Anne of Beaujeu. The Auberge Coupe d'Or, is a seventeenth-century inn with wonderful stone and wrought-iron work.

Whether you use Belleville of Villefranche as a base, the first day should be spent travelling north along the N6 leaving at Crêches-sur-Saône to start the tour. The route should cover St Amour, Juliénas, Moulin-à-Vent and Fleurie; with Chiroubles, Morgon and Brouilly after lunch. Including the Côte de Brouilly, these are the nine communes producing the best wines, and the only ones allowed to use these names on their labels. Obviously if you have more time, you can travel at a more leisurely pace and spend longer exploring.

From Crêches it is easy to find the Route de Beaujolais with its instantly recognisable symbol, and after that, it is almost impossible to get lost because the route winds its way through the vineyards back to Villefranche. If your base is at Belleville, simply take the N6 back.

A tour of this nature is immensely rewarding, because it provides the chance to sample the best wines of the nine communes and compare their different styles and characteristics.

Beaujolais is a place for the wine lover rather than the casual tourist. The most interesting buildings are often those associated with wines — the farms, *chais* and cellars. Many of the farms are at least 200 years old, and in the eighteenth century there was a trend towards building massive outdoor cellars, or *chais*, away from the main farmhouse. Traditionally, the farms were always built with the cellars occupying the ground floor, and the family's accommodation above.

Tour of the Beaujolais Villages and Vineyards

The first port of call should be **Le Plâtre-Durand**, a small village clinging to the top of the hill overlooking St Amour. Here there is an interesting little church and tasting cellar. The vineyards used to be in the control of the Canons of Mâcon, and the village name is said to have derived from their activities when visiting the area and after having drunk the wine!

About 1 mile (2km) to the southwest of St Amour is **Juliénas**. The wines of Juliénas are harder than those from St Amour, with more tannin, so they take longer to mature, but the wait is worth it. The village tasting centre is in a former church (Le Cellier de la Vieille Eglise), and the Château du Bois de la Salle, now a wine cooperative, was formerly a priory. The Maison de la Dîme built in 1647 and famous for its two storeys of arcades, was used as the collecting house for church tithes, which were split equally between the village priest and the Chapter of St Vincent de Mâcon.

Another mile south is **Chenas**, one of the prettiest villages of Beaujolais. The wines of Chenas cause endless battles among the wine experts. Some say they are among the richest in Beaujolais while others have described them as lacking charm. Try them for yourself and make up your own mind. Much of the wine from the commune, however, goes to making Beaujolais sold under the Moulin-à-Vent label, named after the windmill, now a national monument, which stands on top of the hill overlooking the tiny village of Les Thorins. (There is no village called Moulin-à-Vent). The wines are big and fruity and are best after a little ageing.

Continuing south, cross into the commune of **Fleurie**, one of the biggest producers. The wine is soft and light and can be drunk either young or old. The most noted vineyard is Clos de la Roillette, considered by many to be the finest in the whole of Beaujolais. One of the great advantages of the Route de Beaujolais is that once on it, the distance between stops is never more than a mile or two, so most of the time can be spent tasting and admiring the spectacular views, rather than driving.

From Fleurie it is only a stone's throw to the small village of **Chiroubles**, a small commune whose wine is quickly snatched up after each vintage. The most celebrated wine is from Bel-Air. The wines are fresh and fruity and best drunk young.

There is a monument in the town square to Victor Pulliat, a local man and the first wine-maker in Beaujolais to realise the importance of grafting local vines on to disease-resistant American root stock to withstand the *phylloxera* outbreak at the end of the nineteenth century, and which devastated the majority of France's vineyard regions. The vines grow on a natural terrace and the tasting cellars are named La Terrasse.

The road now leads down to the commune producing the Morgon Beaujolais — Villié-Morgon — and with Brouilly to the south, is the largest producing area. **Morgon** was on the Roman road from Lyon to Autun. The wines get their character from the shale on which the vines grow. They mature slowly, developing a rich, fruity nose and mouth-filling flavour. The whole of the area is dominated by the Mont de Brouilly, which rises to about 1,640ft (500m) and is capped by a chapel which acts as a landmark. From Crêches to Morgon the chapel should always be in sight head of you, and from Brouilly to Villefranche it should be behind.

Côte de Brouilly produces big powerful wines although supplies are limited. The wines comes from the vineyards on the slopes of the mountain, while the vines on the plains surrounding it yield the grapes for Brouilly. Brouilly is much lighter, more subtle and fruitier than Côte de Brouilly, and production is about four times greater.

It is obviously foolish to drink too much, and out of the question if you are driving, but a modest tasting of each of these nine wines (even spitting it out if you must) will show just how different they can be.

Villefranche-sur-Saône has a number of interesting sights and many fine old buildings, as well as a good number of pleasant hotels and restaurants considering its size. Many of the cheaper restaurants offer very good local cuisine. About 6 miles (10km) from Villefranche is Lacenas and the Château de Montauzan. It has a magnificent example of the huge eighteenth-century outdoor cellars, popular throughout the region. The château is also the home of the Confrérie des Compagnons du Beaujolais. Although not on the wine route, there is an interesting little wine museum in the Maison Raclet at Romanèche-Thorins.

Belleville is much smaller but again there is a good choice of restaurants, although it is advisable to book a room at either of the two hotels, one near the station and the other a couple of kilometres north of town. The town has Roman origins and used to be called *Lunna*. It was destroyed by the Turks in 732 and was not rebuilt until the eleventh century when it was called **Bellavilla**. It has long been associated with the wine trade and was until recently also famous for its cooperage, but this trade has now died out. The mid-twelfth-century Romanesque church is worth visiting for its tower, apse, carved door and nine-bayed nave. You can also visit the old pharmacy of the Hôtel Dieu, which was run by the Sisters of Martha from the Order of Beaune. Across the river Ardières is **Pizay** where there is the Aero Club de Beaujolais, founded in 1931, and a fourteenth-century château with an ornate square keep and garden by Le Nôtre. The building is now a hotel and restaurant and so can be visited.

Having spent the first day visiting the Crus Beaujolais, the second day should be spent around the

Beaujolais Villages. There are thirty-nine communes and villages who are allowed to use this appellation. The nine crus are only allowed this appellation if production per acre is kept below a certain figure. If a grower (in Chenas for example) prefers to exceed this limit, he is not allowed to use the name of the village by itself, but may call the wine Beaujolais Villages, or Beaujolais Chenas.

The Beaujolais Villages are: Juliénas, Jullié, Emeringes, Chénas, Fleurie, Chiroubles, Lancié, Villié-Morgon, Lantignié, Beaujeu, Régnié, Durette, Cercié, Quincié, St Lager, Odénas, Charentay, St Etienne-la-Varenne, Vaux, Le Perréon, St Etiennes-des-Ouillières, Blacé, Arbuissonas, Salles, St Julien, St Julien-en-Montmélas, Rivolet, Denicé, Les Ardillats, Marchampt and Vauxrenard, all of which are in the Rhône *département*, together with Leynes, St Amour-Bellevue, La Chapelle-de-Guinchay, Romanèche-Thorins, Pruzilly, Chânes, St Vérand, and St Symphorien-d'Ancelles, in the Saône-et-Loire *département*.

The second day can be spent visiting cellars and tasting centres either in the north or south of the region. If you want to take the northern route, drive up again on the N6 to Crêches, and take the road to St Amour. Follow the route down to Chenas and then take the left-hand road to **La Chapelle-de-Guinchay**, where there is a pleasant tasting centre. Your route should then take you south to **Romanèche-Thorins**, with its wine museum dedicated to

Benoît Raclet, through Lancié, and back to **Villié-Morgon**. Both here and at **Beaujeu**, the next village, there are tasting centres. There is also a cooperage exhibition and local crafts museum in Beaujeu. The route should then take you to the tasting centre at **Durette**, and on to Odénas, St Etienne-la-Varenne and Le Perréon, where there are both *co-opérative* cellars and tasting centres to visit. Then head for **Vaux-en-Beaujolais** with its tasting centre, and **Salles** with its fine church and unusual segregated nuns gallery, before driving back to Villefranche through Blacé and St Julien-en-Montmélas.

Places of interest include the thirteenth-century Château de Rigaudière and wine museum at **St Julien** and the nearby classical eighteenth-century château at Blacé; **Salles** with its elegant Louis XVI houses and old Benedictine monastery. You can visit the eleventh-century church and twelfth-century cloisters with their stone statues and **Vaux-en-Beaujolais** made famous by the Clochemerle novels of Gabriel Chevallier. There is a tasting centre and a mineral spring where you can take the waters in Les Balmes, the pump room. The village, built on terraces, has a tiny square on one side of which is the elegant La Pisotterie. There is also a twelfth-century church. Close to and west of Odenas is the **Château de la Chaise**, built in 1675, with a fine 340ft (104m) long vaulted cellar. It was built by a nephew of Père La Chaise, the confessor to Louis XIV. It is now a

Useful Information for Visitors

Hotels and Restaurants in Burgundy

A number of restaurants in Burgundy are signatories to the Bourgognes Découverte Charter, under which they agree to forego a large part of their profit margin on selected Burgundy wines to permit diners to enjoy them at special prices. Each Charter restaurant has its own list, and displays the Bourgognes Découverte sign. These restaurants are highlighted with an asterisk. If a street name is given, it is because the restaurant is located in a small village and its location is obvious. The following price rating is used £ = inexpensive, ££ = medium priced, £££ = expensive but noted for their cuisine. If the restaurant is in a hotel the first name is given.

AISEY-SUR-SEINE 21400
Hotel Du Roy * £-££
☎ 80 93 21 63

ALISE-SAINTE-REINE 21150
Auberge du Cheval Blanc £-££
☎ 80 96 01 55

ALLEREY-SUR-SAÔNE 71350
Les Glycines * £
☎ 85 91 96 60

ALOXE-CORTON 21420
Hotel et Caves des Paulands ££-£££
☎ 80 26 41 05

ANCY-LE-FRANCE 89160
Hostellerie du Centre £-££
Grande Rue
☎ 86 75 15 11

APPOIGNY 89380
Le Marais Revotel * £-££
Route de Bris RN6
☎ 86 53 25 50

Hotel Restaurant Mercure £-££
☎ 86 53 25 00

ARC-SUR-TILLE 21560
Les Marronniers d'Arc * ££-£££
16 rue de Dijon
☎ 80 37 09 62

Hôtel de la Tille £
1 rue de Dijon
☎ 80 37 04 83

ARNAY-LE-DUC 21230
Chez Camille £££
1 place Ed-Herriot
☎ 80 90 01 38

Hotel Restaurant Chez Henri £-££
17 rue St-Jacques
☎ 80 90 14 93

Hôtel Terminus £-££
2 rue de l'Arquebuse
☎ 80 90 00 33

ASQUINS 89540
Les Chandelles * £-££
Route de Vézelay
☎ 86 33 33 30

AUTUN 71400
Golf Hotel * £-££
Route de Chalon
☎ 85 52 00 00

Hotel Saint-Louis £-££
Rue de l'Arbalète
☎ 85 52 21 03

La Tette Noire * £-££
Rue de l"Arquebuse
☎ 85 52 25 35

Le Relais des Ursulines * £
14 rue Rivault
☎ 85 52 68 00

Commerce et Touring Hotel £-££
Ave la République
☎ 85 52 17 90

Restaurant le Chalet Bleu £-££
Rue Jeannin
☎ 85 86 27 30

AUVILLARS-SUR-SAÔNE 21250
L'Auberge de l'Abbaye £-££
☎ 80 26 97 37

AUXERRE 89000
Hotel Les Clairions * £-££
☎ 86 46 85 64

Hotel Normandie £-££
41 boulevard Vauban
☎ 86 52 57 80

Hotel de l'Europe £
Route de Perrigny
☎ 86 46 05 44

Hotel Restaurant le Sainte-Nitasse £
Route de Chablis
☎ 86 46 95 07

Le Trou Poinchy * £-££
34-36 boulevard Vaulabelle
☎ 86 52 04 48

Primavera * £
37 rue du Pont
☎ 86 51 46 36

Le Maxime £-££
Quai de la Marine
☎ 86 52 04 41

AUXEY-DURESSES 21190
Restaurant La Cremailliere ££-£££
☎ 80 21 22 60

AUXONNE 21130
Hotel du Corbeau ££-£££
1 rue de Berbis
☎ 80 31 11 88

AUXONNE-VILLIERS-LES-POTS 21170
Auberge du Cheval Rouge £-££
Eue Armand Roux
☎ 80 31 44 88

AVALLON 89200
Hotel Restaurant le Relais Fleuri ££-£££
RN 6
☎ 86 34 02 85

Hostellerie du Moulin des Ruats * ££-£££
Vallée du Cousin
☎ 86 34 07 14

Hostellerie de la Poste £-££
Place Vauban
☎ 86 34 06 12

Hotel Grill Campanile £
La Cerce RN6
☎ 86 34 06 12

Les Capucins * ££-£££
6 ave Paul Doumer
☎ 86 34 06 52

BALOT 21330
Auberge de la Baume £-££
☎ 80 81 40 15

BEAUNE 21200
Auberge Bourguignonne £££
4 place Madelaine
☎ 80 22 23 53

Hotel Central £££
2 rue Victor Millot
☎ 80 24 77 24

Restaurant de la Cloche * £££
40-42 faubourg Madelaine
☎ 80 24 19 48

Brasserie Les Gourmets £££
6-8 rue Pasumot
☎ 80 22 15 99

Jacques Laine £££
10 boulevard Foch
☎ 80 24 87 10

Bernard Morillon * £££
31 rue Maufoux
☎ 80 24 12 06

La Rotisserie de la Paix * £££
45-47 faubourg Madelaine
☎ 80 22 33 33

Le Relais des Saulx £££
6 rue Louis Véry
☎ 80 22 01 35

Auberge Saint-Vincent * £££
Place de la Halle
☎ 80 22 42 34

Hotel Arcade/Tournebroche * £-££
Avenue Charles de Gaulle
☎ 80 22 75 67

Auberge du Cheval Noir * ££
17 blvd Saint-Jacques
☎ 80 22 07 37

Hostellerie de l'Ecusson ££-£££
Place Malmédy
☎ 80 24 03 82

Le Jardin Des Remparts ££
10 rue de l'Hôtel Dieu
☎ 80 24 79 42

La Rotisserie Fleury * £-££
15 place Fleury
☎ 80 22 35 50

Auberge de la Toison D'Or * £-££
4 boulevard Jules Ferry
☎ 80 22 29 62

Les Chevaliers £-££
3 petite place Carnot
☎ 80 22 32 26

Climat de France/La Soupiere * £
Ave Charles de Gaulle
☎ 80 22 74 10

Dame Tartine £-£££
3 rue Nicolas Rolin
☎ 80 22 64 20

Hotel de France/Le Jardin £-££
35 ave du 8 Septembre
☎ 80 24 10 34

Hotel Abbaye de Maizières £-£££
19 rue Maizières
☎ 80 24 14 25

Hotel Des Arts Et Congres/Le Téméraire £-££
Ave Charles de Gaulle
☎ 80 22 63 34

Caveau des Arches * £-££
10 boulevard Perpreuil
☎ 80 20 10 37

Hôtel Les Balladins £-££
18 rue A.M. Ampère
☎ 80 22 53 17

Beaune Motel/Côte Jardin £
Autoroute A6
☎ 80 21 46 24

Hotel Bellevue £
5 route de Seurre
☎ 80 24 05 10

Cottage Hotel/Pub à Vins * £
Parc Hotelier de la Chartreuse
☎ 80 22 79 58

Hotel Ibis/La Ferne aux vins * £
Ave Charles de Gaulle
☎ 80 22 46 75

Mercure Beaune Central/La Calèche * £
Ave Charles de Gaulle
☎ 80 22 22 00

Novotel/Restaurant Belenoès * £
Ave Charles de Gaulle
☎ 80 24 59 00

Hotel & Restaurant de la Poste * ££-£££
Boulevard Clémenceau
☎ 80 22 08 11

Resthotel Primevere £
Route de Verdun
☎ 80 24 15 39

Samotel * £-££
74 route de Pommard
☎ 80 22 35 55

Restaurant du Hameau * £
Hameau de Gigny
☎ 80 22 05 34

Le Brelinette * £-££
6 rue Madeleine
☎ 80 22 63 94

Le Brasero St-Jacques * £
1 rue du Faubourg St-Jacques
☎ 80 24 12 36

Maxime * £-££
3 place Madeleine
☎ 80 22 17 82

Piqu'Boeuf Grill * £
2 rue Madeleines
☎ 80 24 07 52

Restaurant Des Arts Deco * £-££
25 rue Paradis
☎ 80 24 12 41

Restaurant Pizza Silvio * £
24 rue d'Alsace
☎ 80 22 07 68

Close to Beaune

CHOREY-LES-BEAUNE **21200**
L'Ermitage Corton * £££
RN 74
☎ 80 22 05 28

Le Bareuzai ££-£££
RN 74
☎ 80 22 02 90

Ladoix-Serrigny 21550
Les Coquines ££
RN 74
☎ 80 26 43 58

Le Corton £
RN 74
☎ 80 26 42 37

La Gremelle £-££
RN 74
☎ 80 26 40 56

LEVERNOIS **21200**
Hostellerie de Levernois £££
Route de Combertault
☎ 80 24 73 58

MELOISEY **21190**
La Renaissance £
☎ 80 26 00 76

MEURSAULT **21190**
Le Relais de la Diligence * £
23 rue de la Gare
☎ 80 21 21 32

Motel au Soleil Levant £
5 route de Volnay
☎ 80 21 23 47

Hotel du Centre * £
4 rue de Lattre-de-Tassigny
☎ 80 21 20 75

Hotel des Arts £-££
4 place de l'Hotel-de-Ville
☎ 80 21 20 28

Le Chevreuil * £-££
Opposite Hotel-de-Ville
☎ 80 21 23 25

MONTAGNY-LES-BEAUNE **21200**
Hotel Campanile * £
☎ 80 22 65 50

PULIGNY-MONTRACHET **21190**
Le Montrachet ££-£££
Place des Marroniers
☎ 80 21 30 06

SAVIGNY-LES-BEAUNE **21420**
Hotel l'Ouvrée £-£££
Route de Bouilland
☎ 80 21 51 52

Lud Hotel £-££
31 rue de Cîteaux
☎ 80 21 53 24

BEINE 89800
Le Vaulignot * £-£££
30 route Nationale
☎ 86 42 48 48

BELAN-SUR-OURCE 21570
Hotel Restaurant Du Soleil £-££
Place du Four
☎ 80 93 76 06

BÈZE 21310
Auberge de la Quatr'Heurie £-££
☎ 80 75 30 13

Le Bourguignon £-££
Rue de la Porte de Bessey
☎ 80 75 34 51

Le Relais de Bèze £-££
2 place de Verdun
☎ 80 75 38 75

BLIGNY-SUR-OUCHE 21360
Hostellerie des Trois Faisans £-££
Rue du Pont
☎ 80 20 10 14

Auberge du Val D'Ouche £-££
Place de l'Hotel-de-Ville
☎ 80 20 12 06

BOUILLAND 21420
Hostellerie du Vieux Moulin ££-£££
☎ 80 21 51 16

BRAZEY-EN-PLAINE 21470
L'Esperance * £
1 rue de la Gare
☎ 80 29 93 88

BUXY 71390
**Le Relais du Montagny/Restaurant
Girardot** * £-££
Place de la Gare
☎ 85 92 04 04

CHABLIS 89800
Hostellerie des Clos £-££
☎ 86 42 10 63

Hotel Les Lys
Route Auxerroise £-£££
☎ 86 42 10 62

Hotel Restaurant de l'Etoile £-££
Rue des Moulins
☎ 86 42 10 50

Au Vrai Chablis £-££
☎ 86 42 11 13

CHAGNY 71150
Hotel Bonnard * £-££
☎ 85 87 21 49

Hotel Central * ££
1 rue de la République
☎ 85 87 20 18

Lameloise ££-£££
Place d'Armes
☎ 85 87 08 85

CHAILLY-SUR-ARMANÇON 21320 £-££
**Château de Chailly-Hotel Golf &
Restaurant l'Armançon**
☎ 80 90 30 30

CHAINTRE 71570
Confortinn Primevere Macon * £
☎ 85 37 44 44

CHALON-SUR-SAÔNE 71100
Hotel Arcade * £
Ave de l'Europe
☎ 85 41 04 10

Hotel Mercure ave de l'Europe £-££
☎ 85 46 51 89

Le Saint-Georges * ££-£££
32 ave Jean Jaurès
☎ 85 48 27 05

Restaurant Le Provencal £-££
Place de Beaune
☎ 85 03 65

Restaurant Didier Denis ££-£££
Rue du Pont
☎ 85 48 81 01

Restaurant du Marche * £-££
7 place Saint Vincent
☎ 85 48 62 00

Ripert * £-££
31 rue Saint Georges
☎ 85 48 89 20

Chambœuf 21220
Relais des Hautes-Cotes £-££
☎ 80 51 81 83

Champforgueil 71530
Climat de France * £
☎ 85 46 40 04

Charmoy 89400
Le Relais de Charmoy * £
2 route de Pars
☎ 86 91 23 19

Charnay-les-Macon 71850
Le Moulin du Gastronome * £-£££
540 route de Cluny
☎ 85 34 16 68

Charny 89120
Domaine de Montigny * ££
Perreux
☎ 86 91 62 33

Charolles 71120
Hotel Moderne * ££-£££
14 ave Joanny Furtin
☎ 85 24 07 02

Chassey-le-Camp 71150
Auberge du Camp Romain £-££
☎ 85 87 09 91

Château-Chinon 58120
Hostellerie l'Oustalet £
Route de Lormes
☎ 86 85 15 57

Hotel du Lion d'Or £-££
Rue de Fossés
☎ 86 85 13 56

Châteauneuf-en-Auxois 21320
Hostellerie du Château ££-£££
☎ 80 49 22 00

Châtillon-en-Bazois 58110
Auberge de l'Hotel de France £
Rue Docteur Duret
☎ 86 84 13 10

Châtillon-sur-Seine 21400
Hotel de la Cote d'Or £-£££
2 rue Charles Ronot
☎ 80 91 13 29

Hotel Brasserie Europa £-££
Place de la Résistance
☎ 80 91 04 10

Chenôve 21300
Hotel Comfort Inn l'Escargotière
Route de Beaune
☎ 80 52 15 35

Chevigny-Fenay 21600
Le Relais de la Sans Fond/Le Begin * £-££
Route de Seurre
☎ 80 36 61 35

Clamecy 58500
Hostellerie de la Poste * £-££
9 place Emile Zola
☎ 86 27 01 55

Cluny 71250
Hotel Saint-Odilon £
Belle Croix
☎ 85 59 25 00

Hotel le Moderne/L'Hermitage *
££-£££
Route de Cormatin
☎ 85 59 27 20

Le Potin Gourmand * £-££
Champ de Foire
☎ 85 59 02 06

Corbigny 58800
Hotel la Buissoniere £-££
Place Saint Jean
☎ 86 20 02 13

Château de Lantilly * £-£££
☎ 86 20 01 22

CORCELLES-LÈS-CÎTEAUX **21910**
Le Relais de Cîteaux *£-££*
☎ 80 36 62 41

CORCELLES-LES-MONTS **21160**
Hotel Petit *£*
1 Grande Rue
☎ 80 42 90 04

COSNE-SUR-LOIRE **58200**
Hotel de Grande Cerf *£-££*
Rue Saint Jacques
☎ 86 28 20 21

AUBERGE DE VIEUX RELAIS *£*
Rue Saint Agnan
☎ 86 28 20 21

Le Point du Jour *£-££*
Rue de Maréchal Foch
☎ 86 28 15 28

COUCHES **71490**
Hotel des 3 Maures * *£-££*
Place de la République
☎ 85 49 63 93

La Tour Bajole * *£-££*
Rue St-Martin
☎ 85 45 54 54

COUCHEY **21160**
L'Ecuyer de Bourgogne * *£-££*
9 rue Pierre Curie
☎ 80 52 03 14

CRÉANCEY **21320**
Restaurant du Rond Point *£-££*
☎ 80 90 83 97

CURTIL-VERGY **21220**
Auberge la Ruellee * *£-££*
2 route de Segrois
☎ 80 61 44 11

CUSSY-EN-MORVAN **71550**
Le Cussyssois * *£-££*
☎ 85 54 60 11

DAIX **21121**
Hotel Castel Burgond *££*
Route de Troyes
☎ 80 56 59 72

DIJON **21000**
Jean-Perre Billoux *£££*
4 place Darcey
☎ 80 30 11 00

Breuil La Chouette * *££-£££*
1 rue de la Chouette
☎ 80 30 18 10

Hostellerie du Chapeau Rouge * *££-£££*
5 rue Michelet
☎ 80 30 28 10

Hotel Pullman La Cloche * *£-££*
14 place Darcy
☎ 80 30 12 32

Le Pre Aux Clercs et Trois Faisans * *££*
11-13 place de la Libération
☎ 80 67 11 33

Primavera * *£-££*
11 ave Raymond Poincaré
☎ 80 73 55 84

Mercure Chateau Bourgogne * *££*
22 boulevard de la Marne
☎ 80 72 31 13

Hotel du Nord/Porte Guillaume * *£-££*
Place Darcy
☎ 80 30 58 58

Thibert *£-£££*
10 place Wilson
☎ 80 67 74 64

Restaurant La Toison D'Or *££-£££*
18 rue Sainte-Anne
☎ 80 30 73 52

Ma Bourgogne *££-£££*
1 boulevard Paul Doumer
☎ 80 65 48 06

Le Chabrot £-££
36 rue Monge
☎ 80 30 69 61

Continental/Mayne Rose £
7-9 rue A. Rémy
☎ 80 43 34 67

La Dame d'Aquitaine ££-£££
3 place Boussuet
☎ 80 30 36 23

Hostellerie de l'Etoile * ££
1 rue Marceau
☎ 80 73 20 72

Grésill'Hotel £-££
16 ave R-Poincaré
☎ 80 71 10 56

Le Moulin a vent * ££
8 place François Rue
☎ 80 30 81 43

Le Petit Vatel * £
73 rue d'Auxonne
☎ 80 65 80 64

Restaurant du Port £
5 ave Jean-Jaurès
☎ 80 45 43 30

Hotel de la Poste/Le Grand Cafe £-££
5 rue de Château
☎ 80 30 51 64

Le Rallye £-££
39 rue Chabot Charny
☎ 80 67 11 55

Le Relais de la Gare £-££
next to the station
☎ 80 41 40 35

La Brasserie du Théatre £-££
1a place du Théatre
☎ 80 67 13 59

Le Clos des Capucines £-££
3 rue Jeannin
☎ 80 65 83 03

Café Brasserie La Concorde £-££
2 place Darcy
☎ 80 30 69 43

Le Dome £
16 rue Quentin
☎ 80 30 58 92

Hotel Restaurant KCNIL £-££
11-13 ave Junot
☎ 80 65 30 29

La Pierrade £
24 rue Bannelier
☎ 80 30 86 91

Le Pressoir £-££
Chemin de la Rente de la Cras
☎ 80 41 45 86

Hotel du Stade £
3 boulevard de Strasbourg
☎ 80 65 35 32

La Taverne de Maitre Kanter £
18a rue Odebert
☎ 80 30 81 83

Terminus et Grande Taverne £
22 ave Maréchal Foch
☎ 80 43 53 78

Climat De France/La Soupière * £
15-17 ave Maréchal Foch
☎ 80 43 40 01

Holiday Inn/Le Garden Grill £-££
Parc de la Toison d'Or
☎ 80 72 20 72

IBIS Central/Grill Rotisserie * £-££
3 place Grangier
☎ 80 30 44 00

IBIS (ex Relais Arcade/Le Chanteclair) * £-££
15 ave Albert 1er
☎ 80 43 01 12

Modern' Hotel £
3 rue des Ateliers
80 52 56 46

La Fregate * £
111 rue de la Préfecture
☎ 80 73 58 76

Le Chandelier * £
65 rue Jeannin
☎ 80 66 16 82

Le Faim Palais * £-££
10 rue Léon Mauris
☎ 80 74 33 00

Hotel du Parc de la Colombiere ££-£££
Parc de la Colombiere
☎ 80 65 18 41

Hotel de Paris/First Inn *
9-11 ave Maréchal Foch
☎ 80 43 41 88

Resthouse Primevere £
Rue P. de Coubertin/Mirande
☎ 80 31 69 12

Les Relais Bleus £
12 rue P. de Coubertin/Mirande
☎ 80 66 32 40

Hotel-Grill du Sauvage * £
64 rue Monge
☎ 80 41 31 21

Close to Dijon

CHENÔVE 21300
Hotel Les Balladins £
18 rue Jean Moulon
☎ 80 52 15 11

Hotel au Bon Coin £-££
54 route de Dijon
☎ 80 52 58 17

Hotel Comfort Inn/L'Escargotiere ££
96 route de Beaune
☎ 80 52 15 35

Fimotel/Le Gaulois £
16 rue Jean Moulin
☎ 80 52 20 33

CHEVIGNY-ST-SAUVEUR 21800
Le Clos du Roy £-£££
35 ave du 14 juillet
☎ 80 51 33 66

Hotel au Bon Accueil £-££
17 rue de la République
☎ 80 46 13 40

COUCHES 21160
L'Ecuyer de Bourgogne £-£££
9 rue Pierre Curie
☎ 80 52 03 14

Hermes/Relais de Bourgogne £-££
RN 74 route de Beaune
☎ 80 52 35 36

DAIX 21121
Les Trois Ducs £-££
5 route de Troyes
☎ 80 56 59 75

LONGVIC 21600
La Gourmanderie £
Rue du Port
☎ 80 66 56 16

Climat de France/Louisiane £
7 rue de Beauregard
☎ 80 67 22 22

MARSANNAY-LA-CÔTE 21160
Les Gourmets ££-£££
8 rue du Puits de Tet
☎ 80 52 16 32

Hotel Grill Campanile £
☎ 80 52 62 01

Cottage Hotel £
Route de Beaune RN 74
☎ 80 51 10 00

Novotel Dijon Sud £
Route de Beaune
☎ 80 52 14 22

NORGES-LA-VILLE 21490
Hotel de la Norges £-££
☎ 80 35 72 17

PERRIGNY-LES-DIJON 21160
Hotel IBIS Dijon Sud £
RN 74
☎ 80 52 86 45

PLOMBIÈRES-LES-DIJON 21370
Hotel Restaurant Du Pont de Pany *
£-££
☎ 80 23 60 59

L'Auberge £-££
9 route de Paris
☎ 80 41 69 11

La Combe-aux-Fees £
11 route de Dijon
☎ 80 41 70 87

QUÉTIGNY 21800
Cap Vert £
Rue de Cap Vert
☎ 80 46 11 44

Hotel Climat de France £
14 ave de Bourgogne
☎ 80 46 04 46

SAINT-APOLLINAIRE 21850
Hotel Campanile £
1 rue de la Fleuriée
☎ 80 72 45 38

SENNECEY-LES-DIJON 21800
La Flambee £-££
D905 route de Dole
☎ 80 47 35 35

DONZY 58220
Hotel le Grand Monarque £
Rue de l'Etape
☎ 86 39 35 44

DRACY-LE-FORT 71640
Hotel Le Dracy/La Garenne * £-££
☎ 85 87 81 81

ECHIGEY 21110
Hotel Restaurant Rey £-££
Place de l'Eglise
☎ 80 29 74 00

EPOISSES 21460
Hotel Restaurant de la Pomme d'Or £
Rue des Forges
☎ 80 96 43 01

ETROCHEY 21400
Aux Pecheurs £-££
☎ 80 91 02 39

FAIN-LES-MONTBARD 21500
Hotel Chateau de Malaisy * £-££
Rue de Chateau
☎ 80 89 46 54

FIXIN 21220
Hotel Restaurant Chez Jeanette * £-££
7 rue Noisot
☎ 80 52 45 49

Au Relais de l"Empereur * £
2 rue Magnien
☎ 80 52 45 46

La Courte Paille £-££
☎ 80 52 46 00

Au Clos Napoleon £-££
4 rue de la Perrière
☎ 80 32 45 63

GEMEAUX 21120
Restaurant Tejerina £-£££
Rue de la Liberté
☎ 80 95 01 51

GENLIS 21110
Hotel Restaurant de la Gare * £-££
22 ave de la Gare
☎ 80 31 30 11

GEVREY-CHAMBERTIN 21220
Hotel Les Grands Crus ££
Route des Grands Crus
☎ 80 34 34 15

Le Close Bertin * £
☎ 80 58 51 51

La Rotisserie du Chambertin ££-£££
Rue du Chambertin
☎ 80 34 33 20

Les Millèsimes ££-£££
25 rue de l'Eglise
☎ 80 51 84 24

La Sommellerie £-£££
7 rue Souvert
☎ 80 34 31 48

Hotel Aux Vendanges de Bourgognes * £-££
47 route de Beaune
☎ 80 34 30 24

Gilly-les-Cîteaux 21640
Château de Gilly-les Cîteaux * ££-£££
☎ 80 62 89 98

Grancey-le-Château 21580
Restaurant de la Vieille Porte ££
☎ 80 75 65 88

Hauteville-les-Dijon 21121
Hotel Restaurant La Musarde £-££
7 rue des Riottes
☎ 80 56 22 82

Ivry-en-Montagne
Hotel le Chalet d'Ivry £
RN 6
☎ 80 20 21 18

Izier 21110
Auberge d'Izier * £-££
19 rue du General de Gaulle
☎ 80 31 26 39

La Rochepot 21340
Le Relais du Chateau * £-££
☎ 80 21 71 32

Joigny 89300
Hotel Restaurant Le Rive Gauche £-£££
Rue du Port au Bois
☎ 86 91 46 66

Modern Hotel ££-£££
Rue Robert Petit
☎ 86 62 16 28

Joncy 71460
Hotel du Commerce * £-££
Place Henri Dureault
☎ 85 96 27 20

Labergement-Foigney 21110
Auberge des Mesanges * £-£££
27 rue de Genlis
☎ 80 31 22 33

La Charité-sur-Loire 58400
Hotel Le Grand Monarque £-££
Quai Clemenceau
☎ 86 70 21 73

Hotel Terminus £
Ave Gambetta
☎ 87 70 09 61

La Clayette 71800
Hotel de la Gare * £-£££
38 rue de la Gare
☎ 85 28 01 65

Le Creusot 71200
Le Restaurant * £
Rue des Abattoirs
☎ 85 56 32 33

Hotel le Moulin Rouge £-££
Route de Montcoy
☎ 85 55 14 11

Lamarche-sur-Saône 21760
Hostellerie Le Saint Antoine £-££
☎ 80 47 11 33

La Roche-en-Brenil 21530
Hotel au Bon Accueil £-££
Place de la Danse
☎ 80 64 70 91

Lechâtelet 21250
Auberge de la Fine Gueule £
Quai de Saône
☎ 80 20 42 06

Lery 21440
Hotel Restaurant La Rousotte £-££
Route de Salives
☎ 80 35 11 12

LEVERNOIS 21200
Hostellerie de Levernois £££
Route de Combertault
☎ 80 24 73 58

LEYNES 71570
Au Fin Bec * £-££
☎ 85 35 11 77

LEZINNES 89160
Hotel de la Gare * £-££
4 rue de la Gare
☎ 86 75 66 14

LONGVIC 21600
Hotel Climat de France £
Rue de Beauregard
☎ 80 67 22 22

LORMES 58140
Hotel Perreau £-££
Route d'Avallon
☎ 86 22 53 21

LOSNE 21170
Auberge de lar Marine £-££
☎ 80 29 05 11

LOUHANS 71500
Restaurant La Cotriade £
Rue d'Alsace
☎ 85 75 19 91

Hostellerie du Cheval Rouge £
Rue d'Alsace
☎ 85 75 21 42

LUX 71100
Hotel Les Charmilles £-££
Rue de la Libération
☎ 85 48 58 08

LUZY 58170
Hotel du Centre * £-££
26 rue de la République
☎ 86 30 01 55

MACON 71000
Hotel Altea Bord de Saône * £-££
26 rue Pierre de Coubertin
☎ 85 38 28 06

Hotel Terminus * £-££
91 rue Victor Hugo
☎ 85 39 17 11

La Perdrix * £-££
6 rue Victor Hugo
☎ 85 39 07 05

Hotel Escatel * £
4 rue de la Liberté
☎ 85 29 02 50

Novotel Macon Nord £
A6
☎ 85 36 00 80

Hotel de Geneve £
Rue Bigonnet
☎ 85 38 18 10

Hotel D'Europe et d'Angleterre £-££
Quai Jean Jaurès
☎ 85 38 27 94

Le Poisson d'Or, in the Park £-££
☎ 8538 00 88

Restaurant Pierre * £-£££
7-9 rue Dufour
☎ 85 38 14 23

MAGNY-COURS 58470
Holiday Inn £-££
☎ 86 21 22 33

Hotel du Circuit £
RN7
☎ 86 58 04 88

MALAY-LE-GRAND 89100
Virginia Hotel £-££
Route de Troyes
☎ 86 64 66 66

MARCENAY-LE-LAC 21330
Hotel Restaurant Le Santenoy * £-££
☎ 80 81 40 08

MARCIGNY-SOUS-THIL 21390
La Strada £
☎ 80 64 52 34

MARCILLY-SUR-TILLE 21220
Hotel de la Gare £-££
Place de la Gare
☎ 80 95 06 44

MAREY-LES-FUSSEY 21700
Maison des Hautes Cotes * £-££
☎ 80 62 91 29

MARSANNAY-LA-COTE 21160
Cottage Hotel and Restaurant* £
Route de Beaune
☎ 80 51 10 00

Hotel Ibis
RN 74
☎ 80 52 86 45

MATOUR 71520
Christophe Clement * £-££
le Bourg
☎ 85 59 74 80

MEURSAULT 21190
Motel au Soleil Levant £
route de Volnay
☎ 80 21 23 47

Hotel du Centre * £-££
4 rue de Lattre de Tassigny
☎ 80 21 20 75

Le Chevreuil * £-££
Place de l'Hotel de Ville
☎ 80 21 23 25

Le Relais de la Diligence * £-££
23 rue de la Gare
☎ 80 21 21 32

MIGENNES 89400
Hotel de Paris * £-££
57 ave Jean Jaurès
☎ 86 80 23 22

MIREBEAU-SUR-BÈZE 21310
Hostellerie la Gandeule £-££
Rue de l'Eglise
☎ 80 36 70 79

Auberge des Marronniers £-££
place du Général Viard
☎ 80 36 71 05

MOLOY 21120
Hostellerie de l'Ignon £-££
☎ 80 75 12 33

MONTBARD 21500
Hotel de l'Ecu * ££
7 rue Auguste Carré
☎ 80 92 11 66

Le Cyclamen £-££
6 ave Maréchal Foch
☎ 80 92 06 46

MONTCEAU-ECHARNANT 21360
Auberge Les Chenets * £-££
Rue Moingeon
☎ 80 22 22 00

MONTCEAU-LEWS-MINES 71300
Resthotel Primevre £
Ave du Maréchal Foch
☎ 85 57 49 49

MONTCHANIN 71210
La Tuilerie * £
180 ave de la République
☎ 85 78 49 19

Novotel * £
Route du Pont Jeanne Rose
☎ 85 78 55 55

MONTSAUCHE-LES-SETTONS 58230
Hotel la Morvandelle £-££
Lac des Settons
☎ 86 84 50 62

Hotel Restaurant de la Plage * £-££
☎ 86 84 53 78

Restaurant Les Terrasses £-££
Lac des Settons
☎ 86 84 52 09

MOREY-ST-DENIS 21220
Le Relais Des Grands Crus ££-£££
☎ 80 34 32 57

Restaurant Castel de Tres Girard £££
Rue de Très Girard
☎ 80 34 33 09

M͏OULINS-E͏NGILBERT **58290**
Hotel du Bon Laboureur * £-££
15-17 place Boucomont
☎ 86 84 20 55

N͏EUVY-S͏AUTOUR **89570**
Le Dauphin * £-£££
RN 77
☎ 86 56 30 01

N͏EVERS **58000**
Best Western Hotel Diane £-££
rue du Midi
☎ 86 57 28 10

Hotel Climat de France £
Boulevard Victor-Hugo
☎ 86 21 42 88

Les Jardins de la Porte du Croux £-££
rue de la Porte du Croux
☎ 86 57 12 71

Le Saint-Louis * £-£££
2 place Mossé
☎ 86 57 73 09

La Cour St-Etienne * £
33 rue St-Etienne
☎ 86 36 74 57

N͏ITRY **89310**
Hotel Axis £-££
☎ 86 33 60 92

Auberge la Beurs Beursaudiere * £-££
9 chemin de Ronde
☎ 86 33 62 51

N͏OLAY **21340**
Le Relais de Nolay * £
7 rue d'Aumont
☎ 80 21 85 98

Hotel du Chevreuil £-££
14 place de l'Hôtel Ville
☎ 80 21 71 89

Hotel Sainte-Marie £-££
36 rue de la République
☎ 80 21 71 25

Restaurant Le Burgonde * £-££
35 rue de la République
☎ 80 21 71 25

N͏UITS-S͏AINT-G͏EORGES **21700**
Hotel de la Côte d'Or ££-£££
37 rue Thurot
☎ 80 61 06 10

Hostellerie La Gentilhommiere ££-£££
25 La Serrée
☎ 80 61 12 06

Hotel des Cultivateurs £
12 rue du Général de Gaulle
☎ 80 61 10 41

Hotel de l'Etoile £
5 place de la Libération
☎ 80 61 04 68

Hotel Iris * £
1 ave de Chambolland
☎ 80 61 17 17

La Florentine * £
34 Grande Rue
☎ 80 61 30 69

Le St-Georges £
Carrefour d'Europe
☎ 80 61 15 00

Hostellerie St-Vincent £-££
Rue du Général de Gaulle
☎ 80 61 14 91

P͏ARAY-LE-M͏ONIAL **71600**
Grand Hotel de la Basilique * £-££
18 rue de la Visitation
☎ 85 81 11 13

Hostellerie des 3 Pigeons * £-£££
2 rue Dargaud
☎ 85 81 03 77

Motel-Grill Le Charollais £-££
RN 79
☎ 85 81 03 35

Les Logis de Paray ££
Boulevard Henri de Regnier
☎ 85 81 70 00

Perrigny-sur-Loire 71160
La Cle des Champs * £
Bourg
☎ 85 53 84 52

PLANCHEZ 58230
Le Relais des Lacs * £-£££
Place de la Poste
☎ 86 78 41 68

POISSON 71600
Restaurant de la Poste * ££-£££
☎ 85 81 10 72

PONT-DE-PANY 21410
Chateau de la Chassagne £-££
☎ 80 40 47 50

PONT-ET-MASSENE 21140
Hotel du Lac £-££
☎ 80 97 11 11

PONTIGNY 89230
Le Moulin de Pontigny * £-££
20 rue P. Desjardins
☎ 86 47 44 98

POUILLY-EN-AUXOIS 21320
Hotel de la Poste * £-££
Place de la Libération
☎ 80 90 86 44

Motel du Val Vert £
Route d'Arney-le-Duc
☎ 80 90 82 34

Close to Pouilly-en-Auxois
CHAILLEY-SUR-ARMANÇON 21320
Chateau de Chailly Hotel Golf ££
☎ 80 90 30 30

SAINTE-SABINE 21320
Hostellerie Chateau de Sainte-Sabine £££
☎ 80 49 22 01

POUILLY-SUR-LOIRE 58150
Hotel la Bouteille d'Or £-££
Rue de Paris
☎ 86 39 13 84

Restaurant Chez Memere £
Rue W. Rousseau
☎ 86 39 02 43

PRÉCY-SOUS-THIL 21390
Hotel Restaurant Loriot ££
4 rue de l'Eglise
☎ 80 64 56 33

QUARRE-LES-TOMBS 89630
Auberge des Brizards £-££
☎ 86 32 20 12

Le Morvan * £-££
6 rue des Ecoles
☎ 86 32 24 83

ROMANECHE-THORINS 71570
Hotel les Maritones £-££
☎ 85 35 51 70

ROUVRAY 21530
Hotel Axeal £
RN 6
☎ 80 64 79 79

SAINT-ALBAIN 71260
Hotel Mercure Macon-St-Albain * £
Autoroute 6
☎ 85 33 19 00

SAINT FARGEAU 89170
Le Relais du Chateau £-££
promenade du Grillon
☎ 86 74 01 75

SAINT-FLORENTIN 89600
Hotel Restaurant Les Tilleuls * £-££
3 rue Décourtive
☎ 86 35 09 09

SAINT-HONORE-LES-BAINS 58360
Hotel Bristol Thermal * £-££
16 rue Joseph Duriaux
☎ 86 30 71 12

SAINTE-MARIE-LA-BLANCHE 21200
Relais de Ste-Marie-la-Blanche £-££
☎ 80 26 60 51

SAINT-JULIEN-DE-JONZY 71110
Hotel Restaurant 1 ££
Esperance
☎ 86 33 39 10

SAINT-JEAN-DE-LOSNE 21170
Saonotel/Saony Grill £
☎ 80 29 04 77

SAINT-ROMAIN 21190
Hotel Les Roches £-££
☎ 80 21 21 63

SAINT-SEINE-L'ABBEYE 21440
Hotel de la Posts * £-££
17 rue Carnot
☎ 80 35 00 35

Auberge Campagnarde Chez Guite £
15 rue Carnot
☎ 80 35 01 46

SAINT-USAGE 71500
Auberge de Saint-Usage *
Le Bourg
☎ 85 72 10 95

SALIVES 21580
Le Golf de Salives * £
Larcon
☎ 80 75 66 45

SANTENAY 21590
L'Ouillette £
Place du Jet d'Eau
☎ 80 20 62 34

Le Terroir * £-££
Place du Jet d'Eau
☎ 80 20 63 47

SAULIEU 21210
Hotel De La Borne Imperiale £-£££
14-16 rue d'Argentine
☎ 80 64 19 26

Bernard Loiseau £££
2 rue d'Argentine
☎ 80 64 07 66

Hotel de la Poste ££-£££
1 rue Grillot
☎ 80 64 05 67

Hotel des Quatre Vents/La Louisiane £
47 rue Jules Ferry
☎ 80 64 13 49

Auberge du Relais * £-££
8 rue d'Arginetine
☎ 80 64 13 16

Hotel de la Tour d'Auxois £-££
Square A-Dumaine
☎ 80 64 13 30

La Vieille Auberge £-££
15 rue Grillot
☎ 80 64 13 74

Hotel de Bourgogne £-££
9 rue Courtépée
☎ 80 64 08 41

Hotel le Lion d'Or
7 rue Courtépée
☎ 80 64 16 33

Hotel la Renaissance
7 rue Grillot
☎ 80 64 08 72

SAULON-LA-RUE 21910
Chateau De Saulon-la-Rue £-££
Route de Seurre
☎ 80 36 61 10

SEMUR-EN-AUXOIS 21140
Hotel de la Côte d'Or * £-££
3 place Gaveau
☎ 80 97 03 13

Arcy-sur-Cure 89270
Lac Sauvin
☎ 86 32 41 61

Auxerre 89000
16 blvd Vaulabelle
☎ 86 52 45 38

Auxerre 89000
16 ave de la Résistance
☎ 86 46 95 11

Auxonne 21130
Route d'Athée
☎ 80 37 36 61

Avallon 89200
BP 83 10 ave Victor-Hugo
☎ 86 34 01 88

Bure-les-Templiers 21290
☎ 80 81 01 64

Chalon-sur-Saône
2 rue d'Amsterdam
☎ 85 46 62 77

Cluny 71250
rue Porte-de-Paris
☎ 85 59 08 83

Corbigny 58800
La Collancelle
☎ 86 22 40 13

Dijon 21000
1 boulevard Champollion
☎ 80 71 32 12

Francheville 21440
La Clairière
☎ 80 35 05 11

La Bussière-sur-Ouche 21360
Abbaye de la Bussière-sur-Ouche
and Le Moulin d'Abbaye
☎ 80 49 02 29

Nolay 21340
7 rue d'Aumont
☎ 80 21 85 98

Recey-sur-Ource 21290
3 rue de Beaune
☎ 80 55 54 65

Saint-Léger-des-Vignes 58300
RN 81
☎ 86 25 09 76

Saint-Léger-sous-Bouvray 71990
La Maison du Beauvray
☎ 85 8255 46

Salives 21580
Club des Vacances Vertes le Sacriba
☎ 80 75 62 28

Semur-en-Auxois 21140
1 rue du Champ-de-Foire
☎ 80 97 10 22

Sennecey-le-Grand 71240
Domaine du Château de Ruffey
☎ 85 44 80 34

Les Settons 58230
Station-voile des Settons
☎ 86 84 51 98

Base Nautique de Baye
☎ 86 38 97 39

Base Nautique de Chaumeçon
☎ 86 22 61 35

Tintury 58110
Château de Tintury
☎ 86 84 10 46

Vézelay 89450
Auberge de la Croix Sainte-Marthe
☎ 86 33 24 18

Vissigny Chaumard 58120
☎ 86 57 46 99

BOATING IN BURGUNDY

There are lots of opportunity for boating in Burgundy. You can take a small river or lake cruise, enjoy a luxurious dinner as you sail along, enjoy one of the many hotel boats, or hire a house boat and travel where and when you please.

There are cruises on the Canals of Novernais, Loire and Yonne, on the Lac des Settons, and on the main rivers, especially the Loire and Saône. Trips range from an hour or less to half a day, and there are also lunch, dinner and picnic cruises. Péniches-hôtels, and hotel boats, which offer a very comfortable way of exploring Burgundy. Cruises range from two to seven days and offer full-board services, including evening entertainment and visits to wine cellars. Operators and tour companies offering cruises include:

Abercrombie & Kent Ltd
Sloane Square House
Holbein Place
London SW1 W8N
☎ (171) 730 9600

Abercrombie & Kent Ltd
1420 Kensington Road
Oak Brook
Illinois, USA
60521-2106
☎ (312) 954 29 44

Continentale de Croisieres
9 rue Jean Renaud
21000 Dijon
☎ 80 30 49 20

Croisieres Deilmann
Bruno Maury
11 rue Gentil
69002 Lyon
☎ 78 39 13 06

Le Duc de Bourgogne
Maison de Garde
21370 Velars-sur-Ouche
☎ 80 33 66 49

France Afloat
PO Box 249
Redhill, RH1 2FD
United Kingdom
☎ (171) 704 0700

Peniche Penelope
Quai de la Marine
89000 Auxerre
☎ 86 52 09 90

Quiztour
Bassin de la Villette
19-21 quai de la Loire
75019 Paris
☎ (1) 42 01 11 11

Sonafho
Château La Chassagne
21410 Pont-de-Pany
☎ 80 23 66 20

Fully-equipped house boats (*bateaux habitables*) sleeping between four and twelve people, can be hired for weekends, weeks or longer periods. Prices vary according to size and season. Further information from:

Service de Réservation Loisirs
Accueil (SRLA)
1-2 quai de la République
89000 Auxerre
☎ 86 51 12 05

BOURBILLY 21460
Château de Bourbilly
☎ 80 97 05 02
Open: Tuesday to Sunday 10am-
12noon and 3-6pm.

BRANCION 71700
Castle
Open: March to November 9am-6.30pm

BRAZEY-EN-PLAINE 21470
Parc du Château Magnin
☎ 80 29 91 51
Open: daily.

BUFFON 21500
La Grande Forge de Buffon
☎ 80 89 40 30
Open: daily 10am-12noon and 2.30-
6pm during the summer.

BUSSEY-LA-PIERRE 21330
Living Agriculture Museum
☎ 80 81 41 59
Open: daily April to October.

BUSSY-RABUTIN 21150
Château
Open: April to September, tours at 10
and 11am. October to March tours at
10 and 11am and 2pm and 3pm.

BUSSIÉRE-SUR-OUCHE, LA 21360
Abbaye de la Bussière-sur-Ouche
☎ 80 49 02 29
Open: daily 8.30am-10pm.

BUSSY-LE-GRAND 21150
Château de Bussy-Rabutin
☎ 80 96 00 03
Open: daily 10am-12noon and 2-7pm
during the summer.
Closes: 4pm and all day Tuesday and
Wednesday rest of the year.

Bussy Church
☎ 80 96 05 58
Open: daily 9am-6pm.

CHABLIS 89800
Maison de la Vigne et du Vine de
Chablis
1 rue de Chichée
Open: July to September 9.30am-
12.30pm and 1.30-6.30pm, April to
June and October closes 6pm.

CHALON-SUR-SAÔNE 7100
Denon Museum
Open: daily except Tuesday 9.30am-
12noon and 2-5.30pm.

Musée Nicéphore Niepce
Open: daily 9.30-11.30am and 2.30-
5.30pm except Tuesday.

CHAMPAGNEY 21440
Ecole Musée de Champagny
☎ 80 41 23 82
Open: 3-6pm daily in the summer.

CHATEAU-CHINON 58120
Musée du Septennat and Costume
Museum
Open: May to September daily 10am-
6pm (7pm in July and August),
weekends only at other times.

CHÂTEAUNEUF-EN-AUXOIS 21320
Château de Châteauneuf-en-Auxois
☎ 80 49 21 89
Open: daily 9.30am-12noon and 2-
6pm during the summer. Rest of year
10am-12noon and 2-4pm and closed
Tuesday and Wednesday.

CHÂTILLON-SUR-SEINE 21400
Church of St Vorles
☎ 80 91 24 67
Open: daily during the summer
10.30am-12noon and 2.30-5.30pm.
Hours vary rest of the year.

Archaeological Museum
☎ 80 91 24 67
Open: 9am-12noon and 1.30-6pm.
Closed: Tuesday, September to June.

Chenove 21300
Wine presses of Dukes of Burgundy
☎ 80 52 52 30
Open: daily 2-7pm.

Cîteaux 21700
Abbaye de Cîteaux
☎ 80 61 11 53
Open: Monday to Saturday.

Collonges-les-Bevy 21220
Château de Collonges-les-Bevy
☎ 80 61 40 29
Open: daily 2-6pm.

Commarin 21320
Château de Commarin
☎ 80 49 23 67
Open: April to November daily
10am-12noon and 2-6pm, closed
Tuesday.

Conforgien 21210
Château de Conforgien
Open daily July to September.

Coraboeuf 21340
Château de Coraboeuf
Open: 15 July to end of August daily
10am-12noon and 2-6pm.

Clamecy 58500
Musée d'Art et Histoire Romain
Open: daily except Tuesday 10am-
12noon and 2-6pm. Closed Sundays
November to Easter.

Cluny 71250
Abbey of St Peter and St Paul
Open: 9am-7pm July and August;
9.30am-12noon and 2-5pm October;
9.30am-12noon and 2-6pm April to
June; 10.30-11.30am and 2-4pm
November to March.

Commarin 21990
Château
Open: April to October daily 10am-
12noon and 2-6pm except Tuesday.

Cormatin 71460
Château
Open: year round by appointment.

Courtivron 21120
Château de Courtivron
☎ 80 75 12 42
Open: Mid-July to end of August.

Cosne-sur-Loire 58200
Municipal Museum
Open: daily 10am-12noon and 3-7pm.

Couches 71490
Castle
Open: July and August daily 10am-
12noon and 2-6pm, June and
September 2-6pm, April, May and
October Sunday and public holidays
2-6pm.

Le Creusot 71200
Museum of Man, Metal & Industry
Open: weekdays 9am-12noon and 2-
6pm, weekends 2-6pm.

Curtil-Vergy 21220
Monastery of St Vivant
☎ 80 61 17 31
Open: daily.

Cussigny 21700
Château de Cussigny
☎ 80 62 98 28
Open: mid-July to end of August
10.30am-12.30pm and 2.30-6.30pm.

Dijon 21000
Archaeological Museum
☎ 80 30 88 54
Open: daily except Tuesday and
public holidays

Museum of Sacred Art
☎ 80 30 06 44
Open: daily 9am-12noon and 2-6pm,
except Tuesday and public holidays

Museum of Fine Arts
☎ 80 74 52 70
Open: daily 10am-6pm, except
Tuesday and public holidays.

Grevin Waxworks Museum
☎ 80 42 03 03
Open: daily 9.30am-12noon and 2-7pm.

Natural History Museum
☎ 80 76 82 76
Open: daily 9am-12noon and 2-6pm.
Closed Tuesday and Sunday.

Gardens of L'Arquebuse
☎ 80 76 82 84
Open: daily 7.30am-6pm (8pm in
summer).

Magnin Museum
☎ 80 67 11 10
Open: Tuesday to Sunday 10am-6pm
(closed for lunch 12noon-2pm
October-May).

Rude Museum
☎ 80 74 52 70
Open: June to September 10am-
12noon and 2-5.45pm. Closed
Tuesday.

Museum of Burgundian Life
☎ 80 30 65 91
Open: daily 9am-12noon and 2-6pm,
closed Tuesday.

Mustard Museum
☎ 80 44 44 52
Open: Tuesday and Saturday
mornings

Chapel St-Croix de Jerusalem
☎ 80 29 37 65
Open: Monday to Friday 9am-12noon
and 2-5pm

Chapel of St Bernard
☎ 80 58 23 64
Open: Tuesday 2-4pm, Saturday 3-
6pm

Chartreuse de Champmol
☎ 80 42 48 48
Open: daily 8.30am-7pm

Palais des Etats de Bourgogne
☎ 80 74 51 51
Open: daily except Tuesday

Tour Philippe Le Bon
Town Hall
☎ 80 74 51 51
Open: daily during the summer 9am-
12noon and 2.30-5.30pm

Hôtel le Belin
☎ 80 67 15 65
Open: daily 9am-7pm.

Hôtel Jehanin de Chamblanc
☎ 80 66 65 68
Open: daily 8am-6pm.

Hôtel de Samerey
Open: daily

ECUTIGNY **21360**
Château d'Ecutigny
☎ 80 20 19 14
Open: daily 9am-7pm.

EGUILLY **21320**
Château de Eguilly
☎ 80 90 72 90
Open: daily 10am-12noon & 2.30-6pm.

ÉPOISSES **21460**
Château d'Époisses
☎ 80 96 40 56
Open: daily 9am-7pm gardens only.

FIXIN **21220**
Fixin Church
☎ 80 52 45 52
Open: 9am-6pm daily in summer, by
appointment rest of the year.

Musée Noisot
☎ 80 52 45 52
Open: Wednesday and weekends 2-
6pm June to September.

FLAVIGNY-SUR-OZERAIN 21150
Abbaye de Flavigny
☎ 80 96 20 88
Open: daily 9-11.30am and 2-5pm.

Church of St Genest
☎ 80 96 25 47
Open: 11am-12noon and 2.30-6pm
during the summer, closed Monday
and Sunday, by appointment at other
times.

FLÉE 21144
Château de Flée
☎ 80 97 17 07
Open: by appointment.

FONTENAY 21500
Abbaye de Fontenay
☎ 80 92 15 00
Open: daily 9am-12noon and 2-6pm.

FROLOIS 21150
Château de Frolois
☎ 80 96 22 92
Open: daily 2-6pm.

GEVREY-CHAMBERTIN 21220
Fortress and Château
☎ 80 34 36 13
Open: daily 10am-12noon and 2-5pm
(château 6pm in summer).

HAUTEVILLE-LES-DIJON 21121
Church
☎ 80 56 13 20
Open: by appointment

LA CHARITÉ-SUR-LOIRE 58400
Museum
Open: July and August 10am-12noon
and 2.30-6.30pm. Other times by
appointment.

LAMARGELLE 21440
Moulin de Lamargelle
☎ 80 35 15 06
Open: Sundays July to September.

LANTENAY 21370
Château de Lantenay
☎ 80 35 33 77
Open: 1st and 3rd Thursdays and
Sundays each month 2-6pm.

LANTILLY 21140
Château de Lantilly
☎ 80 97 11 57
Open: July to October 10am-12noon
and 3-6pm, closed Tuesday.

LONGECOURT-EN-PLAINE 21110
Château de Longecourt
☎ 80 39 88 76
Open: June to September 2.30-5.30pm
except Thursday.

LONGVIC 21600
Château de Beauregard
☎ 80 66 20 39
Open: July to September 10am-6pm.

LOUHANS 71500
Hôtel-Dieu and Apothecary
Open: daily except Tuesday.

LUX 21220
Château de Lux
☎ 80 75 37 18
Open: daily by appointment.

MÂCON 71000
Musée des Ursulines
Open: 10am-12noon and 2-6pm.
Closed Tuesdays & Sunday mornings.

Lamartine Museum
Open: April to October 10am-12noon
and 2-6pm, except Tuesdays and
Sunday mornings. November,
December and March 2-6pm.

MÂLAIN 21410
Château de Mâlain
☎ 80 23 60 73
Open: 2-7pm daily during the
summer, Sunday only during the rest
of the year.

Gallo-Roman Excavations
☎ 80 23 60 73
Open: daily 8am-12noon and 2-7pm during the summer, by appointment during the rest of the year.

MARIGNY-LE-CAHOUËT 21150
Château de Marigny-le-Cahouët
☎ 80 97 07 28
Open: June to October Wednesday and weekends 9am-12noon and 2-6pm.

MARSANNAY-LA-CÔTE 21160
Maison du Patrimoine et du Tourisme
☎ 80 52 12 70
Open: 3-7pm.

MENESSAIRE 21430
Château de Menessaire
☎ 80 64 15 88
Open: daily 9am-5pm July and August.

Maison du Siegle
☎ 80 64 28 65
Open: daily by appointment.

MEURSAULT 21190
Château de Meursault
☎ 80 21 22 98
Open: mid February to mid December 9.30am-12noon and 2.30-6.30pm.

MILLY-LAMARTINE 71960
Manor of Lamartine
Open: April to November, guided tours daily except Tuesday.

MOLESMES 21330
Abbaye de Molesmes
☎ 80 81 44 47
Open: April to October daily 3-6pm.

MONTBARD 21500
Musée Anciennes Ecuries de Buffon
☎ 80 92 01 34
Open: April to September 10am-12noon and 2-6pm, closed Tuesday.

Museum of Fine Arts
☎ 80 90 01 34
Open: June to August 10am-12noon and 3-6pm, rest of the year 3-6pm, closed every Tuesday.

Parc Buffon
☎ 80 92 01 34
Open: daily 10am-12noon and 2.15-5pm (6pm in summer).

MONTIGNY-SUR-AUBE 21520
Château de Montigny
☎ 80 93 55 25
Open: daily 9am-12noon and 2-5pm.

MONTMOYEN 21290
Château de Montmoyen
☎ 80 81 02 04
Open: mid-July to mid-September daily 11am-12noon and 2-5pm, by appointment.

MONT-ST-JEAN 21840
Château de Mont-St-Jean
Open: daily.
Church
☎ 80 84 30 70
Open: July and August 3-6pm daily.

MOUTIERS-ST-JEAN 21500
Jardin de Coeurderoy
☎ 80 96 73 37
Open: 10am-7pm during the summer, by appointment at other times.

NEVERS 58000
St Bernadette Shrine and Museum
Open: April to October 6.30am-7.30pm, 7am-12noon and 1.30-7.30pm at other times.

Frédéric Blandin Municipal Museum
Open: May to September 10am-6pm, October to April 10am-12noon and 2-5.30pm. Closed Tuesday.

Nuits-St-Georges 21700
Museum
☎ 80 61 13 10
Open: May to November 10am-
12noon and 2-6pm except Tuesday.

**Chantier des Fouilles Des
Bollards**
☎ 80 65 39 92
Open: daily by appointment.

Orches-Baubigny 21340
Medieval Ruins
Open: daily.

Paray-le-Monial 71600
Relics Chamber
Open: Easter to October 9am-12noon
and 1.30-6.30pm.

Diorama
Open: June to mid-September 9am-
12noon and 1.30-7.30pm, April and
May 1.30-7pm, and mid-September to
end of October 1.30-5.30pm.

Museum of Charolles Porcelain
Open: April to November 10am-
12noon and 2-6pm. Closed Tuesday.

Pierreclos 71960
Castle
Open: daily 9.30am-12noon, 2-6pm.

Pierre-de-Bresse 71270
Castle and Museum
Open: daily 3-6pm.

Pontigny 89230
Abbey
Open: daily except during services.

Précy-sous-Thil 21390
Le Manege
☎ 80 64 51 70
Open: 3-7pm except Monday in
summer, 3-7pm Sunday only during
the rest of the year.

Quemigny-sur-Seine 21510
Château de Quemigny-sur-Seine
☎ 80 93 80 78
Open: daily.

Quincerot 21500
Château de Quincerot
☎ 80 96 75 81
Open: mid July to end of August daily
9.30am-12.30pm and 2.30-4.30pm.

Reulle-Vergy 21220
Church of St Saturnin
☎ 80 61 40 95
Open: daily.

Museum
☎ 80 61 42 93
Open: July to mid-September daily
2.30-6pm, by appointment at other
times.

Rochepot, La 21340
Château de la Rochepot
☎ 80 21 71 37
Open: 10am-12noon and 2-6pm
during the summer, 10-11.30am and
2-5.30pm at other times.

Rosièrs 21610
Château de Rosièrs
☎ 80 75 82 53
Open: daily 9am-7pm.

Saffres 21350
Cliffs
☎ 80 49 67 10
Open: daily.

St Brisson 58230
Maison du Parc Naturel Régional du
Morvan
Open: weekdays 8.45am-12.15pm and
1.30-5.30pm.

Museum of the Resistance
Open: June to mid September daily 2-
6pm.

Herbularium
Open daily.

St Colombe sur Seine 21400
Musée des Canadiens Nord Bourguignons
☎ 80 91 08 46
Open: May to September, Sunday 3-6.30pm

St Fargeau 89170
Château
Open: April to November daily 10am-12noon and 2-6pm.

St Germain-en-Brionnais 21690
Sources de la Seine
☎ 80 35 02 54
Open: daily.

Exposition St Romain
☎ 80 21 28 50
Open: 4-8pm during the summer, at other times by appointment.

Château de St Romain
☎ 80 21 28 50
Open: daily.

Verger Archaeological Site
☎ 80 21 28 50
Open: By appointment.

St Seine-l'Abbaye 21440
Abbey
☎ 80 35 00 20
Open: daily 8am-8pm during the summer, 9am-4pm at other times.

St Thibault 21350
Church of St Thibault
☎ 80 64 66 07
Open: mid March to mid November daily 9am-12noon and 2-6pm.

Salives 21580
Fortifications
☎ 80 75 62 28
Open: daily.

Salmaise 21690
Covered Market
☎ 80 35 84 99
Open: daily.

Santenay 21590
Museum of Wine
☎ 80 20 61 87
Open: May to November weekends 11am-3.30pm.

Church of St Jean- e-Narosse
Open: daily.

Saulieu 21210
Museum François Pompon
☎ 80 64 19 51
Open: 10am-12.30pm and 2-6pm during summer, rest of year open 10.30am-5pm.
Closed Tuesday.

Basilica St Andoche
☎ 80 64 07 03
Open: daily 8.30am-6pm.

Savigny-lès-Beaune 21420
Château
Air and Auto Museum
☎ 80 21 55 03
Open: daily 9am-12noon and 2-6pm.

Semur-en-Auxois 21140
Municipal Museum
☎ 80 97 24 25
Open: 2-5.30pm, Wednesday to Sunday mid-May to end of September, 2-5.30pm, Wednesday, Friday and Sunday rest of the year.

Ramparts
☎ 80 97 11 95
Open: daily 10am-12noon and 2-6pm.

Municipal Library
☎ 80 97 24 25
Open: daily.

Museum
Open: June to September 10am-
12noon and 2-6pm, October to May
Wednesdays and weekends 10am-
12noon and 2-6pm. Monday,
Thursday and Friday 2-6pm.

SEURRE 21250
Ecomusée du Val de Saône
☎ 80 21 09 02
Open: May to September daily 10am-
12noon and 3-7pm.
L'Etang Rouge
☎ 80 21 09 02
Open: May to September daily 10am-
12noon and 3-7pm.

SOLUTRÉ 71960
Museum
Open: daily except Tuesday, March
and April and October to December
10am-12noon and 2-5pm, May 10am-
12noon and 2-6pm, June to
September 10am-1pm and 2-7pm.
Closed January and February.

TALMAY 21270
Château de Talmay
☎ 80 36 13 64
Open: Tuesday to Sunday 3-5pm, by
appointment rest of the year.

TANLAY 89430
Château
Open: daily April to end of October
except Tuesday. Guided visits from
9.30-11.30am and 2.15-5.15pm.

Centre of Contemporary Art
Open: June to September daily 11am-
7pm.

TIL-CHÂTEL 21120
Church
☎ 80 95 08 41
Open: daily 8am-6pm.

TONNERRE 89700
Hôtel-Dieu and Hospital Museum
Open: June to September 10am-
12noon and 1-7pm. April, May and
October, weekends and public
holidays 1-6pm.

VAL DES CHOUES À ESSAROIS 21290
Abbaye du Val des Choues
☎ 80 81 01 09
Open: 10am-7pm. Closed Tuesday
September to June.

VÉZELAY 89450
St Madelaine Basilica
Open: off season, sunrise to sunset, in
season 7am-7pm.

VILLAINES-EN-DUESMOIS 21450
Château Ducal
☎ 80 89 03 10
Open: mid-June to mid-September 3-
6pm, rest of the year by appointment.

VILLENEUVE-LES-CONVERS 21450
Agricultural Museum
☎ 80 96 21 08
Open: March to November Sundays

The Vineyards of Burgundy

There are hundreds of opportunities
for tasting the wines of Burgundy as
you travel through the region. Many
of the vineyards and wineries offer
tastings advertise the fact widely.
The following wineries and tasting
cellars, however, are all members of
the 'From Vineyards to Cellars'
Hospitality Charter'. The signatories
are all pledged to give you a warm
welcome, and are proud and happy
to present their products. At least
one wine of the range available will

be offered for free tasting, and if a charge is made for more extensive tastings this is indicated in the following entries. There is no obligation to buy, although shipment and take-away sales are easily arranged. Generally, you will come across three types of tasting cellar in the region — those owned by the *viticulteur* (V) or wine grower, those owned by *coopératives* (C) and those owned by *négociants* (N). Most Burgundy estates are small family concerns, about 10 acres (4 hectares) on average, and the work in the vineyard is usually done by the owner. The estate produces most of its wine in bottle and labelled with a local appellation. There are around 4,500 individual wine growing estates in Burgundy. Cave coopératives are joint enterprises involving groups of growers who usually deliver their grapes to a central winery. Increasingly, coopératives are handling the marketing and sale of their wines, and most have their own tasting cellars. There are currently twenty-two wine coopératives in Burgundy.

The *négociant-éleveur* selects and buys wine in casks from the growers and then matures and bottles them. There are 120 *négociants-éleveurs* in Burgundy. The vineyards are listed alphabetically in each region which are listed as they would be met if driving north to south.

Only the wineries, caves and tasting centres included in this section are open to the public. Not all of the vineyards mentioned elsewhere in this book can be visited.

Vineyards of Chablis

Beine

Domaine la Bretauche
Louis and Pascal Bellot (V)
45 Grande Rue
89800 Beine
☎ 86 42 41 66
4 miles (6km) from the Auxerre-South tollgate. Fifteenth century half-timbered farmhouse. Open weekends 11am-7pm all year round, and weekdays 2-7pm from 1 June to 1 October. English spoken.

Domaine Jean-Marie Naulin (V)
6 rue du Carouge
89800 Beine
☎ 86 42 46 71
4 miles (6km) from Chablis this vineyard is run by Madame Yvette Naulin who offers free tastings in her small cellar. Open daily from 9am-1pm and 2-8pm.

Chablis

Domaine Jean Collet et Fils (V)
15 ave de la Liberté
89800 Chablis
☎ 86 42 11 93
The vineyard was founded in 1792 and is on the Auxerre side of Chablis. The tastings are in the beautiful vaulted cellars. Open Monday to Friday 9am-12noon and 2-6pm. Closed last two weeks of August. English spoken.

Caves Jean Dauvissat (V)
3 rue de Chichée
89800 Chablis
☎ 86 42 14 62
Wines from five vintages always available in the seventeenth century cellars. Open Monday to Saturday 8am-9pm, Sunday and public holidays 9am- 8pm.

Domaine William Fèvre (V)
14 rue Jules Rathier
89800 Chablis
☎ 86 42 12 06
A charming Renaissance style farmhouse only 100yds (91m) from the town hall. The full range of Chablis wines is available for tasting. Open daily from 8am-12noon and 1.30-5.30pm. Closed on public holidays. English spoken.

S.C.A. La Chablisienne (C)
8 boulevard Pasteur
89800 Chablis
☎ 86 42 11 24
The *coopérative* represents 280 growers and a wide range of Chablis and Bourgogne crus and vintages are available for tasting. Open daily Monday to Saturday 8am-12noon and 2-6pm. Sundays and public holidays 9.30am-12noon and 2-6pm. Video presentation available.

Le Cellier Chablisier
7 rue Jules Rathier
89800 Chablis
☎ 86 42 15 64
Bernard Guyot had the idea to group together several producers wines for tasting in the eighteenth century cellar near the Petit Pontigny. The vineyards can also be visited. The first wine tasted is free, then 38F for four wines. Open daily 9am-7pm. Closed Wednesdays between 30 November and 1 March.

Domaine Guy Robin (V)
13 rue Berthelot
89800 Chablis
☎ 86 42 12 63
A good opportunity to try the whole gamut of Chablis. Open Monday to Saturday 8am-12noon and 2-6pm, Sunday and public holidays 8-11am and 3-6pm. English spoken.

Domaine Vocoret et Fils (V)
40 route d'Auxerre
89800 Chablis
☎ 86 42 12 53
The chance to sample several Premiers and Grands Crus. Open Monday to Saturday 8am-12.30pm and 1.30-5.30pm. Closed on Sundays and public holidays.

Chapelle-Vaupelteigne, La

Domaine Jean Goulley et Fils (V)
22 vallée des Rosiers
89800 La Chapelle-Vaupelteigne
☎ 86 42 40 85
The house is only 50yds (45m) from the church and you can visit the cellars before tasting. Open Monday to Saturday 8am-12noon and 1.30-5.30pm. English spoken.

Courgis

Domaine de la Conciergerie (V)
12 rue Restif de la Bretonne
89800 Courgis
☎ 86 41 40 28
The 42 acre (17 hectares) estate has been in the Adine family for many generations, with 12 acres (5 hectares) being cultivated for organic production. The estate also has three guestrooms. Open Monday to Saturday 9am-12noon and 1.30-7.30pm, Sunday 9-11am.

Fleys

Domaine de la Meuliere (V)
89800 Fleys
☎ 86 42 13 56
Two-and-a-half miles (4km) from Chablis in a tiny village. The grapes are picked traditionally by hand. Open daily from 9am-12.30pm and 2-7.30pm. Appointments preferred for weekend visits.

Domaine Landrat-Guyollot (V)
Les Berthiers
58150 St Andelain
☎ 86 39 11 65
Traditional wines from the Val de Loire and Nivernais. Take part in *Le Trivinal*, a game about the history of the vineyard and area. Open Monday to Saturday 9am-12noon and 1-7 pm. Sunday and holidays by appointment. English spoken.

Domaine de Maltaverne (V)
RN7
58150 Pouilly-sur-Loire
☎ 86 26 13 57
5 miles (8km) north of Pouilly-sur-Loire in attractive rustic settings. Open daily 8am-7pm. English spoken.

Maison Jean Pabiot et Fils (N)
Les Loges
22 rue St Vincent
58150 Pouilly-sur-Loire
☎ 86 39 10 25
One of the largest wine growing estates in the area, in Les Loges, 3 miles (5km) from Pouilly. Open daily 8am-12noon and 2-6pm.

Domaine Hervé Seguin (V)
Le Bouchot
58150 Pouilly-sur-Loire
☎ 86 39 10 75
A specialist wine producer offering tastings in the cellars in rue Louis Joseph Gousse on the D28 in Le Bouchot. Open 9am-12noon and 2-7pm.

Vineyards of the Côte de Nuits

Chambolle Musigny

Domaine Henri Felettig (V)
21220 Chambolle-Musigny
☎ 80 62 85 09

This is a family run winery with a number of plots in the area offering the chance to taste some local wines. Open Monday to Friday 2-7pm, Saturday 9am-12noon and 2-7 pm, Sunday and public holidays 9am-12noon.

Domaine Sigaut (V)
21220 Chambolle-Musigny
☎ 80 62 80 28
Traditional wine making methods still used and the wine is matured in barrels for fifteen to eighteen months. Open daily. English spoken.

Château André Ziltener (N)
21220 Chambolle-Musigny
☎ 80 62 81 37
In the centre of village in beautiful grounds is the Ziltener château. There are tastings and guided tours. There is a museum in part of the converted cellars based on the Cîteaux monks. Open daily 9.30am-6.30pm. English spoken. First tasting free then 40F for six additional wines.

Corgoloin

Domaine Bernard Chevillon et Fils (V)
21700 Corgoloin
☎ 80 62 98 79
On the outskirts of the village about 500yds from the RN74. Open daily.

Domaine du Clos des Langres (V)
21700 Corgoloin
☎ 80 62 98 73
A large 125 acre (50 hectare) estate with an eighteenth century wine press that is a national monument. Open daily 10am-6pm. Closed weekends out of season. English spoken.

Domaine Jean Petitot (V)
21700 Corgoloin
☎ 80 62 98 21
A wine making family for generations

who enjoy sharing their passion for wine with visitors. Open Monday to Friday 8am-8pm. English spoken.

Fixin

Domaine Vincent et Denis Berthaut (V)
9 rue Noisot
21220 Fixin
☎ 80 52 45 48
The cellars are named after Napoléon who figured prominently in the history of the village. Tastings take place opposite the offices near the Post Office. Open Monday to Friday 8am-12noon and 2-7pm, Saturday 8am-12noon, and Sunday and public holidays 10am-12noon and 2-6pm. Closed from 21 November to 15 March.

Domaine du Cos St Louis (V)
Rue Abbé Chevalier
21220 Fixin
☎ 80 52 45 51
In the hamlet of Fixey north of the village on the route des Grands Crus. There is a small museum in the seventeenth century farm house and winery. Open daily from 10am-7pm. Closed 1 November to 15 April, English spoken.

Domaine Philippe Joliet (V)
Manoir de la Perrière
21220 Fixin
☎ 80 52 47 85
The manor house was built by the monks of Cîteaux Abbey in the twelfth century. There is a very old wine press in the tasting cellars near Noisot Park. Open Monday to Saturday 9am-12noon and 2-6pm. Sunday and public holidays by appointment.

Gerland

Domaine Gachot-Monot (V)
21700 Gerland
☎ 80 62 50 95
The cellars are 8 miles (13km) from the vineyards near Cîteaux Abbey on the D road between the A31 and A36. Open Monday to Saturday 9am-12.30pm and 3.30-7.30pm. Sunday and public holidays 10am-12noon. English spoken.

Gevrey-Chambertin

Caveau du Chapître (V) (Group of Producers)
1 rue de Paris
21220 Gevrey-Chambertin
☎ 80 51 82 82
A chance to taste many of the best red, white and sparkling wines of the area. Open daily from 9.30am-12noon and 3-7pm. Closed on Tuesday.

Domaine Esmonin Pere et Fille (V)
1 rue Neuve Cos-St-Jacques
21220 Gevrey-Chambertin
☎ 80 34 36 44
The tasting cellar is near the church and Michel Esmonin and his daughter Sylvie welcome visitors. Open Monday to Friday 11am-12noon, Saturday 10am-12noon, Sunday and public holidays by appointment. Closed August and Christmas week. English spoken.

Domaine Jean-Claude Fourrier (V)
7 route de Dijon
21220 Gevrey-Chambertin
☎ 80 34 33 99
A superb range of wines is offered for tasting in this beautiful house. Open Monday to Friday 9am-12noon and 2-6.30pm, weekends 10am-12noon and 2-6pm. Visits by appointment during the wine harvest and first eighteen days of August. English spoken.

Domaine Heresztyn (V)
27 rue Richebourg
21220 Gevrey-Chambertin
☎ 80 34 30 86
Between the school and church, the tastings are in a specially converted room although the cellars can also be

visited. Open Monday to Friday 9am-12noon and 2-7pm, Saturday 9am-12noon and 1.30-7pm, Sunday 9am-12noon, and public holidays 9am-12noon and 1.30-7pm. Visits on Sunday afternoon by appointment. English spoken. The first tasting is free and 25F for the next four wines.

Domaine Vachet-Rousseau (V)
15 rue de Paris
21220 Gevrey-Chambertin
☎ 80 51 82 20
The thirteenth-century house in the centre of the village stands on a site occupied since Roman times. Open Monday to Friday 9am-12noon and 2-7pm. Saturday 9am-12noon and 2-6pm, Sunday and holidays 10am-12.30pm. First tasting free then 35F for four wines.

Gilly-les-Cîteaux

Maison l'Heritier-Guyot (N)
rue des Clos Prieurs
21640 Gilly-les-Cîteaux
☎ 80 62 86 58
Founded in 1845 this winery is also noted for its fruit liqueurs. Open Monday to Friday 8am-12noon and 2-6pm. Closed first two weeks of August.

Marsannay-la-Côte

Domaine Jean-Pierre Guyard (V)
4 rue du Vieux Collége
21160 Marsannay-la-Côte
☎ 80 52 12 43
The seventh generation of wine growers in a beautiful eighteenth century home with vaulted cellars. Open Monday to Saturday 9am-8pm, Sunday 9am-12noon.

Morey-St-Denis

Domaine Robert Gibourg (V/N)
17 rue de Ribardot
21220 Morey-St-Denis
☎ 80 34 36 51

There is a vineyard museum with tools next to the tasting cellar and around 18,000 bottles in stock. Open Monday to Friday 9am-12noon and 2-6pm. Closed second and third week of August. English spoken.

Domaine Jean Raphet et Fils (V)
45 route des Grands Crus
21220 Morey-St-Denis
☎ 80 34 31 67
In the centre of the village, the Domaine started thirty years ago and much of the production is sold whole-sale. There is a large range of wines available in the tasting cellars. Open daily by appointment.

Domaine Jean Taupenot (V)
21220 Morey-St-Denis
☎ 80 34 35 24
The estate can trace its history back to the fifteenth century and it still follows the age-old traditions of wine making while utilising the best of modern techniques. Grapes are picked by hand, enjoy long fermentation and ageing in oak casks. Open Monday to Friday 9am-12noon and 2-7pm.

Nuits-St-Georges

Caveau du Beffroi (wine shop)
5 rue Sonoys
21700 Nuits-St-Georges
☎ 80 61 32 43
The chance to taste many fine wines from estates and small owners in this wine shop next to the tourist office. Park nearby in front of the covered market. Open daily from 9am-12.30pm and 2.30-7.30pm. Closed 1 November to 15 March. English spoken.

Maison Dufouleur Père et Fils (N)
17 rue Thurot BP27
21700 Nuits-St-Georges
☎ 80 61 21 21

A large wine merchants with extensive and impressive tasting cellars. Park in front of the police station. Open daily 9am-7pm except Tuesday. Closed 24 December to 31 January. English spoken. First wine free.

Domaine Philippe Gavignet (V)
36 rue Docteur Louis Legrand
21700 Nuits-St-Georges
☎ 80 61 09 41
A family estate opposite the sports centre. There is a small museum in the tasting cellar. Open Monday to Saturday 8am-12noon and 2-6pm. Sunday and pubic holidays by appointment.

Maison Pierre Gruber (N)
49 rue Henri Challand BP56
21700 Nuits-St-Georges
☎ 80 61 02 88
In the heart of the village offering many excellent wines. Open Monday to Saturday 8am-12noon and 2-6pm. Closed on public holidays. English spoken.

Domaine Henri et Gilles Remoriquet (V)
25 rue des Charmois
21700 Nuits-St-Georges
☎ 80 61 08 17
Fourth generation wine makers offering fine wines, including a number of Premiers Crus. Open Monday to Friday 10am-12.30pm and 2-7.30pm. Saturday 9am-12noon and 2-7pm. Sunday and public holidays 9am-12noon and 2-4pm.

Domaine René Tardy et Fils (V)
32 rue Caumont Bréon
21700 Nuits-Saint-Georges
☎ 80 61 20 50
The tasting takes place in the winery and cellars, next to the thirteenth century Church of St Symphorien.

Open daily from 8.30-1130am and 2-6pm (8pm during the summer). Closed 25 December to 1 January.

Prémeaux-Prissey

Maison Bertrand Ambroise (V/N)
rue de l'Eglise
21700 Prémeaux-Prissey
☎ 80 62 30 19
A family with a long wine-making tradition. The house is next to the thirteenth century church. Open Monday to Friday 2-7pm, Saturday 9am-12noon and 2-7pm, Sunday and public holidays 9-11.30am. English spoken.

Domaine R. Dubois et Fils (V)
RN74
21700 Prémaux-Prissey
☎ 80 62 30 61
Wine makers for three generations although there is now a very modern winery. Follow the signs from the church. Open daily 8-11.30am and 2-6pm. Sunday and public holidays by appointment. English spoken.

Vosne-Romanée

Domaine Robert Arnoux (V)
3 route Nationale
21700 Vosne-Romanée
☎ 80 61 09 85
The tasting room is in a specially converted vaulted cellar on RN74. The family has been making wine for five generations. Park in the courtyard. Open daily from 9am-12noon and 2-6pm. English spoken.

Domaine Pascal Chevigny (V)
route de Boncourt
21700 Vosne-Romanée
☎ 80 61 17 42
A prime vineyard site producing very good wines. Open Monday to Saturday 9am-12noon and 2-6pm. Holidays

9am-12noon. Visits by appointment 15 July to 20 August and 1 January to 20. English spoken. First glass free.

Domaine Bruno Clavelier (V)
RN74
21700 Vosne-Romanée
☎ 80 61 12 01
A family with a long wine making tradition and Bruno Clavelier is a respected oenologist. Open Monday to Saturday 8am-12noon and 1.30-6pm. Sunday 9-11am, public holidays 9am-12noon and 2-6pm. Sunday and public holiday visits preferably by appointment. English spoken. First glass free then 25F for three wines.

Domaine François Gerbet (V)
2 RN74
2170 Vosne-Romanée
☎ 80 61 07 85
The estate and maturation cellar is on the RN74 on entering the village although the tasting cellar is in the place de la Mairie. Open Monday to Friday 8am-12noon and 2-6pm. Weekends and public holidays 10am-12noon and 2-6pm. Closed first two weekends in January.

Domaine François Lamarche (V)
9 rue des Communes
21700 Vosne-Romanée
☎ 80 61 07 94
A charming tasting room and an opportunity to visit the cellars. Open Monday to Saturday from 8am-12noon and 2-6pm, Sunday 8am-12noon. Closed last two weeks of August and first week of September. English spoken. First wine free then 30F for three wines.

Domaine Denis Mugneret et Fils (V)
14 route Nationale
21700 Vosne-Romanée
☎ 80 61 28 36

Traditionally made wines matured in oak casks and grapes from many of the best Côte de Nuits vineyard sites. Open daily 9am-12noon and 2-6pm.

Domaine Armelle et Bernard Rion (V)
8 route Nationale
21700 Vosne-Romanée
☎ 80 61 05 31
Mostly red wines traditionally made. Open Monday to Saturday 9am-7pm. English spoken.

Domaine Robert Sirugue (V)
3 avenue du Monument
21700 Vosne-Romanée
☎ 80 61 00 64
Founded at the end of the nineteenth century, this estate is reached along an impressive tree-lined drive. Fine vaulted cellars. Open Monday to Friday 9am-12noon and 2-7pm. Saturday 9am-12noon and 2-6pm. Sunday by appointment.

Vougeot

Domaine du Château de la Tour (V)
Clos de Vougeot
21640 Vougeot
☎ 80 62 86 13
The only way to be completely harvested, vinified and bottled within the walls of Clos de Vougeot. Open Monday to Friday 8am-7pm. Weekends and public holidays 10am-7pm. Closed Tuesdays and weekends and public holidays during the winter. English spoken.

Domaine C. Confuron et Fils (V)
rue du Vieux Château
21640 Vougeot
☎ 80 62 86 80
The estate has parcels of vineyards in many of the best Côte de Nuits areas, and this is a good opportunity to taste a selection of good wines. Open daily

from 10am-12noon and 2-5pm. Closed last two weeks of August and Christmas week. English spoken.

Le Grande Cave (N)
21640 Vougeot
☎ 80 62 87 13
Although the château in the centre of Vougeot was demolished a long time ago, the cellars remain and are now used to store and age wine. There is a tasting room offering a very wide range of the region's wines. Open daily 8am-12.30pm and 2-7pm. First wine free then 30F for three wines.

Vineyards of the Hautes Côtes de Nuits

Marey-les-Fussey

Domaine Thevenot Lebrun et Fils (V)
21700 Marey-les-Fussey
☎ 80 62 91 64
One of the family's that has contributed greatly to re-establishing the reputation of this appellation. Good wines and good prices. Open Monday to Friday 9am-12noon and 2-6pm. Saturday 9am-12noon.

Villars-Fontaine

Domaine du Château de Villars-Fontaine (V/N)
21700 Villars-Fontaine
☎ 80 61 17 31
In the centre of the village with eighteenth century buildings. The ruins of the Abbaye St Vivant, now a historic monument are owned by the château and can be visited. Open Monday to Friday 9.30am-12noon and 2.30-7pm. English spoken.

Domaine de Montmain (V)
21700 Villars-Fontaine
☎ 80 62 31 94

Lovely views from this estate and modern winery buildings designed by owner Bernard Hudelot. Open Monday to Friday 8.30am-12noon and 1.30-6pm. Saturday 9am-12noon and 2-6pm. Closed Sunday and public holiday. English spoken.

Villers-la-Faye

Maison Bouhey-Allez (N)
21700 Villers-la-Faye
☎ 80 62 91 35
Founded in 1885 the present owner makes his own wines and sells those of other growers. There is a large range to taste. Open Tuesday to Friday 8am-12noon and 2-6pm. Saturday 8am-12noon and 2-5pm. Closed Sunday and Monday. English spoken.

Vineyards of the Côte de Beaune

Aloxe-Corton

Château de Corton André (V)
21420 Aloxe-Corton
☎ 80 26 44 25
The only Côte de Beaune Grand Cru château and the chance to taste wines from both the Côte de Beaune and Côte de Nuits. Open daily 10am-6pm. English spoken.

Auxey-Duresses

Domaine André et Bernard Labry (V)
Melin
21190 Auxey-Duresses
☎ 80 21 21 60
An excellent chance to see how different soil types produce different characteristics in Burgundy wines. Open Monday to Saturday 9am-7pm, Sunday and public holidays 9am-12noon and 2-7pm. English spoken.

Domaine Jean-Pierre Prunier (V)
21190 Auxey-Duresses
☎ 80 21 23 91
In the centre of the village. Jean-Pierre
and Andrée or their son Pascal present
the wines which have been made by the
family on the estate for many generations. A beautiful tasting cellaret and
vaulted cellars. Open Monday to
Saturday 8am-12noon and 1.30-8pm.
Sunday and public holidays 9am-
12noon and 2-7pm. English spoken.

Domaine Prunier-Damy (V)
rue du Pont Boillot
21190 Auxey-Duresses
☎ 80 21 60 38
Philippe and Anne-Marie Prunier-
Damy come from a long line of wine
families and present their wines in a
vaulted cellar next to the church noted
for its unusual belltower and steeple.
Open Monday to Friday 8am-12noon
and 1.30-7.30pm, Saturday 8am-12noon
and 1.30-8pm, Sunday and public
holidays 9am-12noon. English spoken.

Beaune

Domaine Gabriel Bouchard (V)
4 rue du Tribunal
21200 Beaune
☎ 80 22 68 63
The cellars are in the town centre
opposite the St Etienne car park. The
opportunity to taste wines from many
of Beaune's most prestigious areas.
Open daily.

Domaine Cauvard (V)
34a rue de Savigny
21200 Beaune
☎ 80 22 29 77
On the outskirts of Beaune but well
signposted. A wide range of fine wines
available for tasting in the cellars.
Open Monday to Saturday 9-1130am
and 2-6.30pm. Closed Christmas week.

Maison Champy Père et Ce (N)
5 rue du Grenier à Sel
21202 Beaune Cedex
☎ 80 22 09 98
In the heart of the old quarter near the
Town Hall, the tastings are held in a
1720s house with a large network of
cellars. Every appellation of Burgundy
wine is available for tasting,. Open
Monday to Friday 8am-12noon and 2-
6pm. Saturday and public holidays
9am-12noon and 2-5pm. English
spoken. First wine tasted free, then 30F
for four wines.

Cave des Cordeliers (N)
6 rue de l'Hotel-Dieu
21200 Beaunbe
☎ 80 22 14 25
A wide range of fine Burgundy wines is
available for tasting in the superb
cellars of this house in the centre of
Beaune. Open Monday to Saturday
9am-12noon and 2-7pm. Sunday and
public holidays 9.30am-12noon and
2.30-7pm. English spoken.

Demeure St Martin (wine collection)
4 boulevard Maréchal Foch
21200 Beaune
☎ 80 22 38 00
The cellars house an exceptional
collection of great wines with special
tastings of wines from the Hospices de
Beaune and Hospices de Dijon. You
can also visit the apartments of the
Marquis de Santenay as they would
have been in the 18th century. Open
daily 10am-6pm. Closed last two
weeks of December and all January.
English spoken. First wine tasted free.

Caves Exposition de la Reine Pédauque (N)
2 faubourg St Nicolas
21200 Beaune
☎ 80 22 23 11
Reine Pédauque is one of the great

wines merchants of Burgundy. There is a guided tour of the cellars and a free tasting of four wines. Dinners with entertainment are also available in the cellars. Open Monday to Saturday 9-11.30am and 2-5.30pm, Sunday and public holidays 10-11.30am and 2-5pm. English spoken.

Les Caves des Hautes Côte et de la Côte (Group of producers)
Route de Pommard
21200 Beaune
☎ 80 24 63 12
The largest winery set up by a group of growers with 1,200 acres (480 hectares) of vineyards covering 60 different appellations. Open Monday to Friday 8am-12noon and 2-6pm, Saturday 9am-12noon and 2-6pm. Sunday and public holidays 9am-12noon. First wine tasted free.

Lycée Viticole De Beaune (V)
16 ave Charles Jaffelin
BP215, 21206 Beune
☎ 80 26 35 81
This college has been training wine-growers since 1884 and sells the wines made by students and researchers. Follow the green signs for Auxerre from Beaune. Open Monday to Friday 8am-12noon and 2-6pm. Saturday 8am-12noon. English spoken. First wine tasted free then 20F for four wines.

Le Marché Aux Vins (Office de diffusion de Bourgogne)
rue Nicolas Rolin
21200 Beaune
☎ 80 22 27 69
In the setting of the ancient Cordeliers Church, and opposite the Hospices, a chance to taste many of the best wines found from Chablis to Beaujolais. Many of the buildings date from the thirteenth and fourteenth centuries. Open daily from 9.30-11.30am and 2.30-5.30pm (6pm in summer). English spoken. First wine tasted free.

Domaine Albert Morot (V)
Château de la Creusotte
Ave Charles Jaffelin
21200 Beaune
☎ 80 22 35 39
The château offers a chance to visit a traditional fermenting room and cellars and taste fine wines. Open daily 9am-12.30pm and 2-7pm (Saturday until 7.30pm). English spoken. First wine tasted free then 25F for three wines.

Maison Patriarche Père et Fils (N)
7 rue de Collège
21200 Beaune
☎ 80 24 53 78
The largest of Burgundy's cellars extending more than 15,000yds (13,790m) and housing several million bottles. The cellars date from the fourteenth and seventeenth centuries in the former Dames de la Visitation Convent. There is a free tasting of twenty one wines. Open daily 9-11.30am and 2-5.30pm. Closed last two weeks of December and all January. English spoken.

Maison Albert Ponnelle (N)
38 faubourg St Nicolas
21200 Beaune
☎ 80 22 00 05
Outside Beaune a chance to taste many of the area's finest crus. The cellars date from the fourteenth century. Open Monday to Friday 8am-12noon and 2-6pm, weekends 9am-7pm.

Clos St Bernardin (N)
15 rue de l'Hotel-Dieu
BP30
21201 Beaune Cedex
☎ 80 22 25 68

The opportunity to taste the best wines from seven family estates in magnificent cellars close to the Hospices. Open Monday to Friday 9am-12noon and 2-6pm. English spoken. First wine tasted free then 40F for three wines.

Bligny-lès-Beaune

Domaine de Château de Bligny-lès-Beaune (V)
Grande Rue
21200 Bligny-les-Beaune
☎ 80 21 47 38
About two-and-a-half miles (4km) south of Beaune, the tastings are in the cellars of the fifteenth century set in very attractive grounds. The winery processes grapes from the estate's 50 acres (20 hectares) of vineyards. Open Monday to Friday 9am-12noon and 2-6pm. Closed last two weeks of August and Christmas week. English spoken.

Domaine Gabriel Fournier (V)
6 rue de l'Eglise
21200 Bligny-lès-Beaune
☎ 80 21 46 50
Third generation wine makers offer tastings in a beautiful nineteenth century vaulted cellar. Open Monday to Friday 12noon-2pm and 7-9pm. Saturday 9am-12noon and 2-8pm, Sunday 10am-12noon and 2-8pm. Closed last two weeks of August. English spoken.

Cheilly-lès-Maranges

Domaine Chevrot (V)
Located in the most southerly Côte de Beaune village, the cellars were built in 1798. Good wines and great views. Open Monday to Friday 10am-12noon and 2-6pm, Saturday 9am-12.30pm and 2-6pm, Sunday and public holidays 10am-12.30pm. English spoken.

Domaine René Martin
La Cave de Cheilly (V)
Au Pont du Canal D974
71150 Cheilly-lès-Maranges
☎ 85 91 14 51
The cellars are alongside the D974 and the canal, and the Martin family has been making wines here for ten generations. There is a video about working in the vineyards. Open Monday to Saturday 9.30am-12noon and 2.30-6.30pm, Sunday and holidays 10am-12noon and 3-7pm. English spoken.

Chorey-lès-Beaune

Domaine Arnoux Père et Fils (V)
rue des Brenots
21200 Chorey-lès-Beaune
☎ 80 22 57 98
Follow the signs from the village to reach the estate which has been farmed by the same family for many generations. Open daily but visits preferably by appointment. English spoken.

Domaine Dubois d'Orgeval (V)
21200 Chorey-les-Beaune
☎ 80 24 70 89
Dominique and Fabienne d'Orgeval welcome you in their tasting cellar. Open Monday to Saturday 9am-12noon and 2-7.30pm. Sunday and public holidays by appointment. Closed middle two weeks of August.

Ladoix-Serrigny

Domaine Edmond Cornu et Fils (V)
Le Meix Gobillon
21550 Ladoix-Serrigny
☎ 80 26 40 79
Located in a very narrow street, the winery was built in 1870 the present owners great grandfather. The estate covers 32 acres (13 hectares) almost exclusively of Pinot Noir. Open Monday to Saturday 9am-12noon and 2-8pm. Closed Sunday.

Domaine Bernard Lobreau (V)
rue des Barrigards
21550 Ladoix-Serrigny
☎ 80 26 41 77
The tasting cellars are about 800yds
(730m) from the station. Open daily
from 7am-8pm. English spoken.

Meursault

Domaine Thierry Bernard-Brussier (V)
1 rue du Moulin Judas
21190 Meursault
☎ 80 21 60 34
The tastings take place in a charming
rustic room in the house 150yds (137m)
from the town centre. Thierry, and his
wife Claire, will welcome visitors.
Open Monday to Friday 9am-8pm,
Saturday 9am-7pm, Sunday and public
holidays 9am-12.30pm and 3-6.30pm.

Domaine Guy Bocard (V)
4 rue de Mazeray
21190 Meursault
☎ 80 21 26 06
The great white Meursault and Côte de
Beaune reds of this estate are matured
in the eighteenth century cellars in the
centre of the village. Open Monday to
Friday 10am-12noon and 3-6pm,
Saturday 10am-6pm, Sunday and
public holidays 10am-12noon. Closed
last two weeks of August.

Domaine Michel Bouzereau et Fils (V)
3 rue de la Planche Meunière
21190 Meursault
☎ 80 21 20 74
Taste the wines in the vaulted cellars of
the house situated in the centre of town
between the two main squares. The
family has been making wines for
many generations. Open Saturday
9am-12noon and 2-7pm. Visits on
weekdays and Sundays by
appointment.

Domaine Pierre Bouzereau-Emonin (V)
7 rue Labbé
21190 Meursault
☎ 80 21 23 74
Wine makers for six generations. Pierre
and his sons offer their wines for
tastings in their vaulted cellars behind
the Town Hall. Open daily 9am-
12noon and 2-7pm. Sunday visits
preferably by appointment. English
spoken.

Domaine Daniel Chouet-Clivet (V)
4 route de Volnay
2190 Meursault
☎ 80 21 27 99
A complete range of red and white
appellations is offered for tasting in the
tasting room north of the village and
near the campsite. Open Monday to
Friday 1-2pm, Saturday 8am-12noon
and 1-6pm, Sunday and public
holidays 10am-12noon and 2-7pm.

Domaine Bertrand Darviot (V)
Domaine de la Velle
17 rue de la Velle
21190 Meursault
☎ 80 21 22 83
The Durviot has made wine on this
beautiful estate for eight generations.
Their home is a former thirteenth
century manor house. The tasting
room contains a seventeenth century
wine press. Open Monday to Saturday
10am-12noon and 2-6pm. Closed
Sunday. English spoken. First wine
tasted free, then 10F for four wines.

Maison Jean (V/N)
11 rue de Lattre de Tassigny
21190 Meursault
☎ 80 21 63 67
A chance to taste great white wines and
some very good reds. There are two
floors of cellars built over one hundred
years ago. Open Monday to Friday

from 2-6pm, Saturday 3-7pm. Sunday and public holiday visits by appointment. English spoken.

Domaine Patrick Javillier (V/N)
Place de l'Europe
21190 Meursault
☎ 80 21 65 50
The house once owned by the church, is in the centre of the village and named after St Nicolas, patron saint of Meursault. Open Saturday and public holidays 10am-12.30pm and 3-7pm. Sunday 10am-12.30pm. Closed December to February.

Domaine Monceau-Boch (V)
2 rue du Moulin Judas
21190 Meursault
☎ 80 21 23 65
The estate has many prime vineyard sites in the area and the tasting cellars are in the village among a number of seventeenth and eighteenth century buildings. Open Monday to Saturday 9am-12noon and 2-6pm. Sunday and public holidays to 11am and 2-6pm.

Domaine René Monnier (V)
6 rue du Docteur Rolland
21190 Meursault
☎ 80 21 29 32
The estate was founded in 1723 and now uses the very latest vinification techniques. Almost two-thirds of all production is exported. Open Monday to Friday 9am-12noon and 2-6pm. Saturday 9am-12noon. Other times at weekends by appointment.

Domaine Pascal Pouhin (V)
20 rue Pierre Joigneaux
21190 Meursault
☎ 80 21 29 02
Pouhin makes great white wines but also offers several very good reds for tasting. Open daily 9am-12noon and 1-7pm.

Monthélie

Domaine Jacques Boigelot (V)
21190 Monthélie
☎ 80 21 22 81
One of the prettiest villages in the Côte, between Meursault and Volnay. The domaine has vineyards in four main sites in the area and the house and tasting centre are in the centre of the village. Open daily 8am-12noon and 2-7pm.

Domaine Changarnier (V)
place du Puits
21190 Monthélie
☎ 80 21 22 18
The estate has been farmed by the Changarnier family for twelve generations and Pierre continues the strong commitment to tradition today. Open Monday to Friday 9am-6pm, weekends 10am-6pm, public holidays 10am-7pm. English spoken.

Pernand Vergelesses

Domaine Denis Père et Fils (V)
Chemin des Vignes Blanches
21420 Pernand Vergelesses
☎ 80 21 50 91
A new winery just outside the old village on the Echevronne hillside. A wide range of red and white available for tasting. Open Monday to Saturday 9am-12noon and 2-7pm. Sunday and public holidays 10am -12noon.

Domaine P. Dubreuil-Fontaine Père et Fils (V)
21420 Pernand-Vergelesses
☎ 80 21 55 53
A large range of red and white wines are available for tasting. The domaine is in the village which clings to the Corton hillside, 4 miles (6km) from Beaune. Open Monday to Friday 9am-12noon and 2-6.30pm Sunday 9am-12noon.

Pommard

Domaine Michel Arcelain (V)
rue Mareau
21630 Pommard
☎ 80 22 13 50
Some lovely wines available for tasting from this highly regarded estate. Open Monday to Friday 8am-12noon, Saturday 8am-12noon and 1.30-7pm, Sunday and public holidays by appointment.

Domaine du Château de Pommard (V)
21630 Pommard
☎ 80 22 07 99
The eighteenth century farmhouse is in the centre of the 50 acre (20 hectare) enclosed vineyard, the largest continuous estate in Burgundy owned by one person. Open March to November daily 8.30am-6.30pm. Visiting by appointment during the winter. First wine tasted free.

Domaine Coste-Caumartin (V)
rue du Parc
BP19
21630 Pommard
☎ 80 22 45 04
An old family estate with parts of the house dating from 1641. Tastings take place in the beautiful vaulted cellar. Open Monday to Saturday 9am-7pm, Sunday and public holidays 10am-5pm.

Domaine Jacques Frotey-Poifol (V)
rue des Poutures
21630 Pommard
☎ 80 22 47 59
Visit the vineyards before enjoying a tasting in the cellars. Open Monday to Saturday 9am-12noon and 2-6pm. Sunday and public holidays 9am-12noon by appointment. Closed last two weeks of August.

Domaine Jean-Luc Joillot (V)
rue de la Métairie
21630 Pommard
☎ 80 22 47 60
The domaine is near the church and Jean-Luc and his mother Simone are proud to present their wines from their Pommard, Beaune and Haute-Beaune vineyards. Open Monday to Friday 9am-1pm and 6-8pm. Saturday and public holidays 9am-12noon and 1-6pm, Sunday 9am-1pm.

Domaine Raymond Launay (V)
rue des Charmots
21630 Pommard
☎ 80 24 08 03
Charming tastings are held in the vineyard cellars. Open daily 9am-12noon and 2-7pm.

Domaine Lejeune (V)
La Confrérie
21630 Pommard
☎ 80 22 10 28
This small family estate built in 1865 is sited on the former St Sacrament Confraternity, opposite the church. The wine warehouse contains a rare old wine cask made from birch strips. Open for visits by appointment only. Closed mid-August to mid-September. English spoken.

Domaine André Mussy (V)
rue Dauphin
21630 Pommard
☎ 80 22 05 56
The tasting is beyond the green gate next to the bakery. Park in the square. The estate has been in the family since 1746. Open 9am-8pm. English spoken.

Les Domaines de Pommard (Group of producers)
Place de l'Europe
21630 Pommard
☎ 80 24 17 20

A group of sixteen producers have combined to present their wines in these cellars off the village square. Open daily 9.30am-12.30pm and 2.30-7pm. Closed Christmas week.

Domaine Jean et Pierre Tartois (V)
21630 Pommard
☎ 80 22 11 70
The estate has 15 acres (6 hectares) of vineyards in the Pommard commune. Open daily from 8am-12noon and 2-7pm.

Domaine Virely-Rougeot (V)
Place de l'Europe
21630 Pommard
☎ 80 24 96 70
The domaine is a member of the Caves Particulières, a group of winemakers dedicated to using traditional methods. Open Monday to Friday 10am-12.30pm and 2-6.30pm, Saturday 9.30am-12.30pm and 2-7pm, Sunday 10am-12.30pm and 2-7pm, public holidays 9am-7pm.

Puligny-Montrachet

Domaine Jean Charton/
Maison Chartron et Trébuchet (V/N)
21190 Puligny-Montrachet
☎ 80 21 32 85
The domaine is noted for its white Côte d'Or and Macon wines. Open Monday to Friday 8am-12noon and 2-6pm.

Domaine Henri Clerc (V)
place des Marronniers
21190 Puligny-Montrachet
☎ 80 21 32 74
The domaine offers great whites and red for tasting in their cellars in the village square. Open Monday to Friday 8am-12noon and 1.30-6pm. Weekends and public holidays 9am-12noon and 1.30-6pm.

St Aubin

Domaine Hubert Lamy (V)
21190 St Aubin
☎ 80 21 32 55
The family have been making wine since 1648 and their 40 acres (16 hectares) are spread among some of the finest vineyards in the region. The tasting cellar is decorated with many antique tools used in the vineyards and winery. Open Monday to Saturday 9am-12noon and 2-6pm. Sunday afternoon and public holiday visiting by appointment. English spoken.

St Romain

Domaine Henri et Gilles Buisson (V)
21190 Saint-Romain
☎ 80 21 27 91
A wide range of wines including Corton Grand Cru can be tasted in the converted cellaret. The family has been making wine for three generations. Open Monday to Saturday 8am-12noon and 1.30-7pm. Sunday and holidays 10am-12noon and 3-7pm.

Domaine Germain Père et Fils (V)
21190 St Romain
☎ 80 21 22 11
A wine making family for many generations, the tasting cellar is on the Orches road from the centre of the village. Open Monday to Saturday 8am-12noon and 1-7pm. Sunday and public holidays 8am-12noon by appointment.

St Marie-La-Blanche

Domaine Jean Allexant (V)
21200 St Marie-la-Blanche
☎ 80 26 60 77
Although on the Beaune plain, Jean Allexant offers red and white wines for tasting from his famous Côte de Beaune estate. The wine is matured in

new vats. Open Monday to Friday 9am-6pm. English spoken.

Santenay

Domaine Joseph Belland (V)
rue de la Chapelle
21590 Santenay
☎ 80 20 61 13
This estate extends over many of the finest vineyards in the area, the vines are cultivated traditionally, the grapes picked by hand and the wines matured in oak in the eighteenth century vaulted cellars. Open from 8am-12.15pm and 1.30-7.30pm. English spoken.

Domaine Roger Beland (V)
3 rue de la Chapelle
25190 Santenay
☎ 80 20 60 95
Wine makers for five generations offering great wines grown and made from their southern Côte d'Or estate. Open Monday to Saturday 8am-12noon and 1.30-7pm. Sunday 9am-12noon, public holidays 9am-12noon and 2-7pm. English spoken.

Domaine Brenot (V)
17 rue de Lavau
21590 Santenay
☎ 80 20 61 27
Just outside the village on the Nolay road set among the vines. You can visit the cellars where the wines are matured before the tasting. Open Monday to Friday 8-11am and 2-6pm, Saturday 8-11am and 2-5pm, Sunday and public holidays 10-11.30am and 2-5pm. Closed over Christmas and New Year. English spoken. First wine tasted free.

Domaine de la Buissière
Jean Moreau (V)
21590 Santenay
☎ 80 20 61 79
Jean Moreau, his wife and children take turns to greet visitors at the tasting cellars near the Castle of Philip the Bold. Open Monday to Friday 8am-12noon and 2-8pm, Saturday 8-11am and 2-8pm, Sunday and public holidays 9-11 am and 2-8pm.

Domaines Françoise et Denis Clair (V)
14 rue de la Chapelle
21590 Santenay
☎ 80 20 61 96
A new estate with recently-planted vineyards but already showing great promise. Open Monday to Saturday 8am-7pm. Sunday and public holidays by appointment. English spoken.

Domaine Chapelle et Fils (V)
Le Haut Village
21590 Santenay
☎ 80 20 60 09
A Jacobin cellar and great wines. Open Monday to Friday 8am-12noon and 2-6pm, Saturday 9am-12noon and 2-7pm. Sunday and public holidays visits by appointment. English spoken.

Domaine Mestre Père et Fils (V)
12 place du Jet d'Eau
21590 Santenay
☎ 80 20 60 11
The Mesre family live in the centre of the village near the fountain, and have been making wines for five generations which can be tasted in the fine vaulted cellars. Open Monday to Saturday 8am-12noon and 1.30-6pm, Sunday and public holidays 10am-12noon. English spoken.

Domaine Olivier Père et Fils (V)
5 rue Gaudin
21590 Santenay
☎ 80 20 61 35
The vineyard has been completely replanted in the last few years as Hervé

Olivier works to restore the Domaine's fortunes after an inactive generation. There are good wines in the cellars and great views around it. Open daily 8am-12noon and 1.30-7pm. English spoken.

Domaine Prieur-Brunet (V)
rue de Narosse
21590 Santenay
☎ 80 20 60 56
The family have lived here in magnificent surroundings since 1804. The vaulted cellars and the small wine growers museum can be visited before the tasting in a converted cellaret. Open Monday to Friday 9am-12noon and 2-7pm. Saturday 10am-12noon and 2-5pm. Closed Sunday and public holidays. English spoken.

Savigny-lès-Beaune

Maison Doudet-Naudin (N)
3 rue Henri Cyrot
21420 Savigny-lès-Beaune
☎ 80 21 51 74
The house was founded in 1849 and specialises in maturing old wines. Visitors are received in the vaulted cellars built between 1830 and 1840. Open Monday to Friday 11am-12noon and 2-5pm. Closed over Christmas and New Year. English spoken.

Maison Henri de Villamont (N)
rue du Docteur Guyot
21420 Savigny-lès-Beaune
☎ 80 21 52 13
A lovely red- and grey-brick house with typical slate roof in the middle of the vineyard. Open daily from 10am-7pm. Closed 30 November to 31 March. English spoken.

Domaine Jacob-Girard et Fils (V)
2 rue de Cîteaux
21420 Savigny-lès-Beaune
☎ 80 21 52 29

At the Bouilland crossroads. New modern winery buildings stand beside the typical Burgundy home and original cellars. Open Monday to Saturday 9am-12noon and 2-7pm. Sunday and public holidays 10am-12noon and 2-6pm.

Domaine du Prieuré (V)
1 place Fournier and 23 route de Beaune
21420 Savigny-lès-Beaune
☎ 80 21 54 27
The estate is in the old priory built by the Cîteaux monks in the eighteenth century. Wines are presented in the former cloisters. Open Monday to Saturday 9-11.30am and 2-7pm. Sunday and public holidays by appointment.

Maison Seguin-Manuel (N)
15 rue Paul Maldant
21420 Savigny-lès-Beaune
☎ 80 21 50 42
The estate was founded in 1720 and the fermenting room is in a building built by the Cîteaux monks in the thirteenth century. Open Monday to Saturday 8am-12noon and 2-7pm, Sunday 2-6pm and public holidays 10am-12noon and 2-6pm. Closed first three weeks of August. English spoken.

Volnay

Domaine Henri Delagrange-et-Fils (V)
rue de la Cure
21190 Volnay
☎ 80 21 61 88
Growers for six years, the Delagrange family are proud to present their fine range of wines. Open Monday to Saturday and public holidays 10am-12noon and 3-6pm. Sunday 10am-12noon.

Domaine Michel Poulleau et Fils (V)
rue du Pied de la Vallée
21190 Volnay
☎ 80 21 62 61
Some excellent reds available for
tasting. Open Monday to Friday 6-
8pm, Saturday 9-11am and 2-7pm,
Sunday and public holidays 9-11am.

Domaine Rossignol Féevrier (V)
rue du Mont
21190 Volnay
☎ 80 21 62 69
A range of exceptional wines and
exported worldwide. Open daily 8am-
7pm, public holidays 8am-6pm.
Appointments preferred especially
during the harvest.

Domaine Christophe Vaudoisey (V)
21190 Volnay
☎ 80 21 20 14
Wine growers for many generations,
the family offers a wide range of
Burgundy wines in the converted
cellaret. Open Monday to Saturday
10am-7pm, Sunday and public
holidays 11am-12noon.

Vineyards of the Haut Côte de Beaune

Baubingy

Domaine François Rocault (V)
21340 Baubingy
☎ 80 21 78 72
Great views and good wines, especially the Domaine's Rosé d'Orches.
Open Monday to Friday 10am-12noon
and 2-7pm, Saturday 10am-7pm,
Sunday and public holidays 10am-
12noon. English spoken.

Cirey-les-Nolay

Domaine Nicolas Père et Fils (V)
21340 Cirey-les-Nolay
☎ 80 21 76 15

The family has 25 acres (10 hectares) of
vineyards and the tastings are in the
cellaret and barrel and bottling cellar.
Open daily 8am-8pm.

Echevronne

Domaine Jean Fery et Fils (V)
Le Village
21420 Echevrone
☎ 80 21 598 60
A 25 acre (10 hectares) vineyard with
many old vines producing high quality
grapes. Open Monday to Friday 2-
6pm, Saturday 9am-12noon and 2-
6pm, Sunday and public holidays
9am-12noon. English spoken.

Marcheseuil

Domaine Claude Nouveau (V)
21430 Marcheseuil
☎ 85 91 13 34
A warm welcome in this specially converted tasting cellar, and some great
wines. Open Monday to Saturday 8am-
8pm. Sunday 10am-12noon and public
holidays 9am-8pm. English spoken.

Nantoux

Domaine Joliot (V)
route de Pommard
21190 Nantoux ☎ 80 26 01 44
Claire and Jean-Baptiste Joliot are part
of a long wine making tradition and
their love of their wines is infectious.
Open daily 8am-9pm.

Paris l'Hôpital

Maison Pail Compain (V)
71150 Paris l'Hôpital
☎ 85 91 10 32
The house has vineyards from Chablis
to Beaujolais and you can taste their
many crus in the tasting cellars by the
village square. Open Monday to Friday
8am-12noon and 2-6pm.

Domaine A. Goubard (V)
Cocelle
71150 Paris l'Hôpital
☎ 85 91 10 81
The hamlet overlooks the village of Paris l'Hôpital. The tastings which take place in the vaulted cellars are of wines from the Chenevières vineyards. Open Monday to Friday 10am-7pm, Saturday 10am-12noon and 4-7pm, Sunday and public holidays 10am-12noon. English spoken.

Domaine Marie Lafouge (V)
71150 Paris l'Hôpital
☎ 85 91 12 66
The estate is run by Marie Lafouge and has been in her family for many generations. The wines are made and matured using traditional methods and tasted in a classic Burgundy cellaret. Open Monday to Friday 9-11.30am and 2-8pm. Saturday 9am-8pm, Sunday and public holidays 9am-12noon. Closed November and first week of December.

Vineyards of the Côte Chalonnaise

Autun

Le Cellier de Jean-Patrice Laly (N)
14 rue de la Grange-Verru
71400 Autun
☎ 85 52 24 83
Visitors can taste wines from the bottle and the barrel in the cellars of this house which has produced wine for five generations. There is a small, but fascinating wine museum. Open Tuesday to Saturday 8am-12noon and 2pm-6.45pm. Closed Saturday afternoon January to March, and Sunday and Monday year round. English spoken.

Buxy

Cave des Vignerons de Buxy (C)
Les Vignes de la Croix
71390 Buxy
☎ 85 92 03 03
More than 200 growers are members of the cooperative. They are almost entirely small family vineyards with a strong commitment to traditional production. Open Monday to Saturday 8am-12noon and 2-6pm. Closed Sunday and public holidays. English spoken. There is a fee for a tour which includes two glasses of wine.

Chagny

Domaine de la Folie (V)
Owned by the Noël-Bouton family for more than 200 years, the estate is on the outskirts of Chagny. There is a very old wine press. Open Monday to Saturday 9am-12noon and 2-5pm. Sunday and public holiday 11am-1pm. English spoken.

Domaine Pagnotta Père et Fils (V)
19 ave Général Leclerc
71150 Chagny
☎ 85 87 10 29
The latest technology is used to produce the wines and you should take time to view the French-style ceilings in the winery and maturation cellars. Open Monday to Friday 11am-8pm. Saturday 10am-8pm, Sunday and public holidays 9am-12noon. English spoken.

Chalon-sur-Saône

Maison des Vins de la Côte Chalonnaise (Group of producers)
Promenade St Marie
71100 Chalon-sur-Saône
☎ 85 41 64 00
In the centre of the town, an oppor-

tunity to taste a large range of red and white wines, chosen by the producers themselves twice a year. Open Monday to Saturday 9am-12.30pm and 1.30-7pm. Sunday and public holidays by appointment. English spoken. First wine free then 25F for three wines.

Chamilly

Château de Chamilly (V)
71510 Chamilly
☎ 85 87 22 24
The glorious house was once the home of Noël Bouton, Marquis of Chamilly, and Lieutenant-General of the Royal Armies. The wines are tasted in the former kitchens of the seventeenth-century château. Open daily but appointments preferred. English spoken.

Chassey-le-Camp

Domaine Jean-Hervé Jonnier (V)
Hameau de Bercully
71150 Chassey-le-Camp
☎ 85 87 21 90
The estate is about 500yds (457m) south of the village at the foot of a hill on which a stone-age camp has been discovered. Open daily from 8am-8pm. English spoken.

Domaine Philippe Milan et Fils (V)
71150 Chassey-le-Camp
☎ 85 87 19 73
The tasting cellar is close to a classified Roman encampment. The family-owned domaine offers red and white crus, all of which are aged in oak. Open Monday to Friday 9-11.30am and 1.30-6.30pm, Saturday 9am-12noon and 1.30-7pm, Sunday and public holidays 9am-12noon.

Domaine la P'Tiote Cave (V)
71150 Chassey-le-Camp
☎ 85 87 15 21

The cellars date back to the fifteenth century and the Mugnier family offer a warm welcome in the tasting cellaret and fine vaulted cellars. Open Monday to Saturday 8am-8pm, Sunday and public holidays by appointment.

Culles-les-Roches

Domaine Noël Perrin (V)
Ecole
71460 Culles-les-Roches
☎ 85 44 04 25
The southernmost village of the Côte, and the chance to taste their own wines plus others from the area and the Mâcon. Open Monday to Saturday 9am-12noon and 2-7pm. Sunday and holidays by appointment. English spoken.

Givry

Domaine Chofflet-Valdenaire (V)
Russilly
71640 Givry
☎ 85 44 34 78
A family estate since 1710 in the small hamlet of Russilly. Tastings in the cellars. Open Monday to Saturday 9am-12noon and 2-7pm. English spoken.

Domaine François Lumpp (V)
Le Pied du Clou
36 ave de Mortières
71640 Givry
☎ 85 44 45 57
A modern winery making mostly reds in oak barrels replaced every five years. About a fifth of the production is white and a fifth of this is aged in barrels. Open Monday to Saturday 9am-12noon and 2-7pm. Sunday 9am-12noon. English spoken.

Domaine Parize Père et Fils (V)
18 rue des Faussillons
Poncey
71640 Givry
☎ 85 44 38 60

The family has been making wine for five generations in this small hamlet and the tasting takes place in their 19th century winery and cellars. Open daily 8am-8pm.

Mercurey

Domaine de la Croix Jacquelet (V)
71640 Mercurey
☎ 85 45 14 72
The huge cellars hold 1,200 barrels, one of the largest in Burgundy. The tasting cellars are in the centre of the village. Open Monday to Friday 8am-12noon and 2-6pm. Weekend and holiday visits by appointment. English spoken.

Domaine Jeannin-Naltet Père et Fils (V)
Rue de Jamproyes
71640 Mercurey
☎ 85 45 13 83
The family acquired the estate in 1858 and this is the fifth generation of wine makers here. There are 20 acres (8 hectares) of vineyards of which 15 acres (6 hectares) are Premier Cru. Open Monday to Friday 8am-7pm, weekends and public holidays 10am-7pm. English spoken.

Domaine Michel Juillot (V)
Grande Rue
71640 Mercurey
☎ 85 45 27 27
The vaulted cellars are beneath an elegant eighteenth century house. The family has been making wines here for many generations. Open Monday to Saturday 9am-12noon and 2-6pm. Sunday and public holiday visits by appointment. First wine tasted free.

Domaine Juillot & Theulot (V)
Clos Laurent
Rue de Mercurey
71640 Mercurey
☎ 85 45 13 87

The estate is behind the Hostellerie du Val d'Or, and John Claude Theulot and his wife receive visitors in their tasting cellaret or the cellar. Open Monday to Friday 8.30am-12.30pm and 1.30-7pm, Saturday 9am-12.30pm and 1.30-6.30pm, Sunday and public holidays 9.30am-12noon. English spoken.

Domaine Maurice Protheau et Fils (V)
Château d'Etroyes
71640 Mercurey
☎ 85 45 25 00
Wine growers since 1720, the Protheau family combine old and new wine making techniques. Open Monday to Friday 9am-12noon and 2 -5pm, Saturday 9am-12noon, Closed Sunday. English spoken.

Domaine Antonin Rodet (V/N)
Grande Rue
71640 Mercurey
☎ 85 45 22 22
The former home of Antonin Rodet and the opportunity to taste a wide range of wines from both the local area and the region. Open Monday to Friday 9am-12.30pm and 1.30-6pm.

Moroges

Domaine Alain Berthault (V)
71390 Moroges
☎ 85 47 91 03
Lovely views from the winery, and a fine collection of coopers' tools. Open Monday to Saturday 10am-12noon and 2-5pm. Sunday and public holiday visits by appointment. Closed last two weeks of August and first week of September. English spoken.

Rully

Domaine Jean-Claude Brelière (V)
Place de l'Egise
71150 Rully
☎ 85 91 22 01

The estate was founded in 1948 and covers 18 acres (7 hectares) of vineyards, most of it devoted to white production using both old and modern wine-making techniques. Open Monday to Saturday 8am-12noon and 2-6pm. Closed Sunday. English spoken.

Domaine Michel Briday (V)
89 Grande Rue
71150 Rully
☎ 85 87 07 90
An interesting new estate established in 1976 covering 25 acres (10 hectares) and many appellations, and using the most natural principles possible. Open Monday to Friday 10am-12noon and 1-7pm, Saturday 9am-12noon and 1-7pm, Sunday 9am-12noon.

Maison André Delorme (N)
2 rue de la République
71150 Rully
☎ 85 87 10 12
The house was established in the village in 1900 and specialist in sparkling wines made according to the Champagne method. It now produces very good red and white still wines as well. Open Monday to Friday 8.30am-12noon and 1.30-6pm, Saturday 8.30am-12noon and 2-5pm. Closed Sunday and public holidays.

Domaine Raymond Dureuil-Janthial (V)
Rue de la Bruisserolle
71150 Rully
☎ 85 87 02 37
A small 18 acre (7 hectares) estate with traditional winery and wooden vats in which the grapes are crushed by foot, and then slowly fermented on their skins. There is a nineteenth-century vaulted cellar. Open Monday to Saturday 8am-12noon and 2-7pm. Sunday and public holidays by appointment.

Domaine de l'Ecette Jean Daux (V)
21 rue de Geley
71150 Rully
☎ 85 91 21 52
The estate, to the north of Rully near the D981, has been in the family for many generations and produces red and whites from Rully and other appellations. Open Monday to Saturday 9.30 to 11.45am and 1 to 8pm. Sunday and public holidays by appointment.

Domaine Pierre-Marie Ninot (V)
Le Meix Guillaume
Rue de Chagny
71150 Rully
☎ 85 87 07 79
The 20 acre (8 hectares) vineyard has been in the family for several generations, and wines, classically matured in oak, have won many awards. Open daily 9am-12noon and 3-7pm.

St Martin-sous-Montaigu

Domaine du Cray Roger Narjoux (V)
71640 St-Martin-sous-Montaigu
☎ 85 45 13 17
Roger Narjoux's family has made wine here since 1640, and he and his wife Michèle receive guests in their 16th century home. You can also visit the cellars. Open daily 8am-8pm.

The Vineyards of Couchois

Couches

Domaine de la Chapelle (V)
Eguilly
71490 Couches
☎ 85 49 66 65
One-and-a-half miles (2km) from the village towards Creusot for the opportunity to taste good red, white and rosé Burgundies. Open Monday to Friday 6-8pm. Saturday 9am-12noon and 2-

7pm. Sunday and public holidays 9am-12noon. English spoken.

Dracy-les-Couches

Château de Dracy (V)
71490 Dracy-les-Couches
☎ 85 49 62 13
The wines are tasted in the château just outside the village. The house dates back to the fifteenth century an the 100yd (90m) long cellars and fermenting room date from the seventeenth century. Open Monday to Saturday 8am-12noon and 2-7pm. Sunday and public holidays from 2-6pm, preferably by appointment. English spoken.

Domaine Jean et Geno Musso (V)
71490 Dracy-les-Couches
☎ 85 49 66 72
An organic producer whose wines have found national and international acclaim. Open Monday to Saturday 8am-12noon and 1.30-6pm by appointment. English spoken.

St Maurice-les-Couches

Domaine Gadant & François (V)
71490 St Maurice-les-Couches
☎ 85 49 66 54
Taste the wines in the beautiful sixteenth-century vaulted cellar in the centre of the village. The family has been making wines here for several generations. Open daily 8am-12noon. Appointments for afternoon visits.

Domaine Viticole de la Tour Bajole (V)
Le Grand Quartier
71490 St Maurice-les-Couches
☎ 85 49 67 60
The estate has been in the family since 1742 and traditional methods of growing and wine making are scrupulously preserved. Open Monday to Saturday 9am-12noon and 2-7pm. Closed Christmas week. English spoken.

Vineyards of the Mâconnais

Burgy

Domaine des Chevron Albert Goyard et Fils (V)
71260 Burgy
☎ 85 33 22 07
The vineyards are still cultivated in the traditional manner and the grapes picked by hand, although the latest vinification techniques are used. Open Monday to Saturday 9am-12noon and 1-7pm. Sunday and public holidays 9am-12noon. English spoken.

Bussières

Domaine la Hys de Montrevost (V)
71960 Bussières
☎ 85 37 71 64
Lamartine the poet was taught here by his tutor Abbé Dumont. Tasting is in the cellar in the centre of the village. Open Monday to Saturday 10am-12noon and 2-7pm. Sunday and public holidays 10am-1pm. English spoken.

Chaintré

Cave Coopérative de Chaintré (C)
Le Moulin d'Or
71570 Chaintré
☎ 85 35 61 61
Founded in 1928 the cooperative has a total of 200 members. Open Monday to Saturday 10am-12.30pm and 2-7.30pm. English spoken.

Domaine Mathias (V)
71570 Chaintré
☎ 85 35 60 67
A wide range of Mâcon and Beaujolais wines can be tasted. There is an old wine press. Open Monday to Saturday 8am-12noon and 2-6pm.

Chapelle-de-Guinchay, La

Maison Paul Beaudet (N)
place de la Gare
71570 La Chapelle-de-Guinchay
☎ 85 36 72 76
The cellars were built in 1869 by Joseph Beaudet to be near the new railway. His descendants continue the business which has won many awards for its wines. Open Monday to Friday 9am-12noon and 2-6pm. Closed first three weeks of August. English spoken.

Chardonnay

Cave de Chardonnay (C)
71700 Chardonnay
☎ 85 40 50 49
This village is the birthplace of the Chardonnay grape, and was first settled around 3200BC. Open Monday to Friday 8am-12noon and 2-6pm, Saturday 8am-12noon and 2-5.45pm, Sunday and public holidays 10am-12noon and 3-7pm. English spoken.

Charnay-les-Mâcon
Maison Chevalier (N)
Les Tournons
71850 Charnay-les-Mâcons
☎ 85 34 26 74
Close to the Romanesque church with the wine shop next on the edge of the vineyard. Beautiful views. Open Monday to Friday 2-5.30pm, Saturday 9am-12noon.

Clessé

Cave Coopérative de Clessé (C)
71260 Clessé
☎ 85 36 93 88
Still wines and Champagne method sparklers are sold. The tasting cellars are in the centre of the village, 150yds (90m) from the Romanesque church. Open Monday to Saturday 8am-12noon and 2-6.30pm. English spoken.

Davayé

Domaine Gaillard (V)
Les Plantes
71960 Davayé
☎ 85 35 83 31
Noted especially for its elegant white wines, the domaine is on the road leading to the Roche de Vergisson. Open Monday to Friday 9am-1pm and 5-7pm. Saturday 9am-6pm, Sunday and public holidays 10am-6pm.

Fuissé

Maison Paul Burrier (N)
71960 Fuissé
☎ 85 35 61 75
A white wine specialist, particularly Pouilly-Fuissé. The house was funded by Georges Burrier in 1945 and is now run by his son Guy, Mayor of Fuissé. Open Monday to Friday 8am-12noon and 2-6pm. Closed last week of July and first three weeks of August and Christmas week. English spoken.

Domaine du Château de Fuissé (V/N)
71960 Fuissé
☎ 85 35 61 44
A beautiful little château with fifteenth century porch and unusual pentagonal tower, and two bottle-shaped yew trees. A great range of prestigious wines available for tasting. Open Monday to Friday 9am-12noon and 2-5.30pm. Saturday 9am-12noon. Closed over Easter, Christmas and first three weeks of August. English spoken.

Domaine Roger Luquot (V)
71960 Fuissé
☎ 85 35 60 91
The tasting cellars are in the centre of town and the wines are offered by many of the country's top restaurants. Open Monday to Saturday 8am-12noon and 1.30-7pm. Sunday and public holidays 9am-12noon.

Igé

Les Vignerons de Igé (C)
71960 Igé
☎ 85 33 33 56
A brand new winery with the nearby former Romanesque church converted into a tasting cellar and wine museum. Open Monday to Friday 8am-12noon and 1.30-6pm, Saturday 8am-12noon and 2-7pm, Sunday and public holidays 2-7pm. English spoken. First wine free, 10F charge for two wines.

Leynes

Domaine Sangouard (V)
Le Bourg, 71570 Leynes
☎ 85 35 13 26
The cellar is next to the home of Annie-Claude and Vincent Sangouard, and close to the church which dates back to the eleventh century. Open Monday to Friday 10am-12noon and 4-7pm, Saturday 9am-12noon and 2-6pm, Sunday and public holidays 10am-12noon. English spoken.

Lugny

Cave de Lugny (C)
rue des Charmes
71260 Lugny
☎ 85 33 22 85
The largest cooperative producers in Burgundy offering a wide range of wines. Open Monday to Saturday 8am-12noon and 1.30-5.30am (6pm in the summer), Sunday and public holidays 2-5.30pm. English spoken.

Mâcon

Maison Mâconnaise des Vins
484 ave de Lattre-de-Tassigny
71000 Mâcon
☎ 85 38 36 70
The restaurant offers regional specialities served with selected local crus,

and these can also be tasted and bought in the adjoining converted cellaret. Open 7.30am-9pm. English spoken.

Péronne

Domaine des As (V)
The estate was founded in 1985 by Christian and François Grenot who were joined by Annie and Guy Prost in 1992. They have 15 acres (6 hectares) of vineyards around the house outside the village on the Burgy road. Open by appointment. English spoken.

Domaine du Bicheron Daniel Rousset (V)
Saint-Pierre de Lanques
71260 Péronne
☎ 85 36 94 53
There are more than 20 acres (8 hectares) of vineyards and traditional wine making methods are used. Open Monday to Friday 11am-1pm and 6-8pm, Saturday 8am-1pm and 1.30-8pm, Sunday 8am-12noon. Visits on Sunday afternoons and public holidays by appointment. English spoken.

Prissé

Domaine de la Feuillarde (V)
La Feuillarde
71960 Prissé
☎ 85 34 54 45
The grapes from the 38 acre (5 hectares) estate are all picked by hand and great whites and good reds are offered for tasting in the eighteenth century cellar. Open daily 8am-8pm. English spoken.

Groupement des Producteurs de Prissé (C)
71960 Prissé
☎ 85 37 88 06
Over 250 growers are members of this cooperative, founded in 1928, with more than 1,100 acres of vines, seventy per cent of which is Chardonnay. Open daily 9am-12noon and 2-6.30pm.

Roche-Vineuse, La

Domaine du Château de la Greffière (V)
71960 La Roche-Vineuse
☎ 85 37 79 11
The original house was built in 1585
and the present château dates from
1830 with the cellars built in 1780.
Open Monday to Saturday 8am-
12noon and 1.30-7pm. Sunday and
public holidays 9am-12noon and 1.30-
6pm. English spoken.

Domaine Sante-et-Fils (V)
Hameau de Somméré
☎ 85 37 80 57
This is the fourth generation of wine
makers who specialise in Mâcon
whites and Passe-Tout-Grains, although they do make reds. Open
Monday to Friday 8am-12.30pm,
Saturday 8am-12.30pm and 1-7pm,
Sunday and public holidays 8am-
12.30pm and 1-3pm. English spoken.

Romanèche-Thorins

Maison Georges Duboeuf (N)
71570 Romanèche-Thorins
☎ 85 35 51 13
Another famous Burgundy name and
an opportunity to taste all the wines of
Mâcon and Beaujolais. Also visit Le
Hameau du Vin, and discover all about
vines and wines. Open for tasting
Monday to Friday 8am-12noon and
1.30-5.30pm. Saturday 8am-12.30pm.
The exhibition is open daily 9am-6pm
and a tasting is included in the price of
the visit. English spoken.

Solutré-Pouilly

Caveau de Pouilly-Fuissé (group tasting
centre)
71960 Solutré-Pouilly
☎ 85 35 83 83
Run by the Union des Producteurs des
Grands Vins de Pouilly-Fuissé, the

tasting cellars are at the foot of the
famous Roche de Solutré. Open daily
May to October, and afternoons only in
March and April, November and
December. Closed January. First wine
tasted free.

Domaine Bressand (V)
La Roche, 71960 Solutré-Pouilly
☎ 85 35 80 96
The wines are tasted in the home of the
Bressand family, about 100yds from
the museum car park. Their vineyards
are close by. Open daily 8am-8pm.
English spoken.

Tournus

Cave de l'Abbaye (wine shop)
48 rue de la République Centre
71700 Tournus
☎ 85 51 02 39
Near the town hall, you can enjoy a
tutored tasting with owner Jean-Yves
Tillon, who is also vice-president of the
Association des Sommeliers de
Bourgogne. Open Tuesday to Saturday
9am-12noon and 2-7pm. Sunday and
public holidays 9am-12noon.

Cave des Vignerons de Mancey (C)
RN6, 71700 Tournus
☎ 85 51 00 83
The cooperative was founded in 1929
and now has 150 grower members.
There are two tasting cellars, one in
Tournus and the other in Mancey.
Open Monday to Saturday 8am-
12noon and 2-6pm. Sunday 9am-
12noon and 3-6pm. English spoken.

Uchizy

Domaine Sallet (V)
rue du Puits
71700 Uchizy
☎ 85 40 50 46

Follow the 'chambres d'hôtes' signs for the estate. Open Monday to Friday 6am-8pm, Saturday 10am-12noon, Sunday 10am-12noon and 5pm-7pm, public holidays 10am-12noon.

For further information about the vineyards and wineries of the area contact:

Bureau Interprofessional Des Vins de Bourgogne
12 boulevard Bretonnière
BP150
21204 Beaune Cedex
☎ 80 24 70 20

Délégation Régionale de Chablis
1 rue de Chichée BP31
89800 Chablis
☎ 86 42 42 22

Délégation Régionale de Beaune
Rue Henri-Dunant
BP150
21204 Beaune Cedex
☎ 80 22 31 35

Délégation Régionale de Mâcon
502 ave du Maréchal-de-Lattre-de-Tassigny
71000 Mâcon
☎ 85 38 20 15

Hotels and Restaurants in Beaujolais

Hotels

BEAUJEU
Hotel Anne de Beaujeu £-££
rue de la République
☎ 74 04 87 58

BELLEVILLE
Hotel Ange Couronné £-££
16 rue de la République
☎ 74 66 42 00

CHAROLLES
Hotel Lion d'Or ££
6 rue Champagny
☎ 85 24 08 28

CORCELLES-EN-BEAUJOLAIS
Hotel Restaurant Gailleton £-££
☎ 74 66 41 06

COURS
Hotel Le Pavillon ££
Col du Pavillon
69470 Cours
☎ 74 89 83 55

Nouvel Hotel £-££
rue Georges-Clémenceau
☎ 74 89 70 21

FLEURIE
Hotel Grand Vins ££
69820 Fleurie
☎ 74 69 81 43

JULIÉNAS
Hotel des Vignes £-££
route St Armor
69840 Juliénas
☎ 74 04 43 70

Chez la Rose
☎ 74 04 41 20

Mâcon
Hotel Bellevue ££-£££
416 quai Lamartine
71000 Mâcon
☎ 85 38 05 07

Quincie-en-Beaujolais
Hotel Mont-Brouilly ££
69430 Quincie-en-Beaujolais
☎ 74 04 33 73

Romanèche-Thorins
Hotel Maritennes £££
71570 Romanèche-Thorins
☎ 85 35 51 70

Villié-Morgon
Hotel le Villon
69910 Villié-Morgon
☎ 74 69 16 16

Villefranche-sur-Saône
Hotel Plaisance
96 ave Libération
69400 Villefranche-sur-Saône
☎ 74 65 33 52

Restaurants

Beaujeu
Anne de Beaujeu ££
69430 Beaujeu
☎ 74 04 87 58

Beauregard
Auberge Bressane ££
01480 Beauregard
☎ 74 60 93 92

Blacaret
Beaujolais £-££
69460 Blacaret
☎ 74 67 54 75

Chénas
Daniel Robin ££
69840 Chénas
☎ 85 36 72 67

Cours
Chalets des Tilleuls £-££
Thel, 69470 Cours
☎ 74 64 81 53

Fleurie
Auberge du Cep £££
place Eglise
69820 Fleurie
☎ 74 04 10 77

Odenas
Christian Mabeau
69460 Odenas
☎ 74 03 41 799

St Georges-de-Reneins
Hostellerie St Georges ££
69830 St Georges-de-Reneins
☎ 74 67 62 78

St Vérand
Auberge St Vérand £-££
71570 St Vérand
☎ 85 37 16 50

Tarare
Jean Brouilly £££
3 Terrace Paris
69170 Tarare
☎ 74 63 24 56

Villefranche-sur-Saône
La Fontaine Blue ££
18 rue Moulin
69400 Villefranche-sur-Saône
☎ 74 68 10 37

Viry
La Monastère
71120 Viry
☎ 85 24 14 24

Castles, Museums, Sights and Monuments of Beaujolais

ANSE
(Gallo-Roman town and medieval fortifications)
Château des Tours
Open: guided visits Saturday 2.30pm, and by appointment.

Tourist Mini-Railway
☎ 74 60 26 01
Open: weekends and public holidays, Easter to All Saints Day.

AMPLEPUIS
Barthélemy Thimonnier Museum (*Sewing Machine Museum*)
☎ 74 89 08 90
Open: Wednesday, Friday and weekends in July and August 2.30-6.30pm, open mornings by request.

BEAUJEU
Marius Sudin Arts and Crafts Museum
☎ 74 69 22 88
Open: April to June, October and November daily except Tuesday, 2.30-6pm, also 10am-12noon weekends July to September daily 10am-12noon, and 2.30-6pm.

CHAZAY D'AZERGUES
Vieilles Pierres Museum
☎ 78 43 68 19

Corcelles
Castle
☎ 74 66 00 24
Open: daily except Sunday and public holidays 10am-12noon and 2.30-6.30pm.

GLEIZÉ
Château de Vaurenard
☎ 74 68 21 65
Open: by appointment.

ROMANÈCHE-THORINS
The Order of Winemakers Museum
☎ 85 35 52 48
Open: Easter to All Saints Day, Sunday and public holidays 9.30-11.30am and 2-5pm. At other times by request.

Guild Museum
☎ 85 35 52 48
Open: by request if closed.

Zoo
☎ 85 35 51 53
Open: daily.

ST BONNET-LE-TRONCY
Jean Claude Colin Museum
☎ 74 02 03 80
Open: check at Town Hall.

ST CHRISTOPHE LA MONTAGNE
Rural Museum
☎ 74 04 76 06

ST GEORGES-DE-RENEINS
Ludna Archaeological Museum
☎ 74 67 61 45
Visits by appointment.

ST JEAN-DES-VIGNES
Espace Pierres Folles (geological site and museum)
☎ 78 43 72 89
Open: daily.

ST JULIEN-EN-BEAUJOLAIS
Claude Bernard (*father of experimental medicine*) **Museum**
Open: November to February 10am to noon and 2.30 to 5pm, April to October 10am-12noon 2.30-6pm except Monday. Closed Christmas week and all March.

THEIZÉ
Château Rochebonne
Open: Sunday and public holidays May to November 3-7pm.

VAUX-EN-BEAUJOLAIS VINE AND WINE MUSEUM
☎ 74 03 26 58

VILLEFRANCHE (RENAISSANCE COURTYARDS)
Espace d'Arts Plastique
☎ 74 68 33 70
Open: daily.

Vineyards and Tasting Cellars to Visit

The nineteen caves coopératives of Beaujolais

Beaujolaise du Bois-d'Oingt
69620 Le Bois-d'Oingt
☎ 74 71 62 81

Beaujolaise de la Region de Bully
69210 Bully
☎ 74 01 27 77

Cave du Château de Chenas
69840 Chenas
☎ 74 04 48 19

Maison des Vignerons Cave Coopérative
69115 Chiroubles
☎ 74 69 14 94

Des Grands Vin de Fleurie
69820 Fleurie
☎ 74 04 11 70

Intercommunale de Gleize
69400 Gleize
☎ 74 68 39 49

Château du Bois de la Salle
69840 Juliénas
☎ 74 04 42 61

Cave Coopérative Beaujolaise
69480 Lachassagne
☎ 74 67 01 43

Intercommunale de Letra
69620 Letra
☎ 74 71 30 52

Vignerons de Liergues
69400 Liergues
☎ 74 68 07 94

Cave Beaujolaise du Perreon SCA
69460 Le Perreon
☎ 74 03 22 83

Beaujolaise de Quincie
69430 Quincie
☎ 74 04 32 54

Coteaux du Lyonnais
69210 St Bel
☎ 74 01 11 33

Des St Étienne
69460 St Etienne-des-Oullières
☎ 74 03 43 69

De Bel Air
69220 St Jean-d'Ardières
☎ 74 66 35 91

De St Julien
69640 St Julien
☎ 74 67 57 46

Cave Coopérative Beaujolaise
69620 St Laurent-d'Oingt
☎ 74 71 20 51

Cave Coopérative Beaujolaise
69620 St Verand
☎ 74 71 73 19

Cave Coopérative du Beau Vallon
69630 Theizé
☎ 74 71 75 97

Tasting Cellars

ARNAS
Caveau Degustation des Sarments
☎ 74 60 39 61

BEAUJEU
Le Temple de Bacchus
☎ 74 04 81 18

Caveau des Beaujolais Villages
place de l'Hotel de Ville
☎ 74 04 81 18

CHATILLON D'AZERGUES
Le Pavilion des Pierres Dorées
☎ 78 47 98 15

CHENAS
Caveau du Cru
☎ 74 04 44 33

CHESSY-LES-MINES
Caveau des Vins Mathelin
☎ 78 43 92 41

CHIROUBLES
La Terrasse de Chiroubles
☎ 74 04 24 71

Maison des Vignerons
Le Bourg
☎ 74 69 14 95

COGNY
Les Voûtes
☎ 74 67 33 25

CORCELLES
Château de Corcelles
☎ 74 66 00 24

FLEURIE
Caveau de Fleurie
Le Bourg
☎ 74 04 16 63

GLEIZÉ
**Cooperative Vinicole
Intercommunale de Gleize**
1471 route de Tarare
☎ 74 68 39 49

JULIÉNAS
Le Cellier de la Vieille Eglise
Le Bourg
☎ 74 04 42 98

LEYNES
Relais Beaujolais Mâconnais
☎ 85 35 11 29

REGNIÉ-DURETTE
Caveau des deux Cochers
☎ 74 04 38 33

ROMANÈCHE-THORINS
Caveau du Moulin à Vent
RN6
☎ 85 35 58 09

ST AMOUR
Caveau de St Amour
Le Plâtre
☎ 85 37 15 98

ST JEAN-D'ARDIÈRES
Maison des Beaujolais
RN6
☎ 74 66 16 46

ST JEAN-DES-VIGNES
Refuge des Pierre Dorées
☎ 78 43 72 03

ST LÉGER
Cuvage des Brouilly
Le Bourg
☎ 74 66 82 65

VAUX
Caveau de Clochmerle
Le Bourg
☎ 74 03 26 58

VILLIÉ-MORGAN
Caveau des Morgon
Bourg
☎ 74 04 20 99

Facts for Visitors
Burgundy and Beaujolais

ACCOMMODATION

Burgundy is popular as a tourist destination and reservations are strongly advised if you plan to travel during the summer months.

Hotels

Hotels are star rated according to the quality of comfort and service provided. This is usually, but not always, reflected in the prices charged. The system is:

****	Luxury
****	First Class
***	High Standard
**	Good Hotel
*	Average

This guide suggests a large number of hotels to suit all tastes and pockets, and there are a number of free hotel booklets if you want an even greater choice.

These include *Hotels in Bourgogne* free from the Comité Départemental de Tourisme de la Côte d'Or, BP 1601, 21035 Dijon Cedex ☎ 80 63 66 00, and *The Logis de France de Bourgogne*, also free from L'Union Régionale des Logis de France de Bourgogne, Chambre Régionale de Commerce et d'Industrie de Bourgogne, BP209, 21006 Dijon Cedex ☎ 80 63 52 52

Farm Inns

There are fifteen traditional farm inns in Burgundy offering comfortable accommodation and the opportunity to taste authentic regional cooking usually prepared from home grown produce.

Further information is available from: Chambre d'Ariculture de la Côte d'Or, Service 'Accueil à la Ferme', 42 rue de Mulhouse, 21000 Dijon ☎ 80 72 57 13

Bed and Breakfast

The Chambres d'hôtes are the Burgundian equivalent of bed and breakfast establishments, and they are becoming more popular throughout the region. There are about 300 guest rooms available and standards are set by the Charte Nationale des Chambres d'hôtes, which determines the size and furnishings of the room, as well as bathroom facilities, and the level of service which must be provided.

Further details from: *Burgundy Chambres d'Hôtes Guide*, Gîtes de France, 27 rue Auguste Comte, 21000 Dijon ☎ 80 72 06 05

Gîtes de Group (Gîte d'Étape)

There are a number of *gîtes* which cater specially for individuals or small groups. Rooms are comfortable with their own toilet, and can have four to six beds, and there may aso be dormitory accommodation.There are usually facilities for cooking although breakfasts are provided.

Further details are available from Gîtes de France de Côte-d'Or, 27 rue Auguste Comte, 21000 Dijon ☎ 80 72 06 05

Youth Hostels

To stay at a youth hostel it is essential to be a member. It is advisable to join your national association before departure and make advance reservations for your accommodation if travelling during busy periods.

Further information can be obtained from Centre de Rencontres Internationales et de Sejour de Dijon, 1 boulevard Champollion, 21000 Dijon ☎ 80 71 32 12.

Apartments

If planning a lengthy stay it may be worthwhile considering leasing an apartment. The 'gîte rural' is a comfortably furnished and well equipped apartment intended for letting in the summer. They can be leased from one week. There is also Gîtes de France Country Accommodation which offer more basic facilities, and holiday chalets in very rural areas, often close to lakes or the mountains.

For further information contact Gîtes de France de Côte-d'Or, 27 rue Auguste Comte, 21000 Dijon ☎ 80 72 06 05

Huttes de France

This is a relatively new innovation, and copied from Scandinavia where they have proved very popular. You can spend a weekend, week or fortnight in a wooden mini-chalet with all the facilities needed.

Further details available from: Huttes de France, 46 boulevard Pasteur, BP360, 63010 Clermont-Ferrand ☎ 73 34 18 48.

Camping

There are fifty-six officially classified campsites throughout the region, two naturist campsites, and ten on-farm campsites, five members of the Gîte de France, and the other five members of the Bienvenue à la Ferme association.

For a free booklet about about campsite locations and services, contact: Comité Départemental de Tourisme de la Côte d'Or, BP1601, 21035 Dijon Cedex ☎ 80 63 66 00

Burgundy also offers a number of 'youth campgrounds' where young people travelling alone or in small groups can stay very inexpensively. Each site offers washroom facilities and a warden who oversees the camp and can advise about activities in the area and things to see and do. The camps are open to travellers between the ages of thirteen and twenty-five and stays are limited to a maximum five consecutive nights per campground.

There are youth campgrounds

at: Arcenant, Chaux, Fixin, Grancey-le-Château, Pouilly-en-Auxois, Recey-sur-Ource, St-Romain, Selongey and Vieux-Château.

For further information contact: Centre Information Jeunesse de Bourgogne, 22 rue Audra, 21000 Dijon, ☎ 80 30 35 56.

ANNUAL FAIRS AND EVENTS

January
St Vincent Tournament Festival in honour of the patron saint of winemakers on the third weekend of the month. Location changes annually

February
Chiché: Fete of St Vincent, normally the first weekend

March
Dijon: Les Grand Jours de Bourgogne wine fair
Chalon-sur-Saône: carnival

April
Magny-Cours: Grand Prix
Nolay: fair and bring and buy

May
Mâcon: Wines of France Fair
Semur-en-Auxois: medieval fair
Chalon-sur-Saône: Montgolfiades

June
Dijon: Music festival
Tournus: Tournus Passions — concerts and events
St Jean-de-Losne: Blessing of the River Boats

July
Anzy-le-Duc: Music Festival
Autun: Choir festival
Château de la Clayette: Son et lumière
Beaune: International Music Festival
Magny-Cours: Grand Prix-Formula 1 and Motor Racing Championship events
Chalon-sur-Saône: National Arts Festival
Meursault: Festival of Music and Wine
Vézelay: Pilgrimage of Madeleine
St Fargeau: Historical pageant

August
Cluny: Music Festival
St Fargeau: Historical pageant
Autun: Grand Summer Fair
Coulanges-sur-Yonne: Regatta
St Léger-sous-Beuvray: traditional country fair
Saulieu: Fête du Charolais
St Honoré-les-Bains: Flower festival

September
Dijon: International Folklore and Wine Festival
Gevrey-Chambertin: Wine Festival
*Semur-en-Auxoi*s: Opera Festival

October
Dijon: International Food Fair

November
Le Trois Glorieuses: Burgundy's biggest wine celebration, at Clos de Vougeot, Chapitre, Beaune, Meursault and La Paulée
Chablis: Wine Festival

BANKS

Opening times vary enormously, but most banks are open weekdays between 9.30am and 4.30pm, and some close for lunch. Automatic teller machines are available outside many main branches.

BOATING

There are almost 750 miles (1,207km) of rivers and canals in Burgundy, and huge stretches of quiet waterway away from commerical traffic. The area has relied on water for transportation for centuries because of its special geographical siutation, at the watershed of three major river systems — the Seine, Loire and Rhône. Beginning in the seventeenth century and continuing over three centuries, a huge network of canals was built to connect the three rivers and speed up transport of goods between the south of France and Paris. Three other rivers, the Saône, Yonne and Seille, are also navigable, and connected to the system. Together these rivers and canals plus many lakes provide a delightful way to explore Burgundy.

The main waterways are

River Yonne: From Auxerre to Montereau, the Yonne crosses the gently rolling countryside of lower Burgundy and the Ile-de-France region. It flows through Auxerre, Joigny, Villeneuve-sur-Yonne, Sens, Pont-sur-Yonne and Montereau, where Napoléon fought one of his last battles.

Burgundy Canal: Joins the the valleys of the Yonne and the Saône, flowing first through the valley of the Armançon, before arriving at the 'Gateway of Burgundy' where it travels through a 725ft (221m) long tunnel near Pouilly-en-Auxois. The canal moves through hilly countryside which is why there are so many locks. Areas covered include Tonnerre and the châteaux of Tanlay and Ancy-le-Franc; the Auxois region with Fontenay, the site of Alesia and the medieval village of Châteauneuf; the Ouche valley to Dijon, and finally the plains of the River Saône.

The Nivernais Canal: The central part of the canal, which runs for 38 miles (61km) between Cercy-la-Tour and Sardy, is inaccessible to the long commercial barges so is almost exclusively the domain of pleasure boats. From Auxerre to Clamecy and Corbigny, the canal follows the Yonne, and then by means of a remarkable series of locks at Sardy and the tunnels at La Colancelle, it reaches the lakes of Vaux and Baye, the highest part of its course. The canal descends gently towards the Loire valley crosssing the plains of the Bazois by Châtillon and Cercy-la-Tour.

The Settons Lakes: These are in the heart of the magnificently scenic Morvan and offer a wide range of boating and water activities.

Marne to Saône Canal: This stretch of water is known locally as the 'Burgundy-Champagne canal'. It southern section travels through the Côte-d'Or, and then follows the beautiful Vingeanne valley passing the châteaux of Talmay, Beaumont-sur-Vingeanne and Fontaine Française.

The Saône and Seille: The Saône is one of France's most beautiful rivers and in its highest reaches, marked what was once the boundary between France and the Austrian Empire. This is the reason why there are so many fortified towns in the area, such as Auxonne, Verdun-sur-le-Doubs and St Jean-de-Losne. The Lower Saône from Chalon-sur-Saône to Tournus, Mâcon and Lyon, flows along the foot of the hills that make up the Chalonnais, the Mâconnais and Beaujolais regions, all noted for their vineyards. The Seille is a tributary of the Saône, offering in the 25 miles (40km) between Tournus and Louhans, a magnificent journey through the quiet and fertile Bresse area.

Centre Canal: Of all the Burgundy canals, this is the busiest with plenty of commercial traffic, especially on the Saône section between Montceau-les-Mines and Chalon-sur-Saône, where, because of the volume of traffic, the locks are automatic. It is, however, still a very attractive section of waterway, especially between Chagny and Santenay where you cruise between famous Burgundy vineyards, and the delightful area known as Le Creusot. It passes through the rich plains of the Charollais before arriving at Digoin, via Paray-le-Monial, renowned for its Romanesque art and as a place of pilgrimage.

Roanne to Digoin Canal: The canal continues the southerly course of the Canal du Centre and the Canal Lateral à la Loire, crossing the Brionnais, an area of Burgundy famous for its many Romanesque churches, and the gently, rolling countryside.

Canal Lateral à la Loire: Built close to the left bank of the Loire, the canal crosses Digoin by a rare canal bridge. It is a pleasant stretch of water without many locks, and passing through the vineyards areas of Sancerre. Decize, Nevers, and La Charité-sur-Loire are all worth visiting.

The Briare and Loing Canals: The Briare Canal was the work of Sully, the famous Minister of Henry IV and construction started in 1604 and took 38 years to complete. It was the first major canal project in France, and the Loing canal was built a hundred years later. Both are still used to transport cereals through the peaceful countryside of the Gâtinais. Of interest are the canal bridge and the seven locks at Rogny, which date from the seventeenth century, and although now unused, classified as a national historic monument.

House boats are available for hire from many operators throughout the region.

For further information contact:

Service de Réservation Loisire Accueil
3 rue du Sort
58000 Nevers
☎ 86 59 14 22

Port au Bois
89300 Joigny
☎ 86 91 72 72

Bateaux de Bourgogne
3-4 quai de la République
89000 Auxerre
☎ 86 52 18 99

Le Grand Bassin
Castelnaudary
☎ 68 23 17 51

Rive de France
172 boulevard Berthier
75017 Paris
☎ 46 22 10 86

Hotel barges

Continentale de Croisieres
9 rue Jean Renaud
21000 Dijon
☎ 80 30 49 20

Château La Chassagne
21410 Pont-de-Pany
☎ 80 40 47 50.

Canoeing and Rafting

River Yonne — Olympic Auxerrois
Ave Yver Prolongée
89000 Auxerre
☎ 86 52 13 86

Avallon-Morvan Canoe Kayak
3 route de Paris
89200 Avallon
☎ 86 34 13 03

Canoe Kayak Senonais
Quai Schweitzer, 89100 Sens
☎ 86 65 52 30.

Canal de Bourgogne
Club Nautique Dijon Bourgogne
47 quai Galliot, 21000 Dijon
☎ 80 41 39 99

ASPTT Dijon Canoe Kayak
Base nautique du Lac Kir
21000 Dijon
☎ 80 42 08 32.

River Saône
Etoile Auxonnaise C.K.E.A.
21130 Auxonne
☎ 80 31 06 53

Club Canoe Kayak
71400 Dracy-St-Loup
☎ 85 82 82 46

A.S.B.V.D. rue du Camping
21170 St Jean-de-Losne
☎ 80 29 16 36.

River Loire Canoe Club Nivernais
Quai de la Médine
58000 Nevers
☎ 86 61 32 66.

Loire and Morvan
Service Loisire Accueil Nievre
3 rue du Sort, 58000 Nevers
☎ 86 59 14 22

Point Rivière Rafting
Auberge des Michaux
58230 St Agnan
☎ 86 78 72 30

Office Departemental des Bases de Plein Air de la Nievre
58230 Montsauche-les-Settons
☎ 86 84 51 98

CLIMATE

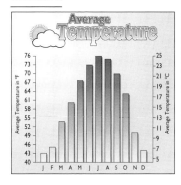

CURRENCY AND CREDIT CARDS

The French *franc* comes in paper denominations of 20, 50, 100, 200 and 500, and in 1, 2, 5 and 10 *franc* coins. There are 100 *centimes* to the *franc*, and 5, 10 ,20 and 50 *centime* coins.

All major credit cards are widely accepted, and most hotels and large stores accept traveller's cheques. Cash machines are available in large towns and cities and can be used for withdrawals if your credit or checking card is a member of one of the international networks.

DISABLED HOLIDAYMAKERS

The French Government Tourist Office issue a special information sheet for disabled visitors to France. This is available on application with a stamped addressed envelope.

The Liason Committee for the Transport of Disabled Persons (Comité de Liaison pour le Transport des Personnes Handicapées) 34 Avenue Marceau Paris 8e and the Ministry of Equipment, Housing, Transport and the Sea (Ministère de l'Equipment, du Logement, des Transports et de la Mer) 92055 Paris La Defense cédex 04 publish a transport guide for the disabled.

A list of *gîtes* which accommodate for disabled travellers and regional numbers of the APF (Association des Paralyses de France) can be obtained from:

Association des Paralyses de France Central Office
17 Boulevard Auguste-Blanqui
75013
Paris
☎ 140 78 69 00

Another useful address to contact for information is

Red Cross
Croix Rouge Paris
1 Place Henri Dunant
75384
Paris
☎ 1 44 43 11 00

ELECTRICITY

220 volts, 50 cycles AC. If visiting from the UK a continental adapter is required. If visiting from the USA a converter to reduce the voltage to the appliance and a converter is needed, unless your appliance is dual-voltage.

EMBASSIES AND CONSULATES

Foreign Embassies and Consulates in France are:

Australia
Embassy and Consulate
4 Rue Jean-Rey
75015 Paris
☎ 40 59 33 00

Canada
Embassy-Chancellery
35 av Montaigne
75008 Paris
☎ 47 23 01 01

United Kingdom
Embassy
35 Rue du Faubourg Saint-Honoré
75008 Paris
☎ 42 66 91 42

British Consulate
16 Rue d'Anjou
75008 Paris
(same telephone number)

United States of America
Embassy-Chancellery
2 Avenue Gabriel
75008 Paris
☎ 42 96 12 02

The Foreign Office leaflet *Get it Right Before you Go* provides advice about how to behave in France, and gives information about the services offered by the Consulate. This is obtainable from the French Government Tourist Office.

INSURANCE

Make sure you have comprehensive health and travel insurance, and if you are driving, that you and your passengers are fully covered. UK residents are covered by a reciprocal health agreement with France, but you may still have to pay for treatment and recover it on your return. Always keep all receipts.

MAPS

The *Michelin Motoring Atlas of France* is recommended for its detail (1:200,000). If you do buy the Michelin atlas, make sure you get the spiral-bound version, as it is more durable. It contains a planning map, a map of French departments, plans of major towns and cities and a gazetteer.

For route planning, the *Michelin Map 911* is invaluable. It contains information on motorways and alternative routes, distances and journey times, 24-hour service stations, and peak travel periods to avoid. This can be supplemented by the red *Michelin Map 989*, an excellent road map for getting from A to B. Its scale is 1:1,000,000, and it lists all the N (National) and many D (Departmental) roads. It also marks the French *Départements* in black and the detailed Michelin map numbers in blue. The AA also produces a clear and uncluttered road map of France (1:1,000,000), with a folding/colour coding system and showing toll and toll-free motorways. This is also available in 'Glovebox Atlas' form. The AA/Baedeker map is slightly more detailed (1:750,000) and has city-centre plans of main towns.

On arrival at a destination, you may need a more detailed map than the 1:200,000 Michelin yellow. The French equivalent to the British Ordnance Survey map is *Institut Géographique National*, with a scale of 1:100,000. Even larger-scale maps are the IGN Orange (1;50,000) and the IGN Blue (1:25,000). These are useful for walkers and climbers, showing contours, footpaths and many other details. The IGN also has a range of planning maps. to travel around Lyon, a large scale map is essential.

MEASUREMENTS

The metric system is used in France.
Conversions are:
1 kilogram (1,000 grams) = 2.2lb
1 litre = $1^3/_4$ pints
4.5 litres = 1 gallon
1.6km = 1 mile
1 hectare = 2.5 acres approx.

MUSEUMS

Most museums close one day during the week, usually Tuesday and also on public holidays. Visiting times vary enormously during the year, and many are open only in the afternoons and on Sunday.

PASSPORTS AND VISAS

Travellers from the UK, Ireland, USA, Canada, Australia and New Zealand need a valid passport to visit France. Most other travellers from non EC countries require a visa as well, as do most nationals planning to spend more than three months in France. Check well before departure in order to have time to make all the arrangements.

POSTAL SERVICES

French postal and telephone services are state-controlled. The sign for a Post Office is PTT — Poste et Telécommunications. Post Offices are open 8am-7pm on weekdays and 8am-12noon Saturdays. Post Offices in small towns may close for two hours, usually 12noon-2pm, at lunch-times. Letters can be sent to you for collection c/o Poste Restante, Poste Centrale in any French town. It is necessary to have proof of identity in order to collect mail and there is a small fee.

PUBLIC HOLIDAYS

1 January
Easter Sunday and Easter Monday
1 (Labour Day)
8 May (VE Day)
Ascension Day (5 weeks after Easter)
The Monday after Pentecost
14 July (Bastille Day)
15 August (Assumption)
1 November (All Saints)
11 November (Armistice Day 1918)
Christmas Day

Safety

France, and Burgundy in particular, is generally safe but it is sensible to take precautions. Don't wear expensive jewellery or carry large sums of money about. A money belt or pouch worn round your neck is a good idea. It is also sensible to make photocopies of important documents like passports, insurance policy and airline tickets. It will speed up replacement if the originals are lost or stolen. Stay in well-lit areas at night, and if in doubt, always check with hotel staff or tourist officials about areas to be avoided.

Shopping

Wine and luxury food products, particularly cheeses, are the most obvious shopping choices, although non-community citizens will have to watch their customs allowances. Many large stores offer VAT refunds to foreign shoppers, and as this can amount to 18.7 per cent of each purchase.

Shops are generally open from 9am to 6pm, although many stay open later. Smaller shops, especially those selling groceries in rural areas are open longer, often from 8am to 8pm but close for lunch usually from 12noon to 2pm.

Telephones

Pay phones are plentiful and found in post offices, cafés and on the streets. They mainly use 50 centime, 1 and 5 *franc* coins. It is cheaper to ring between 9.30p and 8am weekdays, after 1.30pm on Saturdays and all day Sunday. Lift the receiver, put your money in the slot and dial the number. As unused coins are returned after the call, it is best to use several smaller value coins. Telephone cards are available from post offices and many hotels, shops and so on.

For international calls, dial 19, then the country code, then the area code (less the first 0) and then the number. Have a good pile of coins ready. You can also use international telephone cards such as the UK's British Telecom and USA's AT&T cards to make calls and have them charged to your home phone account.

Time

France is one hour ahead of Greenwich Mean Time, so that it is one hour ahead of London during the winter and two hours ahead during the summmer.

Tipping

Most restaurants add a service charge and this is indicated by the phrase *service compris*. Even when service is included, it is customary to leave a small extra amount, perhaps 50 *centimes* for a beer or glass of wine, and a few *francs* for a meal. When it is not included, tip between fifteen to twenty per cent depending on how good the service was and how much you enjoyed the meal.

It is usual to tip taxi drivers and hairdressers and such like about fifteen per cent, porters about 10F per piece of luggage carried, and you are also expected to leave a small tip when you use a toilet which has an attendant.

TOURIST OFFICES

French Government Tourist Offices are:

United Kingdom
178 Piccadilly
London W1V 0AL
☎ 071-491-7622

United States of America
610 Fifth Avenue
New York, NY 10020
☎ 212 315 0888

645 N Michigan Avenue
Chicago
Il 60611
☎ 312 751 7804

2305 Cedar Springs Road
Dallas, Tx 75201
☎ 214 720 4010

9454 Wilshire Blvd
Suite 303
Beverley Hills, CA 90212
☎ 310 271 2358

Canada
1981 McGill College
Suite 490
Montreal
Quebec H3A 2W9
☎ 514 288 4264

30 St Patrick St
Suite 700
Toronto
Ontario M5T 3A3
☎ 416 593 4723

TRAVEL

Getting to Burgundy and Beaujolais

Driving

The opening of the Channel Tunnel has made it even easier for UK travellers to visit Burgundy, and one can now drive from say Birmingham in the Midlands to Beaune quite easily in a day, stopping off for a leisurely lunch on the way.

If touring in your own car, make sure that it is serviced and running well before departure. You will need to carry your driving license and insurance documents.

If you are flying in and need to hire a car, most of the major airlines offer a fly-drive deal, and if using a car hire company, book as early as possible to take account of discounts which can cut costs up to thirty per cent, especially if you prepay. Hiring cars in France is expensive, and tax is usually on top of the quoted car hire charges.

If you plan to spend a couple of days in Dijon, Beaune or Lyon, you may not need a car, so it may work out cheaper to hire for two shorter periods than for the entire trip. Air-conditioning is not standard with most hire cars, and requests for automatic transmission should request it when booking. Make sure you have adequate insurance, including collision damage waiver. The minimum age varies to the hiring firm but in general you have to be twenty-one.

The main international hire car companies are:

Avis

☎ (1) 46 09 92 12

Hertz

☎ (1) 47 88 51 51

Europcar

☎ (1) 30 43 82 82

Citer

☎ (1) 45 67 97 43

Thrifty

☎ (1) 46 56 08 75

Budget

☎ (1) 46 86 65 65

Mattei

☎ 91 79 90 10 or (1) 43 46 11 50

Eurorent

☎ (1) 45 67 82 17

By road

On the toll motorways — A6 Nord from Paris, A6 Sud from Marseille through Lyon, A26 from Calais to Cambrai, Laon, Reims, Châlons-sur-Marne, Chaumont to Dijon; A31 from Luxembourg to Dijon; A39 from Dole to Dijon, and A40 from Geneva to Mâcon.

On route nationales RN5 from St-Gingolph, Switzerland to Dijon, RN6 from Paris to Auxerre, Mâcon and Lyon, RN7 from Paris to Nevers and Lyon, RN60 from Montargis to Sens and Troyes, RN71 Troyes to Dijon, RN73 Dole to Chalon-sur-Saône, RN74 Lancy to Dijon, RN77 Châlons-sur-Marne to Auxerre, and RN79 Moulins to Mâcon and Bourg-en-Bresse.

By train

TGV from Paris to Montbard and Dijon (1hr 40min), Paris to Beaune and Chalon-sur-Saône (2hrs), Paris to Mâcon and Loché (1hr 40min), Paris to Montchanin (1hr 20min), TGV from Lyon to Montchanin (40min), Train Coral: Paris to Nevers (1hr 50min), Paris Migennes (1hr 15min).

By air

Dijon-Bourgogne Airport (☎ 80 67 67 67) is at Dijon-Longvic, almost 4 miles (6km) south-east of Dijon. There are services to Bordeaux, Nantes, Lille, Tolouse, Clermont-Ferrand and London Stansted. Other airports close to Burgundy: Paris-Charles de Gaulle, Paris-Orly, Lyon Satolas, Mulhouse, Basle and Geneva-Cointrin.

Getting Around in Burgundy Beaujolais

Car, bike or feet are the best ways of getting around the region, while a houseboat allows a more leisurely way of exploring, especially if you hire bikes which allow you to get further afield.

The rail network allows efficient travel between major towns and cities, and if you are doing a lot of travelling, the French Flexipass is a good idea, allowing unlimited train travel on any four days within a four-week period. There is also the France Rail 'n' Drive Pass, which allows three days of unlimited train travel and three days use of a hire car.

Local train services are slow, and bus services, where they exist in rural areas, are not really suitable if you have an itinerary to maintain.

Bicycles can often be hired at railway stations and it is possible to return them to other stations within the same *département* to increase travel flexibility. There are other cycle hire shops in the region, and details of these are available from tourist offices.

Rules of the Road

In France you must drive on the right hand side of the road. You will be reminded by signs, at first in English as you leave channel ports and later by the common and important sign *serrez à droite*. This means both 'keep to the right' and 'keep in the right-hand lane' on dual carriageways.

Another important road sign is *Priorité à droite*. The rule in France is that, unless there is an indication to the contrary, traffic coming from the right always has priority. This applies particularly in built-up areas. The exceptions are either Stop or Give Way signs, where minor roads meet major roads. The sign *passage protégé* means you are on a major road that has priority over side roads.

On a major road, a tilted yellow square means that you have priority; when there is a black bar crossing the diamond, you no longer have priority.

A particular danger occurs at roundabouts. While the *priorité à droite* regulation no longer applies in this region, many Frenchmen still drive as though it does. The law stipulates that drivers must give way to cars on the roundabout. However, they may not and it pays to watch traffic coming from the right at all times.

Other Road Signs

Other common road signs are: *toutes directions*, indicating the route for through traffic; *poids lourds*, the recommended or sometimes *obligatoire* route for heavy vehicles; and *centre ville*, indicating the town centre. It does not always pay to follow 'through traffic' signs — they may take you on a long detour, and you may miss seeing the town centre; but they are useful if you are in a hurry and wish to avoid inner-city congestion. It is best to decide beforehand whether you want to see the town and, if so, ignore the through traffic signs and head for the *centre ville*. Of course, if you are a *poids lourds*, ie if you are towing a caravan or trailer, you should normally follow the sign (except possibly at very quiet periods — lunchtimes, evenings, Sundays).

Caravans are sometimes prohibited from town centres. In towns, watch also for the signs *sens interdit* (no entry) and *sens unique* (one way).

One sign to look out for is *déviation*. The diversion may be brief, or on occasion it may take you miles further than you want to go. Unfortunately there is no way of knowing beforehand about the length of the detour.

Heed signs advising of road hazards. Common ones include: *gravillons* (loose chippings); *chute de pierres* (falling rocks); *chaussée déformée* (uneven or bumpy road, temporary surface); *côtés non stabilisés* (unsafe or uneven road edgings); *sortie de camions* (hidden works entrance — lorries emerging); *nids de poules* (potholes). It is advisable to reduce your speed until the danger is past. Sometimes you are warned of a longer-lasting hazard: *virages sur 5 kilometres* (bends for 5 kilometres). Watch out particularly for the *chaussée déformée* signs if you are towing a caravan — a bumpy road could do serious damage here.

Though French road signs are usually pretty good, pointer-signposts can sometimes cause drivers frustration and confusion. It is not always clear which way they are pointing — they often seem to point across the road indicated, rather than towards it. The best procedure is to take the road nearest to the arrow-head showing your destination. Another problem can be hidden road signs. These can be sited on a wall, often half-way round the corner of the road you are looking for; or they can be hidden by other signs. When you are looking for a road, it is wise to travel slowly enough to be able to respond to a late sighting of a pointer-sign. It helps, too, to study the map well before setting off, or to have a good map-reader with you!

Roads and their Classification

French roads are classified as follows:-

A (*autoroute* or motorway)
N (National road)
D (Departmental road).

Motorway signs are usually blue, while other roads are in green. Take care when approaching motorway entrance points. The signpost may indicate the same destination in two colours, and one should follow the green signs to stay on the trunk road.

Most French motorways are toll roads or *Autoroutes à Péage*. They vary in price per kilometre, but they work out to be expensive, especially if you use them for long distances. They have emergency telephones, 24-hour fuel stations and *aires de repos* (rest-places). These *aires de repos* usually provide picnic facilities and toilets.

You can find short stretches of motorway that are free. These are indicated on the Michelin maps with marker points and distance numbers coloured in blue rather than the normal orange. They can be useful in getting you into or through large towns like Paris, Marseilles or Lyon.

The main trunk roads are National, with the number usually indicating the importance of the road. Thus single number roads (N1 to N9) are usually wider and longer than double, which in turn are more major than three-figure roads. Single-number trunk roads are often almost as fast now as motorways; they are often dual-carriageway for long stretches, by-pass most towns, have restricted entry points and special services. The one drawback though, as with all French roads other than motorways, is traffic-lights. The French have a passion for these, and they can cause considerable delay if you are passing through a large built-up area on an ordinary road.

Departmental roads are often very good — well surfaced and maintained, and relatively traffic-free. They tend to vary in quality according to the prosperity of the department. They are usually narrower, but often better maintained, than three-figure or even sometimes two-figure N roads.

There is often confusion over the numbering of D and N roads. The French Government, are responsible for national roads but have handed over responsibility for many to the Departments, which has led to renumbering. Old maps may carry incorrect numbers. For example, a road numbered N63 on your map may now be D363. Normally the last two numbers have stayed the same, but an additional 3, 6 or 9 has been added or substituted for the first number. Sometimes the numbering changes from N to D from one village to the next, depending on whether a local authority has altered its signposts.

Speed Limits

These are lower in wet weather and low visibility than in dry conditions. In dry, unless otherwise posted, they are:

Dry conditions	Wet conditions
Toll Motorways	
130kmh (81mph)	110kmh(68mph)
Dual carriageways and non-toll motorways	
110kmh (68mph)	100kmh(62mph)
Other roads	
90kmh (56mph)	80kmh(50mph)
In towns	
50kmh (37mph)	50kmh(37mph)

The limit starts with the town name, and the derestriction sign is the town name cancelled with a bar. The warning sign *rappel*, meaning 'slow down', means 'continue the restriction' when used in conjunction with a speed limit. There is a new minimum speed limit of 80kmh (50mph) for the outside lane of motorways, but only in daylight, on level ground and with good visibility. Drivers may not exceed 90kmh (56mph) for the first year after passing their test. Speeding offences may be fined on the spot. Speed limits in town are often lower than 50kmh near schools, hospitals etc.

Fuel and Garage Services

Essence, or fuel, comes as *ordinaire* (two-star), *super* (four-star), *sans plomb* or *vert* (lead-free), or *super sans plomb* (super lead-free). Unleaded fuel is widely available. Diesel fuel (*gazole* or gas-oil) is both widely available and cheaper than normal fuel, the difference being considerably greater than in Britain.

Vehicles equipped to run on LPG gas (Gepel/GPL) may be imported, and many LPG filling stations can be found in France, especially on motorways. You can get a map showing their location free from LPG stations.

Fuel prices vary, being highest on motorways, average in normal garages and lowest in hyper- and supermarkets. While it is more economical, buying fuel in supermarkets has its problems. They may be closed at lunchtimes and on Sundays; they can have awkward access and long waits; they will not have toilets or offer other services, and some supermarkets do not take credit cards. There are no fuel coupons in France.

Most normal filling stations are now self-service, but someone should be available to *vérifier*, or check, the *huile, eau ou pneus* (oil, water or tyres), or to *nettoyer le pare-brise* (clean the windscreen). You are advised to tip for these services and you will usually have to pay for distilled water. Some garages make a small charge for air for tyres.

Winter Driving

This is never severely restricted in France, even in the mountains. Snow chains can be hired from tyre specialist garages or bought in hypermarkets.

To check road conditions, telephone Paris on a twenty-four-hour number C.N.I.R. ☎ (1) 48 94 33 33

CAR OR BICYCLE HIRE

If you go by air, fly-drive arrangements for hiring a car are available with the major airlines. Otherwise, you can make your own arrangements with one of the major car rental companies, which have offices in nearly all towns. It is best to do this in advance from your own country. If it is more convenient, you can usually arrange to collect your car in one place and leave it in another, with no extra charge. To hire a car you must have a valid driving licence (held for at least one year) and your passport. The minimum age varies accordingly to the hiring firm but in general you have to be twenty-one.

Alternatively, you may consider it more healthy and close-to-nature to go by bicycle. Bicycle hire is widely available in France (ask at the local Office de Tourisme or Syndicat d'Initiative for details) or there are facilities at some 200 French railway stations. Some package holidays offer a combined travel and cycling-tour holiday in various parts of France. When hiring for yourself, you are advised to take out insurance before you leave.

INDEX

A

Abbey of Bèze   141
Ajoux   101
Aligoté   134, 157
Alise-St-Reine   21
Alluy   21
Aloxe-Corton   146, 147,
   149, 165
Amplepuis   107
   Monnier Museum   107
Ancy-le-Franc   24
Annonay   118
Anse   96
   Château des Tours   96
Anzy-le-Duc   24
Archéodrome   164
Arcy-sur-Cure   24
Arleuf   25
Arnay-le-Duc   25
   Church of St Laurent   25
Arnay-sous-Vitteaux   25
Autun   25, 180
   Cathedral of St Lazare   26
   Natural History Museum   27
   Rolin Museum   26
   St Nicolas Lapidary
      Museum   26
Auxerre   17, 27
   Art and History Museum   27
   Chapel of the Vistandines   27
   Church of St Eusebe   28
   Church of St-Pierre-en-
      Vallée   28
   Musée Leblanc-Duvernoy   28
   St Etienne Cathedral   28
   St Germain Abbey   27
Auxerrois   132
Auxeu-Duresses   153
Auxey   157
Auxey-Duresses   149
Auxois Lakes   28
Auxonne   28
   Bonaparte Museum   29
   Church of Notre-Dame   29
Avallon   29
   Church of St Pierre   30
   Collegiate Church of St
      Lazare   29
   Costume Museum   30
   Musée de l'Avallonais   30
Avenas   97
Azé   30
   Cave Museum   30

Azolette   101

B

Bard-le-Régulier   30
Bâtard-Montrachet   155
Baubigny   30
Béard   32
Beaujeu   96, 181
   Hospice de Beaujeu   97
   Maison de Pays   97
   Place de l'Hôtel-de-Ville   97
   Temple of Bacchus   97
Beaujolais Nouveau   172
Beaujolais Supérieur   172
Beaujolais Villages   172
Beaumont-sur-Vingeanne   32
Beaune   32, 146, 149, 164,
   165, 168
   Charitable Hospices de
      Beaune   149, 164
   Church of Notre-Dame   33, 164
   Church of St Nicolas   34
   Hôtel Dieu   32, 147, 164
   Les Trois Glorieuses   152, 165
   Musée des Beaux Arts   33
   Museum of Burgundy
      Wine   33
Beaune-Tailly   34
Bellavilla   180
Belleville   96, 101, 178, 180
Berzé-la-Ville   34
   Priory Chapel 34
Berzé-le-Châtel   34
Bèze   34
Bibracte   35
Bissy-la-Mâconnaise   35
Blacé   181
Blagny   167
Blanot   35
Bligny-sur-Ouche   35
Boating   203
Bois d'Oingt   106
Bois-Ste-Marie   35
Bonnes Mares   141
Bourbon-Lancy   35
   Château of St-Aubin-sur
      Loire   36
Bourg-de-Thizy   107
Bourg-en-Bresse   36, 118
   Church of Brou   36, 118
   Church of Notre Dame   37
Bourgneuf-Val-d'Or   157
Bourgogne   132

Bourgogne Aligoté   132, 137,
   158
Bourgogne Aligoté de
   Bouzeron   157
Bouzeron   158
Brancion   37
   Church of St Pierre   37
Bresse   124, 178
Breugnon   37
Brèves   37
Briare   37
Brionnais   40
Brochon   140, 146
Brouilly   173, 176, 177, 178
Pierre-de-Bresse   72
Bussière-sur-Ouche, La   40
   Church of Notre Dame   40
Bussières   40
Bussy-le-Grand   40
Bussy-Rabutin   40

C

Canal de Briare   177
Celle-sur-Loire, La   61
Cenves   100
Cercié   181, 182
Cervon   40
Chablis   41, 132, 133, 135
   Church of St Martin   41
Chagny   157, 168
Chalon   168
   Church of St Peter   169
   Musée Denon   157, 169
Chalon-sur-Saône   41, 157,
   158, 168
   Cathedral of St Vincent   41
   Denon Museum   41
   Nicéphore Niepce Museum   42
Chalonnaise   157, 160, 168
Chambertin   137
Chambolle   162
Chambolle-Musigny   141
Chambost   104
Chambost-Allieres   104
Champallement   42
Champvoux   42
Chânes   181
Chapaize   42
Chardonnay   134, 135,
   148, 154, 157, 158, 160, 172
Charentay   181, 182
Charité-sur-Loire, La   61
Charlieu   42

263

Charnay 105
Charney-les-Macon 44
  Church of St Pierre 44
Charolles 44
  Maison du Charolais 44
Chassagne 156
Chassagne-Montrachet 155, 167
Chassey-le-Camp 44
Château d'Arginy 182
Château de Corcelles,
  Corcelles-en-Beaujolais 182
Château de Jarnioux 106
Château de la Chaise
  Nr. Odenas 181
Château de la Chaize 176
Château de la Palud,
  Quincié 182
Château de la Terrière,
  Cercié 182
Château de Plaige, Luzy 65
Château de Pommard 34, 152
Château de Sermézy,
  Charentay 182
Château de Tholon,
  Lantignié 182
Château La Valsonière
  St Just d'Avray 108
Château St Jean 97
Château-Chinon 44
Châteauneuf-en-Auxois 45
  Church of St Paul 45
Châteaurenard 45
Châtel-Censoir 45
Châtel-Gérard 45
Châtillon d'Azergues 105
Châtillon-Coligny 45
Châtillon-en-Bazois 48
Châtillon-sur-Chalaronne 118
  Church of St André 118
Châtillon-sur-Seine 48
  Archaeological Museum 48
  Church of St Vorles 48
  Source of the Douix 48
Cheese 125, 130
Cheilly 156
Cheilly lès-Maranges 156
Chenas 173, 179
Chénas 174, 181
Cellier de Chénas 174
Chénelette 101
Chenôve 140
Chessy 182
Chessy-les-Mines 105
Chevalier-Montrachet 155
Chevenon 49
Church of St Etienne 49

Chiroubles 173, 176, 177,
  178, 179, 181
Chorey 157
Chorey-lès-Beaune 149, 157
Charité-sur-Loire, La 61
Ciel 49
Cîteaux Abbey 49
Clamecy 49
  Church of St Martin 49
Clayette 50, 61
Clis de la Commaraine 152
Clos de la Roche 137, 141, 162
Clos de Tart 137, 141, 162
Clos de Vougeot 50, 137,
  141, 143, 149, 162, 163
Clos Micot 152
Clos St Denis 137, 141
Clos St Jacques 137
Clos St-Denis 162
Cluny 17, 50, 169
  Abbey of Cluny 141
  Abbey of St Peter
    and St Paul 50
  Church of Notre Dame 51
  Ochier Museum 51
  Parish Church of
    St Marcel 50
Cogny 104
Col de Croix Montmain 101
Col de Dirbize 100
Col de Gerbe 100
Col de la Casse Froide 101
Col des Aillets 108
Col des Cassettes 108
Col des Escorbans 108
Col du Chêne 104
Col du Fût d'Avenas 97
Col du Joncin 104
Col du Pavilon 107
Col du Truges 100
Comblanchien 145
Commagny 51
Commarin 51
Corcelles 101
Corcelles-en-Beaujolais 182
Corgoloin 145, 146
Cormatin 51, 169
Corton 147
Corton Charlemagne 146
Corvol-l'Orgueilleux 51
Cosne-sur-Loire 51
Church of St Agnan 51
  Municipal Museum 52
Côte de Brouilly 177
Côte de Beaune 132, 146,
  149, 156

Côte de Beaune Villages 156
Côte de Brouilly 173, 178, 180
Côte de Chalonnaise 132
Côte de Nuits 132, 137,
  140, 161
Côte de Nuits Villages 145
Côte d'Or 132, 137,
  146, 153, 156, 160, 161, 167
Couches 52
Cours-la-Ville 107
Courzieu 117, 118
Crêches 178, 180
Crêches-sur-Saône 178
Crémant de Bourgogne 137
Cublize 108
Curgy 52
Curtil-sous-Burnand 52

D

Decize 52, 156
Décize-lès-Maranges 156
Denicé 181
Dicy 52
Digoin 52
Dijon 18, 53, 122,
  137, 140, 161
  Archaeological Museum 53
  Cathedral 53
  Church of Notre-Dame 56
  Church of St Jean 54
  Church of St Michel 56
  Church of St Philibert 53, 54
  Espace Grevin 54
  Fine Arts Museum 54, 57
  Horloge à Jacquemart 56
  Hôtel de Vogüé 56
  Jardin de l'Arqueloise 53
  Le Coin du Miroir 54
  Magnin Museum 57
  Maison des Cariatides 56
  Maison Millière 56
  Municipal Library 56
  Palais de Justice 56
  Palais des Ducs et
    des Etats de Bourgogne 57
  Philip the Good's Tower 54
  St Etienne Abbey 56
Donzy 57
Druyes-les-Belles-
  Fontaines 57
Durette 181

E

Echézeaux 162
Échézeaux 144

264

Égreville 57
Emeringes 181
Entrains-sur-Nohains 57
Époisses 57
Escolives-St-Camille 58
Étaules 58
  Chatelet d'Étaules 58

F

Farges-les-Mâcon 58
Ferrières 58
Ferté-Loupière, La 58
Fixin 58, 140, 146, 161
  Church of St Antoine 59
Flagey-Échézeaux 143
  Abbey of St Vivant 143
Flavigny-sur-Ozerain 59
  Abbey of St Pierre 59
Fleurie 173, 176,
  177, 178, 179, 181
Fleurigny Château 59
Fontaine-Française 59
Fontaines Salées Springs,
  St Pierre-le-Moûtier 78
Fontaines-près-Vézelay 59
Fontenay 59
Food Markets 126
Frontenas 104

G

Gallo-Roman art 16
Gamay 134, 154, 160, 172
Game Park, Courzieu 118
Gammay 155
Garchizy 60
Gevrey-Chambertin 60,
  137, 140, 149, 162
Givry 158, 168
Gothic art 17
Gouloux 60
Gourdon 60
Grands Échézeaux 144
Guérigny 60

H

Haut-Beaujolais 172, 173
Haut-Folin, Morvan 69
Hauteville 60

I

Issy-l'Évêque 60

J

Jailly 61

Jarnioux 106
Joigny 61
Juliénas 173, 177, 178,
  179, 181
  Cathedral of St Vincent 174
  Château du Bois
    de la Salle 174, 179
  Maison de la Dîme 174
Jullié 100, 181

K

Kir 121

L

La Chapelle de Mardore 106
La Chapelle-de-Guinchay 181
La Farge 101
La Rochepot 64, 167
La Tâche 144
Lachassagne 106
Ladoix 146
Ladoix-Sérrigny 146, 147
Laduz 64
Laives 64
Lamure-sur-Azergues 101, 106
Château de Pramenoux 101
Lancié 181
Lantignié 181
L'Arbresle 117, 118
Laroche-St-Cydroine 64
Larrey 140
Le Bois d'Oingt 182
Le Creusot 64
Le Gravier 102, 106
Le Parasoir 104
Legny 182
Les Ardillats 100, 181
Les Arvelets 152
Les Dépôts 100
Les Echarmeaux 101, 108
Les Epenots 152
Les Filatures 108
Les Jarollières 152
Les Laforêts 97
Les Pézerolles 152
Les Rugiens 152
Les Sauvages 107
Les Thorins 179
Leynes 181
Ligny-le-Chatel 64
Liqueurs 126
Longefay 97
Lormes 65
Louhans 65
Lower Azergues Valley 104

Luzy 65
Lyon 111, 112, 171, 180
  Amphithéâtre des
    Trois Gauls 115
  Archaeological Gardens 115
  Basilica of Notre-Dame-
    de-Fourvière 113
  Fourvière Hill 113
  Gallo-Roman Museum 113
  Historic Museum of Lyon 116
  Historical Museum 115
  Historical Textile Museum 116
  International Museum
    of the Marionette 115
  Jardin des Plantes 115
  Loge du Change 113
  Maison des Canuts 115, 116
  Maison du Crible 115
  Musée Africain 116
  Museum of Decorative
    Arts 115
  Museum of Fine Arts 115
  Museum of Military
    History 116
  Museum of Printing
    and Banking 115
  Museum of Tele-
    communications 116
  Museum of the History of
    Medicine and Pharmacy 116
  Natural History Museum 116
  Odeon Roman Theatre 113
  Palais de la Miniature 116
  Parc de la Tete d'Or 116
  Roman Amphitheatre 113
  Rue des Trois-Marie 113
  St Jean Cathedral 112
  Tour Métallique 113

M

Machine, La 64
Mâcon 65, 132, 160, 168, 169
  Cathedral of St Vincent 65
  Church of St Vincent 169
  Lamartine Museum 65
  Municipal Museum 65
Mâcon Blanc 160
Mâcon Rouge 160
Mâcon Supérieur Rouge 160
Mâcon Villages 160
Mâconnais 132, 160, 172
Mailly-le-Château 66
Mâlain 66
Marcenay 66
Marchampt 101, 181
Château de Varennes 102

Marcigny 66
Marcy 105
Mars-sur-Aller 66
Marsannay-la-
Côte 140, 161
Massay 66
Massif Central 171
Mazille 66
Mercurey 157, 168
Mersault 146
Metz-le-Comte 66
Meursault 149, 152, 153,
157, 167
Milly-Lamartine 66
Mirebeau-sur-Bèze 67
Monsols 100
Mont Ardoux,
Saône Valley 79
Mont Beauvray,
Morvan 69
Mont Beuvray 67
Mont Brouilly 182
Mont Dardon,
Issy-l'Évêque 60
Mont de Brouilly 180
Mont St Rigaud 100
Mont-St-Jean 68
Mont-St-Vincent 68
Montagny 158, 169
Montargis 67
Montbard 67
Montceau-les-Mines 68
Montceaux-l'Etoile 68
Montenoison 68
Monthélie 149, 153, 166
Montmelas 104
Montréal 68
Monts du Beaujolais 106
Monts du Lyonnais 117
Morey-St-Denis 141, 162
Morgon 173, 176, 178, 180
Morgon Beaujolais 180
Morvan 68
Morvan Hills 132
Morvan National Park 69
Moulin-à-Vent 173, 174,
177, 178, 179
Moulins-Engilbert 69
Musigny 137, 141, 162

N

Nevers 69
Cathedral of St Cyr-
Ste Juliette 69
Church of St Etienne 69
Frédéric Blandin

Municipal Museum 69
St Gildard's Convent 70
Nolay 70
Notre Dame la Rochette 108
Noyers 70
Museum of Art Naïf 70
Nuits-St-Georges 70, 137, 145,
161, 163
Church of St Symphorien 163

O

Odénas 181
Oingt 105

P

Paray-le-Monial 72
Parc des Oiseaux,
Villars-les-Dombes 118
Parc du Morvan 72
Parigny-les-Vaux 72
Church of St Jean Baptiste 72
Parly 72
Church of St Sebastien 72
Pernand-Vergelesses 147, 149
Pérouges 117
Perrecy-les-Forges 72
Petit Chablis 137
Pierre-de-Bresse 72
Pierre-qui-Vire-Abbey 73
Pierreclos 72
Plâtre-Durand, Le 179
Pommard 146, 149, 152, 165
Pontaubert 73
Pontigny 73
Pouges-les-Eaux 73
Pouilly-en-Auxois 73
Pouilly-Fuissé 132, 160, 161,
169
Pouilly-Vinzelles 161
Précy-sous-Thil 73
Prémeaux 145
Prémery 75
Propières 101
Pruzilly 181
Puligny 156
Puligny-Montrachet 154,
167

Q

Quarré-les-Tombes 75
Quincié 181

R

Rapetour 104
Ratilly 75

Regnié 181, 182
Renaissance Art 18
Reulle-Vergy 75
Richebourg 144
Rigaud Massif 172
River Saône 132
River Serein 136
River Vandaine 152
Rivolet 181
Rochetaillée 119
Musée de l'Automobile
Henri Malartre 119
Parc Ornithologique 119
Rochetaillée Motor
Museum 117
Romain 167
Roman Theatre, Vienne 116
Romanèche-Thorins 176, 181
Romanée 144
Romanée-Conti 137, 144, 163
Romanée-St-Vivant 144
Romanesque Art 16
Romenay 75
Roseraie St Nicolas 42
Route de Beaujolais 178, 179
Ruettes 97
Rully 157, 168

S

Sacy 75
Safari Park, Haut Vivarais
Annonay 118
Salles 181
Salles-Arbuissonais-
en-Beaujolais 96
Sampigney-lès-Maranges 156
Sampigny 156
Santenay 79, 132, 156, 165,
167, 168
Santenay-le-Bas 168
Santenay-le-Haut 168
Saône 171, 178
Saône Valley 79
Saulieu 79
Basilica of St Andoche 79
François Pompon
Museum 80
Savigny 146
Savigny-lès-Beaune 148, 149
Seignelay 80
Semur-en-Auxois 80
Church of Notre-Dame 80
Church of St Thibault 81
Couvent des Jacobines 80
Tour de l'Orle d'Or 80
Semur-en-Brionnais 81

Sène   81
Sennecey-le-Grand   81
   Church of St Julien   81
Sens   81
   Cathedral of St Etienne   81
   Cathedral Treasure House   82
   Church of St Savinien   82
St Amand-en-Puisaye   75
St Amour   173, 178
St Amour-Bellevue   181
St André-de-Bage   75
St André-la-Côte   117
St Aubin   155
St Bonnet-des-Bruyères   100
St Bonnet-le-Troncy   106
St Brisson   75
St Christophe   100
St Christophe-en-Brionnais   76
St Clément-de-Vers   101
St Cyr-le-Chatoux   104
St Didier-sur-Beaujeu   101
St Éloi   76
   Church of St Symphorien   76
St Etienne-la-Varenne   181
St Etiennes-des-Ouillières   181
St Fargeau   76
St Florentin   76
St Germain-en-Brionnais   76
St Honoré-les-Bains   77
St Igny-de-Vers   100
St Jacques-des-Arrêts   97
St Jean   168
St Joseph   100
St Joseph Church   100
St Julien   181
St Julien-de-Jonzy   77
St Julien-du-Sault   77
St Julien-en-Montmélas   181
St Just d'Avray   108
St Lager   181
St Laurent-d'Oingt   105, 182
St Léger-Vauban   77
St Magnance   77
St Mamert   97
St Martin-sous-Montaigu   157
St Micaud   77
St Nizier   106
St Parize-le-Châtel   77
St Père   77
   Church of Notre-Dame   77
St Pierre-le-Moûtier   78
St Révérien   78
St Romain   78
St Romain-en-Gal   117
St Saulge   78
St Seine-l'Abbaye   78

St Symphorien-d'Ancelles   181
St Thibault   79
St Vérand   181
St Vérnan   160
St Victor-sur-Rhins   107
St Vincent-de-Reins   106
St. Romain   153
Sully   82

T

Taingy   82
Taizé   84
Talmay   84
Tamnay-en-Bazois   84
Tanlay   84
Tarare   96
Ternand   105
Ternant   84
Theizé   104, 182
   Close de la Platière   104
Thizy   107
   Chapelle St Georges   107
Til-Châtel   84
   Church of St Florent   84
Tonnerre   84
   Church of St Pierre   85
   Hotel d'Uzès   85
   Hôtel-Dieu   84
Toucy   85
Tournus   85, 160, 169
   Church of La Madeleine   86
   Church of St Philibert   85
   Geuze Museum   85
   Museum Bourguignon   85
Truffles   155

U

Uchon   86

V

Vallery   86
Valley of the Azergues   101
Vareilles   86
Varenne l'Arconce   86
Varzy   86
   Chapel of St Lazare   86
Vault-de-Lugnu   86
Vausse Priory   86
Vaux, Le Perréon   181
Vaux-en-Beaujolais   181
Vauxrenard   181
Verdun-sur-le-Doubs   86
Vermenton   86
Verneuil   87
Vertault   87

Vézelay   87
Vienne   116
   Archaeological Museum   117
   Cathedral of St
     Maurice   116
   Church of St Pierre   117
   Temple of Augustus
     and Livia   117
Vignerons de Chiroubles   97
Ville-sur-Jarnioux   106
Villefranche   172, 178
Villefranche-sur-Saône   93, 180
Church of Notre Dame
   des Marais   96
Villeneuve l'Archevéque   88
Villeneuve-sur-Yonne   88
Villié-Morgon   181
Volnay   146, 149, 152,
   166, 167
Vosne-Romanée   144, 163
Vougeot   88, 143, 163